MARTHA

MARTHA

ON TRIAL, IN JAIL, AND ON A COMEBACK

ROBERT SLATER

PEARSON
Prentice
Hall

Library of Congress Cataloging-in-Publication Data

Slater, Robert, 1943-

    Martha : on trial, in jail, and on a comeback / Robert Slater.

        p. cm.

    Includes bibliographical references and index.

    ISBN 0-13-187514-0 (hardback : alk. paper)

    1. Stewart, Martha.   2. Home economists--United States--Biography.

    I. Title.

TX140.S74S77 2006

338.7'6164092--dc22

[B]

2005032631

Vice President and Editor-in-Chief: Tim Moore
Editorial Assistant: Susan Abraham
Development Editor: Russ Hall
Director of Marketing: Amy Neidlinger
International Marketing Manager: Tim Galligan
Cover Designer: Chuti Prasertsith
Managing Editor: Gina Kanouse
Senior Project Editor: Kristy Hart
Copy Editor: Water Crest Publishing
Proofreader: Debbie Williams
Senior Indexer: Cheryl Lenser
Interior Designer: Gloria Schurick
Compositor: Gloria Schurick
Manufacturing Buyer: Dan Uhrig

© 2006 by Pearson Education, Inc.
Publishing as Prentice Hall
Upper Saddle River, New Jersey 07458

Prentice Hall offers excellent discounts on this book when ordered in quantity for bulk purchases or special sales. For more information, please contact U.S. Corporate and Government Sales, 1-800-382-3419, corpsales@pearsontechgroup.com.
For sales outside the U.S., please contact International Sales, 1-317-581-3793, international@pearsontechgroup.com.

Company and product names mentioned herein are the trademarks or registered trademarks of their respective owners.

Printed in the United States of America

First Printing January 2006

ISBN 0-13-187514-0

Pearson Education LTD.
Pearson Education Australia PTY, Limited.
Pearson Education Singapore, Pte. Ltd.
Pearson Education North Asia, Ltd.
Pearson Education Canada, Ltd.
Pearson Educación de Mexico, S.A. de C.V.
Pearson Education—Japan
Pearson Education Malaysia, Pte. Ltd.

CONTENTS

ACKNOWLEDGMENTS

In March 2004, Martha Stewart mentioned to Larry King that she thought it could be helpful to others for her to write a book about her legal case "just about what lawyer to choose, how to behave, how to attend an interview.... There's no how-to book about this...for anybody who has to go through this process, there should be some guidelines because guidelines would help."

When I read that part of the King-Stewart interview as part of my research for *Martha: On Trial, in Jail, and on a Comeback*, I realized that, although I was also writing a book about her legal case, my goal was entirely different from Stewart's. I was not writing a how-to book. I wanted to write a narrative about one of the most fascinating legal cases of our era, a case that turned America's most famous woman into its most infamous.

I focused on Stewart's legal case for a number of reasons: First, while I had written numerous book-length profiles of American business leaders (Jack Welch, Bill Gates, Lou Gerstner, Donald Trump, etc.), it hardly seemed appropriate to write a business profile of Martha Stewart after all of her legal troubles. She had certainly achieved a great deal as a businesswoman; but it was impossible to write about her continuing business accomplishments after her legal turmoil had put her businesses into disarray.

Second, two previous books on Stewart had covered her life in full and done so with strong negative slants. I did not want to rehash her entire life; nor did I want to produce a negative book about Stewart. Focusing on her legal travails afforded me the opportunity to write about the greatest crisis in her life and career, showing how she had gone through that crisis and had then staged one of the great comebacks of American life.

To research the book, I spoke with numerous people who had something to do with Martha Stewart from the day she took the controversial stock tip on December 27, 2001, to the present: her lawyers and lawyers of others involved in her trial; her public relations advisers and public relations advisers to others involved in her trial; and members of the media who covered the trial. I spoke with people who were familiar with Martha Stewart's experience while she was in jail. I also spoke to a number of Martha Stewart supporters and critics to get a flavor of the kind of emotions whipped up by the trial.

I made a number of attempts to speak with Martha Stewart, and the closest I came were three phone conversations with her spokeswoman, Susan Magrino. In each of the calls, Ms. Magrino grilled me extensively on what the book would be about, whether Martha Stewart would enjoy reading it, and would she feel she had been accurately and fairly portrayed. I took each phone call as a sign that I was getting closer to interviewing Ms. Stewart; but alas no interview took place. It did not surprise me. Martha Stewart had given relatively few interviews to the media from the time she was released from jail in March 2005 to the present. She had barely touched on her legal case in interviews dating back to 2002. Her book, *Martha's Rules*, was due to be published in October of that year. I assumed that after it became clear to Ms. Magrino that I intended to focus on the years of Martha Stewart's legal case, I would have a more difficult time getting the interview because Stewart did not want to discuss that period.

The nature of my research led me to interview many people connected to the case off the record. I was not able to quote them in the book. Nor can I mention their names in these Acknowledgments. I wish to thank them for their help and for their candor.

I do want to thank those who talked to me either fully on the record or largely on the record: Dan Ackman; Douglas Arthur; Kurt Barnard; Kevin Coupe; Howard L. Davidowitz; Lanny Davis; Allen Dodd-Frank; Jim Dowd; Ivan Feinseth; Burt Flickinger; Chrisa Gonzales; Kate Hazelwood; Gordon Joseloff; Elizabeth Koch; Elaine Lafferty; Helen Lucaites; Tom Madden; Lisa Marsh; Dennis B. McAlpine; Gary McDaniel; Lawrence McNaughton; Denise Miller; Peter Montoya; Kevin B. O'Neill; Laurel Parker; Robert K. Passikoff; Stacy Perman; Marvin Pickholz; Penelope Patsuris; Andrew Ritchie; Howard Rubenstein; Seth Siegel; Michelle Soudry; Rochelle Steinhaus; Donald Trump; Troy Wolverton; Nat Worden; and Jacob (Jake) H. Zamansky.

I also want to thank the following for help they gave during the project: Judith Resnik; Dennis Curtis; David Nachman; Amy Shulman; Allen Alter; Michael and Bobbi Winick; Marco Greenberg; Gershon Kekst; and Lissa Perlman.

I want to especially thank Jacob (Jake) H. Zamansky, the securities attorney who attended the Martha Stewart trial every day. He was kind enough to answer my questions on a continuing basis during my research, shedding much light on the intricacies of the case.

I also want to thank Andrew Ritchie, a Canadian journalist who writes often for the SaveMartha.com Web site. Mr. Ritchie constantly supplied me with material that he felt would be of interest to me. I also benefited from numerous insights he made about Ms. Stewart and her legal case.

I want to thank Elizabeth Koch for agreeing to be interviewed; and for allowing me to quote from the notes she took during the Martha Stewart trial, notes that appear on the Reason.com Web site, for which she wrote during the trial.

As usual, the most help that I received for this project came from the closest members of my family: my wife, Elinor; my children: Miriam, Adam, and Rachel; Shimi and Tal; and my grandchildren: Edo, Maya, and Shai, I thank them for providing the encouragement as well as the peace and quiet that enabled me to produce this book.

ABOUT THE AUTHOR

Robert Slater was born in New York City on October 1, 1943, and grew up in South Orange, New Jersey. He graduated from Columbia High School in 1962 and graduated with honors from the University of Pennsylvania in 1966, where he majored in political science. He received a Master's of Science degree in international relations from the London School of Economics in 1967. He worked for UPI and *Time Magazine* for many years, in both the United States and the Middle East.

Slater wrote 17 books about major business personalities before his new book on Martha Stewart:

- *The Titans of Takeover* (Englewood Cliffs, NJ: Prentice Hall, 1987).
- *Portraits in Silicon* (Cambridge, MA: MIT Press, 1987).
- *This ... .Is CBS: A Chronicle of 60 Years* (Englewood Cliffs, NJ: Prentice Hall, 1988).
- *The New GE: How Jack Welch Revived an American Institution* (Homewood, IL: Business One Irwin, 1993).
- *Get Better or Get Beaten! 31 Leadership Secrets from GE's Jack Welch* (Burr Ridge, IL: Irwin Professional Publishing, 1994). This book made the business best-seller list in Japan.
- *SOROS: The Life, Times, and Trading Secrets of the World's Greatest Investor* (Chicago: Irwin Professional Publishing, 1996). This profile of superinvestor George Soros appeared on the *Business Week* best-seller list.
- *Invest First, Investigate Later: And 23 Other Trading Secrets of George Soros, the Legendary Investor* (Chicago: Irwin Professional Publishing, 1996).

- *John Bogle and the Vanguard Experiment: One Man's Quest to Transform the Mutual Fund Industry* (Chicago: Irwin Professional Publishing, 1996). This is a profile of the most important business figure in the mutual fund field.

- *Ovitz: The Inside Story of Hollywood's Most Controversial Power Broker* (New York: McGraw-Hill, 1997). This book made the *Los Angeles Times* and the *New York Times* business best-seller lists.

- *Jack Welch and the GE Way: Management Insights and Leadership Secrets of the Legendary CEO* (New York: McGraw-Hill, 1998). This is an updated look at the business secrets of General Electric's chairman and chief executive officer. It made the *Business Week* and the *Wall Street Journal* best-seller lists.

- *Saving Big Blue: Leadership Lessons & Turnaround Tactics of IBM's Lou Gerstner* (New York: McGraw-Hill, 1999), and *The GE Way Fieldbook: Jack Welch's Battle Plan for Corporate Revolution* (New York: McGraw Hill, 1999).

- *Eye of the Storm: How John Chambers Steered Cisco Systems Through the Technology Collapse* (New York: HarperBusiness, 2003).

- *Magic Cancer Bullet: How a Tiny Orange Capsule May Rewrite Medical History* (New York: HarperBusiness, 2003), co-authored with Novartis CEO Dan Vasella.

- *The Wal-Mart Decade: How a New Generation of Leaders Turned Sam Walton's Legacy into the World's #1 Company* (New York: Portfolio, 2003). A paperback version was published in June 2004.

- *Microsoft Rebooted: How Bill Gates and Steve Ballmer Re-Invented Their Company* (New York: Portfolio, 2004).

- *No Such Thing as Over-Exposure: Inside the Life and Celebrity of Donald Trump* (Upper Saddle River, NJ: Prentice Hall, 2005).

Cast of
Characters

The Judge

Miriam Goldman Cedarbaum—The 74-year-old U.S. District Court Judge, a Brooklyn native, presided over the Martha Stewart trial.

In 1953, she was one of only eight women to earn her law degree from Columbia University. As a federal judge, she was considered erudite, businesslike, prudent, refined, no-nonsense, and above all, fair.

The Defendants

Martha Stewart—Emerging from humble beginnings, she established an entire new industry of homemaking and entertaining; hosting television shows and writing books; she built a business empire around the new industry. For taking a controversial stock tip in 2001, she wound up in jail, after which she began a remarkable comeback.

Peter Bacanovic—Through his friendship with Martha's daughter, Alexis, he met Martha Stewart and became her stockbroker. On vacation on December 27, 2001, he ordered his assistant, Douglas Faneuil, to inform Stewart that ImClone CEO Sam Waksal was selling his company's shares, setting off events that led to Bacanovic's and Stewart's convictions.

The Witnesses

Douglas Faneuil—As the assistant to Martha Stewart's stockbroker, it was he who provided her with the key information that sparked a federal probe against her for taking that tip. Entering into a plea bargain with the feds, he was the Government's star witness and a key cause for Stewart's guilty conviction.

Mariana Pasternak—One of Martha Stewart's closest friends, she was a real-estate broker who came from Westport, Connecticut. She produced the bombshell of the Stewart trial, eliciting from her on their vacation to Mexico the most famous quote of the affair: "Isn't it nice to have brokers who tell you those things?"

Ann Armstrong—Martha Stewart's secretary, she cried on the stand, knowing that her testimony might convict her boss of federal crimes. On the stand, she recounted how Stewart had tried to alter and then change back an e-mail that would have been damaging to Martha Stewart.

THE FEDERAL PROSECUTOR

Karen Seymour—Chief of the criminal division of the U.S. Attorney's office in New York, she was in charge of 150 prosecutors, and in prosecuting Martha Stewart, was trying her first case since taking the job in 2002. Earlier, she had successfully tried an aide to junk bond king Michael Milken and a former AT&T executive.

THE DEFENSE ATTORNEYS

John Savarese—Representing Stewart in the early days of her case was Wachtell, Lipton attorney John Savarese, a former prosecutor who helped convict the bosses of New York's five Mafia families in 1986. He took flak for allowing Stewart to testify before the feds; but she in fact had little choice.

Robert Morvillo—Martha Stewart's trial attorney, at 65, he was close to the end of his career. For 30 years, he had been one of the top white-collar-criminal-defense attorneys in the country. Morvillo had represented such clients as former congressman Robert Garcia and John Zaccaro, husband of former vice presidential candidate Geraldine Ferraro.

John Cuti—Alexis Stewart's husband, John Cuti, was a litigator who sometimes worked for Martha Stewart and her company. A partner at the law firm of Emery Celli Cuti Brinckerhoff & Abady, he attended the trial every day and served as a legal adviser to Stewart.

DAUGHTER OF THE DEFENDANT

Alexis Stewart—The only child of Martha and Andy Stewart, she began dating Sam Waksal, 18 years her senior. Their romance was brief but led to Sam and Martha growing close. Reportedly estranged from her mother in earlier years, Alexis reconciled with Martha and was her constant companion during the Stewart legal case.

THE INSIDE TRADER

Sam Waksal—Sam Waksal, founder of the hot biotech firm ImClone, held a doctorate in immunobiology. After dating Alexis Stewart, he grew friendly with Martha. She acquired ImClone shares and it was her decision to unload them in December 2001 right after Waksal sold his that aroused the feds' suspicions.

THE JOURNALIST

Henry Blodget—The most unusual and most respected journalist at the Stewart trial, he had once been the most famous financial analyst on Wall Street; he was disgraced and barred from the Street after being accused of misleading middle-class investors with faulty research. He showed up at the Stewart trial as a reporter for Slate.com.

PROMOTERS OF THE COMEBACK

Mark Burnett—Known best for producing the television reality program, "Survivor," he went on to co-produce with Donald Trump the hit television reality show, "The Apprentice," starring Trump. One of Martha Stewart's main vehicles of her planned comeback was a television program modeled after Trump's *The Apprentice*, co-produced by Trump and Burnett.

Donald Trump—The real estate magnate worth $2.6 billion, owning one of the nation's great personal brands, he publicly supported Stewart throughout her legal ordeal; then went on to co-produce (along with Mark Burnett) a spin-off of *The Apprentice*, starring Martha Stewart. The show debuted in September 2005.

Susan Lyne—Concerned that the CEO of Martha Stewart Living Omnimedia, Sharon Patrick, was reducing Stewart's role in the company, Stewart handpicked the former Disney executive and founder of *Premiere* magazine to replace Patrick. In the fall of 2005, Lyne was feverishly trying to put Stewart's company back on track.

Charles Koppelman—Martha Stewart handpicked him to help her refurbish her company in 2005. A veteran of the music industry, he became chairman of Martha Stewart Living Omnimedia in 2005 and was given a one-year contract to analyze possible new media and merchandising deals. He also appeared on the new *The Apprentice: Martha Stewart* program.

PREFACE

LEAVING ALDERSON

March 4, 2005, a few minutes after midnight. The temperatures are sub-freezing, maybe even in the teens. Snow covers the ground. Nearby is the Alderson Federal Women's Prison at Alderson, West Virginia. Dubbed "Camp Cupcake" for its easy living, it is more like hell for its 980 inmates.

Soon, its most famous prison inmate will go free.

The rumor mill is churning in full force. Maybe she'll come out in an hour or two, maybe she'll emerge through an entirely different gate. Perhaps she'll make a public statement soon after her release.

Any public utterance that she makes this evening, any facial gesture, will be dissected and analyzed and conveyed immediately around America and the rest of the world.

For the prisoner is both the most famous and infamous woman in America. Many know her simply by her first name, Martha.

Five months earlier, she slipped into jail in the dark of the night just before dawn, silent, secretive, sullen, strident, high and mighty.

Now, she is about to begin her post-prison freedom and she is on a dramatic mission to stage an unprecedented comeback.

Can she pull it off?

Will her fans welcome her with open arms? Can she again become the queen of homemaking? Can she ignite fresh energy into her faltering businesses?

Or will she be scorned as a convicted felon? Will her commercial empire remain a shadow of itself?

All of America is waiting with baited breath for the answer—or so it seems. For, Martha Stewart has risen, and fallen, and now she is trying to rise again.

While journalists stake out the prison, Stewart goes through the routine that every prisoner waits for with the greatest anticipation, handing in her prison khakis, closing out her commissary account, and finally, changing into civilian clothes.

She is like no other prisoner in America. No prisoner, indeed no celebrity prisoner, is watched and analyzed as carefully and constantly as she is.

THE TRACE OF A SMILE

Like every prisoner, she has been counting the days until the hour of her freedom, and now that it is here, the trace of a smile crosses her lips.

Fellow inmates and visitors remark that she is coming off the dreaded experience of five months in prison in remarkably good spirits. The nervous, bemused pre-prison look has given way to a new radiance. Her eyes sparkle. She has a sprightly gait. She emerges kinder, humbler. She seems to have shed her elitist airs by getting close to other prisoners.

This then is the new shiny Martha Stewart, the nicer version, and while there is undoubted orchestration behind her makeover, she still seems genuinely to have put her anger, bitterness, and frustration behind her. She knows she must if mainstream American society and culture will have her back.

As it turns out, Martha Stewart leaves Alderson entirely unnoticed. That is how she and her handlers want it. They are organizing her departure from Alderson and her journey to freedom as if she were a political candidate.

There must be no reminders of her life behind bars. She must convey the image of a leader making a triumphant return, fulfilling her promise, "I will be back." The grimacing, my-life-has-been-a-waste Martha Stewart must be airbrushed out of existence. All photos must show her as a freshly minted heroine.

Hence, her aides do nothing to make life easy for the gaggle of media at the prison gate; but they go out of their way to facilitate television coverage at the Greenbrier Valley Airport in Alderson so that TV crews can shoot Stewart stepping on a plane, whisking her to a new life.

Precisely at 12:30 a.m., she leaves prison and arrives at the airport a half hour later.

"Now we're just waiting for that million-dollar shot," reported a gushing CNN reporter named Deborah Feyerick, "whether it will be a smile, a wave, a wink. What will she be wearing?"

"...We'll have that answer as she leaves West Virginia. I don't know whether she'll ever be back but certainly she's leaving in style."

Martha Stewart is indeed leaving prison in style, accompanied by a brand-new media love-fest. She takes quiet satisfaction that the comeback she so much wants has gotten off to a good start.

She feels that she is finally reading the outside reality in a way that can be helpful to her. She now knows that it had been her own distorted version of that outside reality that had gotten her into such trouble.

But, as she boards the private jet, she knows that cynics and even haters await her, hoping that her comeback will go up in smoke. They do not feel that she should be forgiven for the "small personal matter" (Stewart's phrase) that had turned her life into a nightmare for the past 39 months. They do not regard her as a heroine.

Will the anti-Stewart forces scuttle her comeback? Or will she return to her past glory?

Soon, everyone would know the answer.

PART
I

A MINOR MISTAKE

CHAPTER

1

THAT'S VERY MARTHA

Martha Stewart became the most famous businesswoman in America, a cultural icon whose very name evoked a style and elegance that pervaded all walks of life. She had far greater influence on the way Americans cooked and entertained, and decorated their homes and gardens, than any individual in the nation's history.

She had a knack for knowing how to brighten American households with her food, her flowers, and her gardening; and while many had difficulty articulating precisely what her profession was, millions knew instinctively that her perfectionist emphasis on elegance and simplicity was her unique signature. "Here's how Martha would do it," her loyal fans declared lovingly, as if there were only one way of baking a cake or planting a garden.

She was so good at what she did, she was watched and admired by so many people, that she eventually established standards in a wide variety of homemaking and entertaining spheres affecting the lives of millions of people. By choosing to establish those standards in the most important institution in our lives—our homes—and by helping a newly emerging class of wives and mothers, breadwinners with little time or energy for the home, she came along at just the right time and with just the right message.

She was so good at what she did, she was watched and admired by so many people, that she eventually established standards in a wide variety of homemaking and entertaining spheres affecting the lives of millions of people.

And could she deliver the message! Indeed, she was unique in designing all of her products and then serving as chief spokesperson for them. Ordinarily, designers remain in the background and beautiful models show off the products. But in Martha Stewart's case, she was front and center, a television fixture explaining clearly and simply how to become an ideal homemaker and home entertainer.

ONE OF A KIND

She seemed to have it all, a successful eponymous company, an incredible ability to establish her own personal brand through her products, and a personal authority that gained her wider and wider acceptance with each television appearance and with each book published.

Certainly she was one of a kind.

Who else could say that she began her career in catering and wound up a billionaire? Who else could lay claim to so much celebrity for tossing a salad or arranging a floral display? Who else had so much visibility and so much familiarity that the mere mention of her first name was enough to identify her? Who else had fans that knew her style well enough to say, when someone set a table just right, or nurtured a garden with flair, "That's very Martha."

> *Who else could say that she began her career in catering and wound up a billionaire?*

Nothing was harder in business than to create a personal brand. Only a handful of people had done it: Ralph Lauren, Calvin Klein, Coco Chanel, and Donald Trump come to mind. Martha Stewart did it too, and the more products that bore her name, the smarter she seemed. She fused her name and her personality into the company that she founded and eventually took public—Martha Stewart Living Omnimedia.

Few other business enterprises were as dependent on a single person. The company embodied Stewart's tastes and Stewart's business strategies; she was its major shareholder, its founder, and its chief executive officer. As the company grew and it became an indelible fixture on the business scene, MSLO seemed indestructible and Martha Stewart appeared invulnerable. Sure, a bus might hit her, company executives joked darkly, but the company's future seemed secure: Even if Stewart one day passed from the scene, her iconic stature would serve as the company's anchor forever.

She was a perfectionist. As she went, in her early years, from modeling to trading stocks on Wall Street to a career in catering, she had to be the best. Her fans responded favorably to her setting such high standards for herself. She began to believe that she really did know what was best for everyone. That became her version of reality.

Clinging to that reality, she called herself an educator and took on a didactic demeanor toward everyone. In her version of reality, she was in command of all that she purveyed: her taste, her preferences, her rules prevailed. As the teacher, she was always right, never wrong.

Millions of people sanctioned her view of reality by establishing her as the "domestic diva" and the "queen of homemaking." With so many people fawning all over her, yes-men and yes-women one and all, she had no time for anyone who thought she was less than perfect; she had no time for anyone who did not conform to her view of reality.

She assumed that just being Martha Stewart was enough to ward off any assault on her world. Should anyone dissent from her version of reality, she was armed with a whole set of defense mechanisms: She knew how to marginalize people, to trivialize them, to make them feel inferior to her.

> *She assumed that just being Martha Stewart was enough to ward off any assault on her world.*

To her great shock, some did not share her view of reality. They saw no reason to idealize her or to pay her obeisance. Theirs was a different view of reality, and in their world, there were no queens or princesses who made their own rules. They made the rules.

NO NEED TO FALL

By disconnecting herself from their reality, Martha Stewart fell from power. She had no need to fall. All that she needed to do was to understand their reality and embrace it. But for a long time she could not. When she finally did become sensitive to their reality, when she was no longer disconnected from their reality, she was ready to rise again. *Martha: On Trial, in Jail, and on a Comeback* looks at her fall and her mission to rise again in the first book-length, in-depth examination of the greatest crisis in Martha Stewart's life and career.

It all came to a head for her in the early afternoon of December 27, 2001, when she committed a minor offense, and her world fell apart.

She committed the offense in the spur of the moment on a remote, noisy, busy airport tarmac while on a cell phone, not even certain to whom she was speaking. She did not initiate the alleged crime; the person on the other end of the phone and that person's boss did that. She did not stand to gain a huge amount of money; all she did was avoid losing what amounted to pocket change for her. At first glance, she seemed to be committing the crime of insider trading; but when she was probed the evidence just was not there for an insider trading charge.

And yet this one minor transgression threatened to put an end to all that she had built.

Her critical misstep came about after she learned that a close friend, the co-founder of a major biotech company called ImClone, had been trying to unload his company shares; she then sold all of her stock in that company.

Others had sold stock in that company at the same time as Martha Stewart, but she became the focus of a major investigation undertaken by the Federal Bureau of Investigation, the Securities and Exchange Commission, and the United States Attorney's Office. A Congressional probe went on in parallel with the federal investigation.

Why, if what Martha Stewart had done was indeed minor, had she come under such official scrutiny?

After all, she had not killed anyone. She had not stolen money from a pension fund. She had not put personal items on the company's expense account. Indeed, by acting on a hot stock tip from a stockbroker with connections to the company of the stock, she had done nothing different from what many on Wall Street were doing hour after hour.

Why had the feds singled her out?

True, she had sold her ImClone stock on the eve of an unfavorable FDA decision on the company's highly touted cancer drug called Erbitux; but she was not a senior executive at ImClone, nor did she know that an unfavorable FDA decision was in the offing.

But she was no serial murderer, no child abuser. What had she done to agitate the feds to such a degree?

It was, as it turned out, not what she had done—but what she was.

Martha Stewart was an icon.

She was someone the feds could collar and hold up to public ridicule and put away in jail—and be assured that the entire nation would know of their noble deeds. By taking that stock tip when she did, Martha Stewart provided the feds with a villain at a time when real, honest-to-God corporate villains were roaming the streets free. Ken Lay of Enron and Dennis Koslovsky of Tyco had practically dropped a nuclear weapon on their companies, but their encounter with the criminal justice system was a long way off.

Not only was Martha Stewart iconic, she was available. She was a tantalizing example who could be put under the public spotlight immediately. Unlike the complicated, arcane corporate shenanigans of others, Stewart's tiny little indiscretion could be served up to the media and the public with the kind of immediacy and a panache that could only thrill the feds.

Does the phrase "Kafkaesque" come to mind? You bet it does.

Though far more victim than villain, Stewart fit neatly into the surrealistic world of the feds who cared little about how much actual harm she had done. What they cared about was their resumes.

NEVER LET HER GO

And the feds would never let her go.

Accused of insider trading at the start of the federal probe against her, she was eventually charged with a completely different crime and no insider trading charges were filed. For months the federal authorities looked into Stewart's stock sale, interviewing her twice, talking with her stockbroker and the stockbroker's assistant, hoping to build an insider trading case against her.

But, after 18 months, the authorities were unable to prove that what she did constituted insider trading; but they did catch Stewart committing other alleged crimes: lying to authorities; obstruction of justice, conspiracy, and securities fraud. And so they indicted her on these charges, less venal than insider trading, but still criminal.

Even after she was indicted, no one seriously believed that Martha Stewart would wind up in a courtroom. It all seemed so preposterous, her getting into legal trouble over a stock tip, and over avoiding the loss of such a small ($45,000) amount of money.

But she wound up in a courtroom—and then prison—because she refused to take the feds seriously. In pressing their case against her, they were clearly dissenting from her version of reality—the one in which Martha Stewart could do no wrong.

But she refused to brook any dissenters, and so she came armed for battle against the feds.

Rather than take the feds seriously, she trivialized their efforts. She sought to marginalize what they were doing. She felt that she had done nothing wrong and, at least with respect to her taking that controversial stock tip, she was right about that.

Having done nothing wrong from her perspective, she saw no reason to bend her version of reality.

The problem for her was that she had done something wrong; at least she certainly gave the impression that she had. She had lied to the feds and that was a federal crime.

Thinking that she had done nothing wrong, she fell back on her defense mechanisms; trivialize, marginalize, proclaim your innocence; make it clear that you have better things to do with your time. By taking that tack, she had seriously disconnected herself from reality. She could never defeat the feds with such strategies. But she tried.

The more she became disconnected from reality, the more stiff-necked and nasty she came off. She relied on such traits to overwhelm her rivals. But the feds would not budge. They gave her opportunities to pull the plug on her legal battle. She could have settled her case. She could have avoided a trial and a guilty conviction and jail.

But she insisted on believing that her version of reality would ultimately triumph—and she was wrong. She won no credit for carrying on with her legal struggle. To most people, including the feds, she simply seemed stubborn. And indeed she was.

She became a victim of her stubbornness and made one bad legal decision after another—and all the while the world was watching.

Because she chose to fight rather than to resolve her predicament right away, and because she was the most famous woman in America, she gave the media a dramatic story that at times seemed more important than cataclysmic political events or natural catastrophes.

Though the Martha Stewart legal case came at a time of seemingly constant corporate scandal, she received more media coverage during her courtroom drama than any other celebrity since the 1995 O.J. Simpson trial. Some called Martha Stewart's the first big corporate scandal case of that era, and they drew comparisons between her case and those of Enron, Tyco, Adelphia, and WorldCom. But it was ludicrous to mention her legal case in the same breath with Ken Lay, Bernie Ebbers, and Dennis Koslovsky, corporate leaders who had done far more mischief, and caused far more harm to shareholders and employees.

The feds benefited from the massive media coverage; Martha Stewart did not. She had to preserve her reputation and putting a cloak of secrecy over her case seemed the best way to do that; so she hardly spoke about her case in public; she was thrilled that for the first six months of the probe, the public was kept in the dark.

But the feds wanted to look like white knights in shining armor, dealing a blow to corporate mischief, protecting the little guy against the big, bad scandalmongers. For that they needed all the publicity they could muster. And so they sought to surround the Stewart case with compelling drama: They called press conferences for routine announcements; they turned the trial into a morality play, the good guys (the Government) vs. the bad guys (Martha Stewart and her stockbroker, Peter Bacanovic); and they linked Stewart's alleged crimes with the corporate scandals of the day (Enron, Tyco, and the like).

THE CRUSHED-VELVET CURTAIN

Finally, the feds encouraged the media to believe that the probe into Martha Stewart offered a rare opportunity to give the public a glimpse into the secretive, mysterious world of the upper crust of New York society and to demonstrate that the wealthy played by a different set of financial rules from all others. As *Newsweek* put it in its July 1, 2002 story on the Stewart case: "...l'affaire Martha isn't just about ImClone. It has also pulled back the crushed-velvet curtain on the clubby world of New York's social elite, a place where the rich and powerful pass around insider business gossip as readily as the help passes out smoked-salmon canapés. With post-Enron investors already questioning the fairness of the marketplace, Stewart's case is the most visible reminder yet that folks on the inside get richer while the rest of us watch our 401(k)s shrivel."

But the feds did not have to work too hard to convince the media and the public that the Martha Stewart legal case was one of the most gripping of the era.

It was compelling because the full weight of the Federal Government was taking on one of the nation's most celebrated icons—and all over a minor offense.

It was dramatic because here was someone who had it all yet let it slip away—again over a minor indiscretion.

Finally, it was attention-getting because the main actor in the drama had the ability to put an end to her struggle but chose instead to fight on against heavy odds.

How could such a thing happen?

What was it that impelled Martha Stewart to an indictment and trial, both of which were avoidable?

Once it happened, was her downfall inevitable?

What motivated the federal authorities to pursue her so relentlessly?

How did she stage the most remarkable comeback in modern history?

These are the questions that we take up in this book.

Our story begins in the winter of 2001 when all seemed tranquil and idyllic for Martha Stewart—and her life was about to unravel.

CHAPTER

2

SAVING $45,000

It was early December 2001. For Sam Waksal, founder of ImClone, one of the hottest biotech companies around, it finally looked like he was going to get out from under his financial problems. He had largely kept those problems a secret. Partly, he had felt it was no one else's business; and partly, he had convinced himself that a miracle was about to happen.

The miracle was called Erbitux, the odd-sounding name for the colon cancer drug that ImClone was about to launch. All signs indicated that Erbitux would set the medical world afire: The drug had just appeared on the cover of *BusinessWeek*. The Food and Drug Administration had accelerated its lengthy, frustrating process for approving a drug in order to speed up the birth of the cancer drug. Wall Street was coming on board as well, with ImClone shares peaking at $75.45 on December 6th.

Murmurs of dissent surfaced on occasion, especially within Bristol-Myers Squibb, the large drug company that had manufactured Erbitux, suggesting that FDA approval was not necessarily a slam-dunk. The murmurers were told to recede into their dark corners.

Sam Waksal figured he could go on his well-deserved Christmas vacation with nothing to worry about.

Then on Christmas Day, disaster struck. Someone from Bristol-Myers Squibb was on the phone with Sam's brother Harlan, ImClone's Chief Operating Officer, passing on the devastating news that the FDA intended to reject Erbitux three days hence.

With a trembling hand, Harlan Waksal picked up the phone to Sam, who, as he did every year, was vacationing at the Hotel St. Barth Isle de France in the Caribbean.

Harlan could hardly form any words.

If he felt a strong tie to ImClone, he knew that Sam's connection to the company was so much more personal and emotional. Harlan could not figure out how he would gather the strength to relay the bad news to his brother. He knew he had no choice.

Harlan dialed his brother's number, growing nervous with each second.

Someone picked up the phone at the other end. Harlan recognized Sam's voice. He also heard voices in the background—and, jarringly, he heard laughter. Sam must have been relaxing on the beach with his high-flying business friends.

And now Harlan had to puncture his balloon.

"Sam?"

"Harlan. Is that you? What's going on?"

Harlan paused a second. He wanted to make sure that Sam would hear every word he was about to utter.

"It's the FDA, Sam. It's terrible news. They're rejecting the drug."

Sam listened sadly to what his brother was saying. He went numb. But he had no choice but to pull himself together immediately. He could not let on to his friends that his world had just fallen apart. They would be all over him, asking him questions, wondering if they should sell their ImClone stock.

He dare not share this news—not just yet. He had to think of what to do next.

For a brief moment, he had trouble focusing on the present. He had grown accustomed to the good times: $60 million in 2000; another $70 million the following year—all from ImClone. And now this; how could this be happening?

A FULL-BLOWN NIGHTMARE

Someone asked Sam if everything was all right.

"Yes, nothing's wrong. But I have to leave...."

His friends looked puzzled. What was he talking about, leave the beach, leave the hotel, or was he talking about cutting short his vacation?

Quietly, reining in his emotions, he explained to his friends that he indeed had to rush away from the peace and quiet of the beach; he had some personal business that needed his attention. He was not more specific.

Was he coming back, his friends asked?

"I think so," was all he could say.

The next day, Sam Waksal flew back to New York on his leased jet. Displaying a calm exterior, he was not sure how he would endure the hours before the plane landed. He carried a secret that was sure to evolve into a full-blown nightmare. Only he knew how perilous his financial situation was now: He was in debt to the tune of $80 million, of which fully $65 million was on margin—secured by ImClone stock!

If the FDA did in fact reject Erbitux, his ImClone stock would plummet, and he would be in financial ruin. He arrived home that evening to his 5,000-square-foot mansion-like loft on Thompson Street in New York City's Soho district.

Certainly this was the worst moment of his career; but he could not dwell on that.

He felt a grave responsibility to his family: Not only would the FDA rejection of Erbitux ruin him, it would cause huge financial losses to family members and friends who also owned ImClone stock.

Setting aside that what he was about to do bore an ugly name—insider trading—he began calling around. He got a hold of family members, including his daughter, Aliza, and his parents; as well as friends.

"This is Sam. You better sell your ImClone shares."

When they asked him why, he begged off and simply repeated in as neutral a voice as he could summon, "Sell the shares."

Hanging up the phone, Waksal thought to himself of how far he had come in his life, of how he, the son of Holocaust survivors, had climbed New York's social ladder. That had always been his ambition; and he had achieved it, though it had been a long road for him, dating back to when he obtained a doctorate degree in immunobiology in 1974 from Ohio State.

Here he was now, owner of a $20 million art collection that adorned the walls of his loft; host of monthly salons for artists and writers; of lavish Christmas parties. He was indeed a bon vivant, with not a small reputation as a social climber, but he had loved his life; and now that life was crashing down on him.

He had been born in France after his parents had escaped from a displaced persons camp so that, as the family lore had it, he would not be born in Germany. His first languages were French and Yiddish.

He founded ImClone in 1984 with his brother, Harlan, a physician. They wanted to focus on infectious diseases, cancer, and diagnostics, make some products, get rich, and retire early, according to brother Harlan. It did not quite work that way, taking 10 years for ImClone to come up with what looked like a winning drug—Erbitux. At the height of the economic boom, ImClone shares had peaked at $84 in March 2000.

At one stage, Sam Waksal had dated a young woman named Alexis Stewart. She was eighteen years younger than he was. Their romance was brief, and certainly the most significant aspect of their fling occurred when Alexis introduced her boyfriend to her famous mother—Martha Stewart.

A friendship blossomed between Sam and Martha. They were closer in age to one another than Sam and Alexis; they moved in some of the same social circles; they were both business leaders. Often they spoke on the phone at 6:00 a.m. Becoming a sometime advisor to her, Waksal helped Martha Stewart negotiate her separation from Time Warner in 1997; it was that split that led to her taking her magazine, *Martha Stewart Living*, independent. The split was a key turning point and move upward in Stewart's career. Most likely as a gesture of appreciation to Waksal, she invested in ImClone.

A MINOR FINANCIAL EVENT

In what was surely a minor financial event for her at the time, given her wealth, in January 1999 Stewart purchased 2,500 shares of ImClone at $32 a share. Later that year she took her company, Martha Stewart Living Omnimedia, public, putting her net worth at over $1 billion.

A stock split at ImClone doubled her shares to 5,000; but her ImClone holdings amounted to only .03 of her entire net worth, the proverbial drop in the bucket.

Meanwhile Stewart and Waksal remained close friends. She designed the kitchen in his loft. In 2000, he invited her to be guest of honor at the annual gala at the New York Council for the Humanities, which he chaired.

In October 2001, Bristol-Meyers Squibb invested $1 billion in ImClone, offering $70 a share to all public stockholders. The offer to buy the company seemed attractive to Stewart, and she was willing to dump her shares despite her friendship with Waksal.

But she ran into a brick wall.

The offer was oversubscribed, allowing her to sell only 1,072 of her shares. She still had 3,928 ImClone shares in her portfolio.

Busy running her own company, she had little time or inclination to dwell on her portfolio; she was pleased to turn over responsibility for her stocks to professional stockbrokers, distributing what she owned to Bear Stearns, Morgan Stanley, and Merrill Lynch. At Merrill Lynch, a young man named Peter Bacanovic supervised her account.

Like Sam Waksal, Peter Bacanovic was at ease in New York's social whirl. His Greek-born mother was an anesthesiologist; his Serbian-born father a middle-level banker. Born in Manhattan, Peter grew up on the Upper East Side of Manhattan in the 70s and by the time he was 15, he was partying until 3:00 a.m. at Steve Rubell's infamous Studio 54. Peter's parents owned a home in the Hamptons and he summered there.

Finding himself in the company of the children of bankers and diplomats, he learned to speak French with a nearly perfect accent at the exclusive private school, Lycée Français. "Blind Ambition" was the nickname friends gave him. Even back then, people detected an aggressive, take-no-prisoners approach in him.

He graduated from Columbia University. While there, he became friendly with a woman named Alexis Stewart. In 1988, he graduated from New York University School of Business. He then worked briefly in Los Angeles in the mailroom at the William Morris Agency, a springboard for many great Hollywood careers. Those who knew Bacanovic then sensed that he wanted to become one of the great Hollywood moguls—blind ambition at work. Bacanovic, however, left Hollywood to become a banker in Switzerland for corporate raider Asher Edelman.

Then, in the early 1990s, he became director of business development at ImClone, where his boss was Sam Waksal. By that time, he had been friendly with Alexis Stewart for 20 years. It was Peter Bacanovic who introduced Alexis and her mother to Sam Waksal.

In his off hours, Bacanovic lived the life of a young socialite; at six feet, boyishly handsome, suave, and mysterious, he seemed built for such a life. Equally at home with dowagers and debutantes, he was just as comfortable with tycoons and philanthropists.

Few knew that he was an up-and-coming banker. He rarely talked about stocks on his evenings out. It was a matter of pride to him that he never spoke about his clients. Society columnists referred to him simply as "Peter Bacanovic."

At first glance, it must have seemed odd to some to see him on the arms of wealthy society women whose husbands stayed home rather than attend the various charity events of the New York social set. But it was not odd at all, for Bacanovic was gay. No one could accuse him of trying to steal someone's wife, certainly not if they knew the truth about him.

No THREAT TO HUSBANDS

Later, when it became known that Bacanovic had been a key player in the Martha Stewart legal drama, newspapers began to dissect him, avoiding any direct reference to his sexual preferences; but noting that he was a "walker," a young male escort of older (sometimes married) women. It was the newspapers' sneaky way of "outing" Bacanovic as a gay. The newspapers also hinted that he was trying to win over these women as business clients.

Bacanovic's defenders said that Bacanovic found the "walker" references offensive. "Hanging around, where the money was, was part of Peter Bacanovic's business," insisted Lou Colasuonno, the former editor-in-chief of the *New York Post* and *New York Daily News*, who handled Bacanovic's public relations during the Stewart legal case. "He wasn't a transparent guy who went there for the money."

Certainly, Colasuonno acknowledged, Bacanovic escorted "the Nan Kempners of the world because they had very similar interests in art and culture and charitable events and giving back to those communities. He often hung around in those kinds of society circles. The fact that he's gay was sitting there. So someone who is homophobic and really shallow would say he's a walker. What does that mean? I know what the term implies. That's the code word for oh, he's gay."

Still, if one were to stare enough times at Peter Bacanovic on the arms of these dowagers, it would not take too long to conjure up the image of him on the arm of another wealthy woman, a woman named Martha Stewart.

Peter Bacanovic lived in an Upper East Side townhouse where Holly Golightly dwelled in the popular film, *Breakfast at Tiffany's*. He enjoyed boasting that he lived in such a famous building; but he seemed to dread staying home in the evenings.

Eventually word got out that this quiet, polite, worldly, somewhat mystifying fellow had quite a day job. He was handling hundreds of millions of dollars in investments, and doing a superb job at it. In time, so many blue bloods sought him out that he began turning some away.

Until this point, no evidence existed that Bacanovic broke the law. He seemed an upstanding young man, quite ambitious, but that was no crime; he was eager to surround himself with A-league players, but such "networking" was perfectly above board.

His only "crime" was trying to please and win over as clients the women he was seen with at New York's society events.

None of his clients had as much visibility and celebrity as Martha Stewart. They had obviously begun their relationship on a positive note, for she was impressed enough to "hire" him as her stockbroker at Merrill Lynch. But their relationship was not always smooth. From e-mails that she sent to Bacanovic, it was clear that she found him a tad inexperienced.

In late 2000, she watched the stock market take a nosedive and meanwhile she heard nothing from the young Mr. Bacanovic.

"I think it's time for me to give my money to a professional money manager," she e-mailed Bacanovic, "who will watch it when I am too busy and will take a bit more care about overall market conditions and political and economic problems. We have just watched the slide and done nothing and I'm none too happy."

Here was the unpleasant Martha Stewart, her tone that of a petulant school teacher scolding an errant pupil. It was the tone of a woman who believed that she was right and Peter Bacanovic was wrong; it did not enter her mind that he might have some plausible explanation for what she deemed his failures. It was not part of her outlook that others might be right—and she might be wrong. It was a trait that would eventually cause her immense grief.

She could not have been serious about the threat to fire Peter Bacanovic. Had she wanted to fire him, had she been dissatisfied with him, she would not have written the threatening e-mail. It was not in her nature to be that indecisive. She must have wanted simply to frighten him into performing better for her.

AN IRASCIBLE WOMAN

Bacanovic did not need such pressure.

With an annual income in 2000 of $540,000, he found times were getting tougher: The following year, his income dropped to $350,000, and after the September 11th terrorist attacks, his financial prospects looked bleaker. He could do without lip from Martha Stewart; but there was not much he could do about her. "This is someone who gets irascible," he said resignedly.

No matter how irascible Stewart got, Bacanovic would put up with her. He idolized her. He loved having her as a client. It boosted his self-esteem that he could attract and hold such clients. He knew that he would do almost anything to keep her as a client. He was always looking for ways to please her.

All through the fall and early winter of 2001, Peter Bacanovic and Martha Stewart were watching the daily fluctuations of the ImClone shares. Bacanovic paid special attention to the increasing amount of insider selling of the shares and grew increasingly worried. He urged Stewart to sell her shares. He wanted her to be happy. He could not stand the idea that he would lose money for her.

Aware of Bacanovic's personal relationship with Sam Waksal—he had once been the broker's boss and was now a client—Stewart had every reason in the world to listen attentively to advice from Peter about her ImClone stock. Yet she chose to go deaf upon hearing what seemed to be good, solid advice.

She often listened carefully to the advice of experts—stockbrokers, lawyers, etc.—but she was Martha Stewart and she always had utmost confidence in her own judgment. As a former stockbroker herself, she may have thought that she knew better than Bacanovic. Or, perhaps she felt a sense of loyalty to her close friend, Sam Waksal, and did not want to appear to be abandoning a sinking ship. Whatever the case, she rejected Peter Bacanovic's advice. She did not know it at the time; but it was a fateful decision that took her down a path that led to her fall.

Meanwhile, Sam Waksal was determined to carry on normally despite the advance warning he had received that Erbitux was doomed. He offered no indication to friends or colleagues that his company might be entering a crisis.

On December 6, 2001, his annual Christmas party brought 200 guests together at his Soho loft. Among the guests were Mick Jagger and— Martha Stewart. Also on hand was an Italian millionaire, Jean Pigozzi, owner of a few thousand acres of Panamanian coastal land. Stewart and Waksal planned to attend Pigozzi's 50th birthday party soon after the New Year.

Few paid much attention, but ImClone shares slipped to $70 a share on December 14th. On that day, Waksal joined Stewart and 100 other guests at her Christmas party at the Manhattan restaurant, Chanterelle. Whether and how much Martha Stewart and Sam Waksal spoke on the phone in the next week became of enormous official interest later on; the most that anyone could find out, however, was that people using their phone numbers made brief phone calls to one another. Stewart's associates said the phone calls were innocent enough: She and Waksal were arranging to travel together to the Pigozzi birthday party in Panama.

RISING FEARS

During the afternoon of December 20th, the FDA notified ImClone executives that it had reached a decision on Erbitux that it would announce eight days later. Ordinarily such a heads-up would have been cause for joy; but by now, as the slippage in the ImClone shares suggested, fears rose that the FDA was about to scuttle the drug.

On the following day, four calls went back and forth between Stewart and Waksal's phones, including one in which Martha Stewart told Waksal where she could be reached between December 27th and January 2nd. On that same December 21st, according to Bacanovic, he printed out a worksheet describing the market value of Martha Stewart's stocks. He made some handwritten notations, which appeared in blue ink, in the margins of the worksheet.

On the next day, two more calls were made on phone lines belonging to Stewart or her associates and ImClone. Then on December 23rd, someone from ImClone made a 48-second phone call to Martha Stewart at her home.

Federal officials later intimated that Martha Stewart and/or her associates were staying in close touch with Waksal in order to monitor ImClone's stock and what was causing it to fall.

Close to Christmas, Bacanovic and Stewart held a review session of her portfolio. They again debated what to do about her 3,928 shares of ImClone, forming the same battle lines as in the past: He wanted her to sell; she preferred to hold on to the stock. Bacanovic concluded that Stewart simply did not want to admit that she had been wrong about a stock. Selling ImClone would be an admission that she had been wrong about it, and that she had believed it would climb forever.

There were two contradictory versions of the next part of the Stewart-Bacanovic conversation. One version came from Bacanovic; the other from Federal authorities.

According to Peter Bacanovic, he tried to get from Stewart a sense of when she *would be* willing to sell her ImClone stock. Bacanovic asked: "O.K., if you would not like to sell the stock now, how long are you going to wait before you sell this stock?"

> "We determined that $60 a share would be a suitable price, should it ever fall that low. Of course, she never thought it would."

Stewart grudgingly agreed, according to Bacanovic, to set a price at which she would sell. "We determined that $60 a share would be a suitable price, should it ever fall that low. Of course, she never thought it would."

According to Federal authorities, that latter part of the conversation did not exist.

With that understanding (again, according to Bacanovic), he and Martha Stewart took time off for Christmas.

Stewart and her close friend Mariana Pasternak boarded Martha's private jet for a holiday in Mexico. The two had been close friends for years, largely on the basis of their common background—common to a certain extent: Both had married professionals; both had homes in Westport, Connecticut; and, as it turned out, both had invested in a biotech firm called ImClone.

Borrowing a friend's house in Miami, Bacanovic went off for a week's vacation. He left the office in the hands of a relatively new, young assistant named Doug Faneuil.

Faneuil began his career on Wall Street at the bottom of the totem pole—catering to the administrative needs of his superior, Peter Bacanovic. He got coffee, took messages, every once in a while made a trade.

He was new to the Street, new to the brokerage business, wet behind the ears. He even called himself "Baby."

Other than their both being gay, the two men, Bacanovic and Faneuil, could not have been more different. Whereas Bacanovic was a man of the world, in his early forties, fluent in five languages, a social charmer, Doug Faneuil was 26 years old, baby-faced, and not known as socially adept (he played the part of a nerd in a senior class spoof of *West Side Story*). Faneuil came from an upper middle-class family; he grew up far from New York's social circles, born and raised in Newton, Massachusetts. Whereas Peter Bacanovic was learning French as a youngster, the teen-aged Doug was delivering pizza for Bill's Pizzeria in Newton.

Nor did Faneuil get an Ivy League education as Bacanovic did: After two years studying at Bennington College, he completed his undergraduate degree at Vassar College, where he majored in political science and art. Though he was an aspiring model, Faneuil had a practical bent and spent four years as a financial analyst for D.E. Shaw, a Manhattan-based hedge fund.

Hoping to get on with one of the large Wall Street firms, he obtained his series 7 license that enabled him to process stock trades. In the spring of 2001, six months or so before Bacanovic and Stewart were debating what to do about her ImClone shares, Peter hired Doug Faneuil as his assistant.

No Blind Ambition

No evidence existed to suggest that Faneuil possessed the same blind ambition that Peter Bacanovic did. Doug was simply a young gay man, without the kind of social skills that allowed Bacanovic to frequent the upper crust of society. He had his mind set on getting as good a job as he could on Wall Street. He certainly had nothing in his background to indicate that he might commit a serious crime. Nor did he have any motivation to bring down a business icon. He seemed simply to want to get by.

On the morning of Thursday, December 27, 2001, one of the major players in the unfolding drama was on vacation (Peter Bacanovic); another
(Sam Waksal) was still trying to avert financial disaster; a third (Doug
Faneuil) was innocently sitting in his Merrill Lynch office, a tad distraught
that he had not opted to take this coming Friday off rather than the previous one. The final player (Martha Stewart) was about to depart for her holiday. She could not know it when she began the day, but December 27th
would become the most dramatic day of her career. How she would act
that day had a great deal to do with the way she had grown up.

*She did not grow up in luxury. Embodying gracious living and ele-
gance, as she did as an adult, might have suggested that she came from
well-to-do circumstances.*

*But her parents, Martha and Edward Kostyra, were a schoolteacher
and a pharmaceutical salesman, respectively. Polish-Americans, both
were teachers at first; then her father became a pharmaceutical
salesman.*

*The great depression was coming to an end in 1941; yet times were
still difficult for Edward and Martha. He was having a hard time making ends meet as a high school gym teacher. They lived in a small
apartment in the industrial city of Jersey City, New Jersey, with their
young son Eric. On August 3rd of that year, their second child arrived, a
baby girl, whom they named Martha. She was, her mother remembered,
"a chubby plump little baby, 9 lbs. 1 oz."*

*Martha's father was ambitious and passed along that trait to Martha.
He taught her gardening when she was only three years old. It was said
of him that he planted 80 tomato plants when others were only planting six; and he competed with a neighbor to see who could grow the
longest beans. He corrected misspellings in letters and returned the letters to senders. He insisted that his children be self-sufficient. He
instilled in his children a feeling that they could go farther than others.
Martha's father was super-critical; Martha's mother, very demanding.*

*Another brother and then a sister joined Martha over the next five
years. In 1945, to help make room for their growing family, the Kostyras
moved to the tiny working-class suburb of Nutley, New Jersey, in a
modest house on Elm Place. In time they had six children.*

An Intimidating Figure

*With World War II over, Eddie Kostyra landed a job as a salesman for a
pharmaceutical firm. He traveled around the state but managed to find*

time to introduce his family to musical instruments and the joys of gardening. Martha was quite close to her father, and he inspired her to be quite energetic. But he was an intimidating figure; he ruled the house with an iron fist. Known for his sternness, he gave Martha and the other children chores that they had to do before they could go out to play.

The Kostyra children learned all sorts of things by standing at their father's side. Martha learned how to iron, cook, can, and sew, and how to hold tools for her father, as he did chores around the home. "We all stood there like nurses at an operation and we just stood there until Dad said hand me the Philips head screwdriver, and we had to know what a Philips head screwdriver was."

Later, Stewart critics portrayed her childhood in less than idyllic terms: Her father, in reality, was a hard-drinking bully, her mother cold and disengaged. With five siblings competing for parental attention, Martha, said her critics, possessed a deep insecurity coupled with bitterness and anger.

Martha's mother, known as Big Martha, exhibited a rigidity that led her daughter to impose strict discipline on herself. Big Martha ran the house according to a fixed schedule: Monday was washday, Tuesday ironing day, etc.

With little money available, Martha's parents grew their own vegetables and canned them. Big Martha was also an excellent seamstress. She made most of her daughter Martha's clothes. As the oldest daughter, Martha was expected to learn numerous skills. Standards were high: She had to learn these skills right away—hence, her life-long striving for perfection.

Big Martha believed that she had given her daughter Martha that urge. She "got it from me because I used to be a perfectionist when it came to washing windows and making sure everything was clean and dusted and waxed, and so maybe I'm to blame."

When Larry King asked the younger Martha what she learned from her mother, she could not bring herself to say that she had learned to be a perfectionist or to be disciplined—that might sound too negative; so she said, "Strength, you know, persistence, open mindedness."

These were the character traits that were part and parcel of Martha Stewart's make-up on that fateful December 27th. She was disciplined. She was a perfectionist. She was ambitious. She knew how to take charge. She knew how to do a great many things at once. She believed that her way was the right way.

During that morning Sam Waksal and another member of his family called Doug Faneuil to insist that he sell their ImClone shares.

Sam Waksal had made clear that all of his ImClone stock at Merrill Lynch should be sold, some 79,797 shares, then worth $4.9 million. His written request to Merrill Lynch was marked "Urgent" "Immediate action required"; the transaction had to take place that morning, he wrote.

There was also a request that Aliza Waksal's 39,472 ImClone shares be sold.

At 9:48 a.m., Faneuil put through the Aliza Waksal request.

Selling her shares at $62.64 per share, he obtained $2,472,837 for her in cash.

By 10:00 a.m., Faneuil was on the phone to Peter Bacanovic alerting him that Sam Waksal was trying to dump all of his Merrill Lynch ImClone shares, valued at $7.3 million.

Within minutes of hearing from Faneuil, Bacanovic called Martha Stewart's office.

In calling her to tell her what the Waksals were doing, he was violating fundamental rules at Merrill Lynch. But he wanted to please Martha Stewart and that made him, not her, the villain in this narrative.

Reaching her office, he was told she was in transit and thus not available.

Indeed, it was getaway day for Martha Stewart, two days after Christmas, time for her vacation to begin.

At 9:17 a.m., her private plane took off from a small airport near her Turkey Hill estate in Connecticut for Cabo San Lucas, Mexico. There she would stay at the highly exclusive Las Ventanas resort where a junior suite started at $585 a night. Accompanying her was Mariana Pasternak, her real-estate broker friend from Westport. One writer described her as a "fifty-something well-preserved beauty with high Slavic cheekbones and a perhaps Hungarian accent." Also along was Kevin Sharkey, the decorating editor of *Martha Stewart Living*, and a frequent traveling companion of Stewart's.

Once on board, Stewart served caviar, foie gras, Melba toast, and champagne. She then took up work on a book she planned to write to be called *Homekeeping*, a complete guide to maintenance and home décor.

Unable to reach Martha Stewart, at 10:04 a.m., Peter Bacanovic left a ten-word message for her with her assistant, Ann Armstrong. Those ten words became the most famous phrase in the Stewart legal case.

"Peter Bacanovic thinks ImClone is going to start trading downward."

At that moment, 10:04 a.m., the ImClone stock had dropped to $61.53. Bacanovic ordered Faneuil to inform Martha Stewart about the Waksal stock transaction when she returned the call.

TURNING POINT

In retrospect, it was possible to look back upon certain moments in the Stewart legal case and point to them as turning points. Had one of the protagonists acted differently, more wisely, more sensibly, more ethically—take your choice—it was perfectly plausible to argue that no case would have existed. This was one such moment.

Peter Bacanovic should have known better than to have reached out to Martha Stewart at that precise moment. He had to know—or at least he should have known—that he was conveying inside information to her. For Bacanovic had just learned from Faneuil that Sam Waksal and his family were dumping their own ImClone shares.

So much was made of what Martha Stewart did and did not do in getting herself into such serious legal trouble. What was often overlooked was that on that day, December 27th, she did not initiate the chain of events that led to her fall; nor did she encourage anyone else to commit crimes. And certainly had Peter Bacanovic not instructed Doug Faneuil to contact her on that day, she would have passed the day on vacation uneventfully, keeping clear of harm's way.

Stewart had not asked for the controversial information that Sam Waksal and his family were selling their ImClone stock. But Bacanovic was so infatuated with Martha Stewart, with having her as a client, that he was prepared to do almost anything to make her happy. He was also frightened of her. After all, she had threatened to fire him in that earlier e-mail. Saving her money was one big way of keeping her happy.

It was for all these reasons that it was fair to call what Martha Stewart did—and soon we will see what she did—a minor mistake.

In case any doubt existed about the nefarious Mr. Bacanovic, there was this very damaging exchange between Faneuil and Peter. Faneuil had been asking Bacanovic whether it had been right to get Stewart on the phone.

"Are you sure that's okay? Can I do that?"
"It's not a matter of okay," his boss replied. "Just do it."

"Are you sure that's okay? Can I do that?"

Faneuil waited for the answer nervously.

"It's not a matter of okay," his boss replied. "Just do it."

At 11:07 a.m., ImClone's stock hit $60 a share for the first time.

More than two hours later, Bacanovic sent an e-mail to Faneuil stating: "Subject: IMCL/ Has news come out yet? Let me know."

Three minutes later, at 1:21 p.m., Faneuil responded: "Nothing [sic] yet. I'll let you know. No call from Martha either."

That was because Stewart was still on a plane flying from Connecticut to her vacation spot.

Five minutes after Faneuil's e-mail to Bacanovic, her plane landed in San Antonio, Texas.

At 1:26 p.m., she alighted and stretched after the long flight from Connecticut.

Meanwhile, Mariana Pasternak and Kevin Sharkey walked off to a nearby airport lounge where Pasternak could hear Stewart on the phone speaking in what she called "raised tones"; she had no idea to whom she was speaking or what was being said.

Stewart turned on her cell phone.

She did not have to use the cell at all; she was, after all, on vacation. Still she placed a call to Ann Armstrong to check her messages.

Among the messages Ann Armstrong conveyed to Stewart was the one from Peter Bacanovic.

Nothing in that message conveyed a sense of urgency. To Martha Stewart, it was just one of a number of phone calls that required a reply. She did not even ask Armstrong to put her through to Bacanovic first. Stewart made one other call before asking Armstrong for Bacanovic.

A male voice came on the line. Stewart assumed she was talking to Bacanovic. She was not. She was talking to Doug Faneuil.

All around her there was the usual commotion of a busy airport. Planes were taking off and landing nearby. It was windy and noisy, not the ideal spot from which to make a cell phone call. When Stewart reported to federal authorities later that she believed she was talking to Bacanovic, the feds called that a lie.

That was putting a very sinister construction on what could have been a perfectly natural mistake, given the noise, the wind, just the general din swirling around the tarmac.

Certainly when she picked up the phone, Stewart could not have known it, but she was about to begin the most controversial telephone call of her career. The call lasted 11 minutes.

Stewart asked the person she thought was Bacanovic what was happening with ImClone.

She was told that the price had fallen below $60 a share.

How much ImClone stock was being traded, she asked?

The volume was heavy, came the reply.

That turned out to be an understatement. While 1.5 million shares of ImClone had been traded the previous day, on December 27th the volume was up to nearly 8 million shares, a wave of trading that could only be described as panic selling.

Faneuil told Martha Stewart that Peter Bacanovic wanted her to know that Sam Waksal was selling his ImClone shares.

ANOTHER VILLAIN

At this juncture, Faneuil, the innocent-looking baby-faced kid who just wanted to get by, had broken a fundamental rule at Merrill just as his boss had: He had relayed information to one client about another. Relaying that information made him more of a villain in this piece than Martha Stewart.

Was Sam Waksal selling all of his shares, she asked?

All of them, Faneuil told her.

Upon hearing that, Stewart directed Faneuil to put through the sale of her 3,928 ImClone shares at an average price of $58.43 of ImClone. (This came to $228,000.)

Faneuil then asked Stewart if he should e-mail Heidi DeLuca, Stewart's secretary/accountant, about their exchange.

"Absolutely not!" she replied angrily.

Her voice raised an octave. "You are never allowed to discuss my (personal finances) with anyone! Under any circumstances!"

This was Martha Stewart's own moment of truth.

Just as Peter Bacanovic and Doug Faneuil did not have to alert her that Waksal was selling his shares, she did not have to sell her shares upon hearing about the Waksal stock sale.

She could have done nothing.

She could have simply said, "Well, that's certainly interesting," and given no orders to sell her own shares.

Had she really been on the ball, she might have even said to herself, "Much as I'd like to sell the stock now, it will certainly look bad if I do. People will say I acted on inside information. I better wait."

But she said none of this. Instead, she behaved as if whatever she did, no harm would come to her. In her version of reality, it was perfectly acceptable to sell her stock on the basis of a stock tip that was probably obtained through insider information. After all, she was Martha Stewart. She could do no wrong.

As a former stockbroker and as the head of a publicly-traded company, she knew what insider trading was all about; and however hard it was to define the crime, Martha Stewart should have known that in selling her shares so close to learning that Sam Waksal was selling his, she could be implicating herself in a serious crime.

She should have known better.

Believing that she was untouchable, she was impelled by one of her worst traits—greed.

"She did it," said Lisa Marsh, the reporter for the *New York Post* who covered her during Stewart's legal case, "because she's a killer. She's an aggressive person who if she sees opportunity to make a buck, she'll do it. But she knows the rules, and so she should have known it was improper. She probably did know but saw opportunity to make a quick buck."

But it was more than greed that impelled her to order the stock sale that day. It was hubris as well, a belief that she was above it all, above society's rules that were meant for others—but not for her. She felt free to do whatever she liked. "She had principles," said one Stewart associate, "but she had delusional principles." Meaning, she understood when she was doing something inappropriate; but she deluded herself into believing that she would get away with it. That was all part of her version of reality.

It was her greed, her hubris, and her delusional principles that led her to believe that she had done nothing wrong.

Still, she had committed nothing more egregious than a minor mistake. She had taken the phone call from Doug Faneuil under duress. She was not even sure to whom she was speaking. Conditions on the tarmac were not ideal for cell phone conversation. She was headed for her vacation. She had, by agreeing to sell her shares, not hurt a soul. At worst, it was a minor offense.

It was now that the tale turned Kafkaesque.

For Martha Stewart became the object of a federal investigation. She was indicted for federal crimes. She was tried and convicted. She was sentenced to jail. She spent five months behind bars. Her company suffered dramatic losses. She lost hundreds of millions of dollars when her company's stock faltered. Her once-vaunted reputation was shattered perhaps beyond repair.

Martha Stewart understood that something strange was going on that afternoon of December 27th. She had the presence of mind to get in touch with the one man who might shed some light on what was going on with the ImClone stock.

Immediately after telling Doug Faneuil to sell her ImClone shares, Stewart called Sam Waksal at ImClone. She wanted to get a direct report from him. Instead, she got Emily Perret, Sam's secretary.

Stewart demanded to know what was going on with ImClone. She insisted that Emily locate Waksal at once. (Later, Emily Perret described Martha as "hurried and harsh and direct.")

Stewart, according to Perret, seemed furious with Waksal; she was determined not to be screwed out of her $45,000.

She left a message for Sam: "Something's going on with ImClone, and I want to know what it is."

> "Something's going on with ImClone, and I want to know what it is."

Returning to her plane in San Antonio, Stewart told Mariana Pasternak that she had just sold her ImClone shares and that the Waksals were trying to sell theirs. That was the kind of world Martha Stewart inhabited. She committed crimes and then told her friends. She truly believed that she was beyond reach.

Much of the subsequent investigation into whether Martha Stewart had acted illegally centered on her insistence that she had a preexisting arrangement with Peter Bacanovic to sell her ImClone stock if it fell to $60 a share.

Stewart argued that she had such an agreement—and Peter Bacanovic corroborated her version. As evidence of the agreement, he produced a copy of a Merrill Lynch summary of Martha Stewart's portfolio where he had scribbled "60" next to ImClone.

Further evidence of such an agreement came from Martha Stewart's business manager, Heidi DeLuca, who asserted that she had talked with Peter Bacanovic about his plan to sell the Stewart ImClone stock at $60 a share.

STOP-LOSS ORDER

But the absence of a formal, written stop-loss order raised serious doubts about the Stewart/Bacanovic version. "If there had been a stop-loss order," said Marvin Pickholz, Doug Faneuil's attorney, "it would have been in the Merrill system and it would have been triggered." A stop-loss order permitted brokerage customers to sell a stock automatically once it hit a predetermined level.

Martha Stewart tried to explain, lamely at best, that, while she knew that she could have availed herself of a stop-loss order, she preferred not to turn decision-making over to a computer program. She wanted to be able to make her own judgments about each stock.

Still, whether or not she had an arrangement with Peter Bacanovic to sell her ImClone shares at $60, she had no proof of such an arrangement. She should have understood that the moment she presented that version of the truth—namely, that there was such an agreement—without any real evidence confirming the agreement, she was putting herself into legal trouble.

Arriving in Mexico, Stewart phoned her daughter, Alexis, noting that she had sold her ImClone shares. Mother and daughter speculated about whether Waksal would be angry with Martha for dumping her stock. But that seemed unlikely since it had been Sam Waksal's own sale that had led Martha Stewart to sell her stock. If he were selling his shares, he couldn't be upset with Stewart for selling hers.

That afternoon, a Merrill Lynch biotechnology analyst issued an alert over the squawk box to the firm's 15,000 brokers: Selling pressure on the ImClone stock was acute; an FDA decision was looming; the stock seemed weak.

When the formal notification came that the Food and Drug Administration was turning down Erbitux, it was almost anti-climactic. So much had happened in the previous 24 hours because word had gotten around that the FDA was saying no. Still, the official news, when it came, was shocking.

The fax arrived at ImClone at 2:55 p.m. on December 28th.

The FDA said simply that it could not approve ImClone's application for Erbitux. ImClone waited for the stock market to close that day before making the disappointing announcement. In the wake of the announcement, the stock drifted downward. Martha Stewart's sale a day earlier meant that she had saved a loss of $45,673.

On that same day, Martha Stewart and Mariana Pasternak were talking in their suite in Mexico.

"How's Sam [Waksal]?" Pasternak asked.

"He's disappeared again," Stewart replied. He had not answered her phone call.

Stewart then noted that Sam Waksal was selling or trying to sell his stock. "His stock is going down and I sold mine."

Pasternak sat there bemused, wondering where the conversation was leading.

Then Stewart added, almost parenthetically: "Isn't it nice to have brokers who tell you those things?"

It may have been nice. But it smacked of insider trading.

The most damaging aspect of Stewart's gratuitous remark was the fact that she made it at all. For, if as she later insisted, she and Peter Bacanovic indeed had agreed to sell her ImClone shares if and when the stock reached $60 a share, she had no reason to make the "Isn't it nice" comment.

Why would she feel the need to praise her broker for telling her "these things" (i.e., that Waksal was selling his shares), when she had an agreement in place to sell at $60 a share?

The only possible explanation for Stewart's making the comment to Pasternak is that she (Stewart) simply did not believe anything bad would come of her instructing Doug Faneuil to sell her shares.

She did not construe what she had done as insider trading; and she could not have imagined that anyone else would have either. She simply had a stockbroker who was on the ball—not a crime in her book.

Martha Stewart spent several days in Mexico. She then went to the Pigozzi birthday party in Panama. Sam Waksal arrived a day later with Martha Stewart asking him: "Where the hell have you been? You haven't talked to me since my party."

December 31st was the first day of stock trading after ImClone revealed that the FDA had rejected its application for Erbitux. On that day, the company's stock took a nosedive, dropping 18%, from $55.25 to $45.39 a share.

A man named Brian Schimpfhauser served as an internal auditor at Merrill Lynch. It was his job to monitor the firm's trades to make sure that none of them bore the suspicious look of insider trading. Certainly if someone was selling shares in a company that was about to be greeted with bad news, Schimpfhauser would find that suspicious.

Not surprisingly, in light of the FDA's decision over Erbitux, the Waksals' sales drew the auditor's attention. He asked to talk with Doug Faneuil and Peter Bacanovic.

When on December 31st Doug Faneuil heard that Schimpfhauser was looking for him, he got Bacanovic on the phone, eager for advice on what to say to the Merrill Lynch officer. Faneuil assumed that Schimpfhauser would want to ask him about the Martha Stewart trade.

THAT'S THE REASON

"Tax-loss selling!" Bacanovic screamed at him. "That's what you tell them! That's Martha's reason for selling, tax-loss!" Peter Bacanovic seemed beside himself with anger.

Faneuil was bewildered.

He could not understand why Bacanovic would want him to use tax-loss selling to explain the Stewart sale. To Bacanovic, Faneuil tried to point out that the tax-loss selling explanation was impossible since

Martha Stewart had sold her ImClone shares at a gain. No one would want to take large gains the last day of the year, only losses.

But Bacanovic would hardly let him speak.

That same day the Merrill Lynch internal auditor grilled Peter Bacanovic about the odd timing of the ImClone stock sales vis-à-vis the FDA rejection.

Had he known that ImClone was about to be hit with disastrous news?

Bacanovic stuck to the tax-loss version to explain the sale, leaving Brian Schimpfhauser unsatisfied. All the internal auditor could do was to report the suspicious stock activity to the Securities and Exchange Commission, which then began its own investigation.

Eventually Bacanovic told federal authorities that he and Martha Stewart had a preexisting agreement to sell the ImClone stock if it dipped to $60, which it had done on the day of her stock sale. The agreement, he noted, was verbal. There was nothing in Merrill Lynch's computer system to back up such a claim.

But on December 31st, he uttered not a word of such an agreement.

PART

II

I DID NOTHING WRONG

CHAPTER

3

THE PROBE BEGINS

With the New Year, the wheels of justice began to turn.

The Securities and Exchange Commission, the FBI, and the U.S. Attorney's Office for the Southern District of New York were investigating all of those bizarre coincidences that surrounded the trading of ImClone shares just prior to the FDA's rejection of Erbitux.

In the early part of the investigation, Martha Stewart had little to worry about. The Government had nothing more than a handful of coincidences and no real evidence of insider trading—only suspicions.

At first, however, the coincidences did seem odd.

Those who were investigating had more questions than answers.

In a relatively short time, the investigators put part of the puzzle together, but not all of it.

They discovered quickly enough that Peter Bacanovic, as the broker to both Sam Waksal and Martha Stewart, was key to all these transactions; and what he did and said during the crucial few days in December was crucial to their probe.

As broker to both Waksal and Stewart, Bacanovic knew that Waksal was watching nervously to find out what the FDA would do with Erbitux. He also knew that Waksal's shares—as well as those of Stewart—were vulnerable if the FDA turned down Erbitux.

What the investigators did not know at that point—and this would be the heart of their case, if there was one—was whether Bacanovic had tipped anyone off that Waksal was selling his shares. Any owner of ImClone shares, including Martha Stewart, would find it enormously useful to know that Waksal was selling his company stock.

A Bacanovic tip-off to any of these ImClone shareowners had at least the surface appearance of insider trading.

Though the definition of insider trading was at best murky, the SEC was on the look-out for any "big fish" who engaged in that crime—if only to make an example of that person.

Make no mistake about it.

The federal government wanted to get someone like Martha Stewart. No official would ever admit to singling out a celebrity, to nailing an icon, but the feds certainly had strong motivation to go after Stewart. It was a difficult time for the white-collar prosecutors. Corporate scandal seemed to be spreading through the land; but indictments and prosecutions were slow to come.

Some feminists had a field day arguing that the feds had picked on Stewart because she was a woman. But they missed a key point. Sure she was a woman, a successful businesswoman at that. But she was singled out, pointed out Elaine Lafferty, the editor-in-chief of *Ms. Magazine* at the time of Martha Stewart's legal difficulties, because of the kind of woman she was. She was, quite simply, unlikable. "Anywhere in the law it's always easier and more pleasant for the prosecution to have an unlikable defendant, or an unlikable target."

WOMEN IN POWER

Lafferty argued that there is an "underlying discomfort and hostility toward women" in positions of power. Society is very conflicted in what we want women to be.... Who more than Martha Stewart personifies that conflict? We can revile, but sort of admire, Donald Trump for saying (as he does in his show, *The Apprentice*) "You're fired." "We admire that kind of strength in CEOs or male executives. But the percentage of people who admire that behavior in any kind of woman is dramatically less."

To Stewart's staunchest supporters, what the government was doing was harassment, pure and simple. Andrew Ritchie, one of the main contributors to the SaveMartha.com site and a Canadian journalist, noted that: "It was a personal stock sale and had nothing to do with her employees or her company at all. And to go after her for lying about a crime she was not charged with (insider trading) seemed like persecution to me."

As part of the government's pursuit, the SEC wanted to know whether Peter Bacanovic had told whales or guppies that Sam Waksal and his family were selling their ImClone shares. The guppies could be thrown back in the sea; the whales were worth pursuing. If the SEC pursued the whales, it showed all others how seriously they regarded the crime of insider trading.

As it probed who sold ImClone shares just prior to the FDA's decision against Erbitux, one name stood out to the SEC.

Martha Stewart.

She was a definite whale. What a catch she would make! But before they could prosecute her, they had to know the answers to some vital questions.

WHY AROUSE SUSPICION?

First of all, who was her stockbroker?

Next, did her stockbroker conduct business with anyone who knew that the FDA was about to drop a bombshell on ImClone?

Then, why would Martha Stewart, a former stockbroker and member of the New York Stock Exchange, sell her shares in ImClone on the eve of a negative FDA decision about the biotech firm?

It did not take the feds long to provide answers to the first two questions (her stockbroker was Peter Bacanovic, who also handled Sam Waksal's Merrill Lynch account); but the feds could not figure out why Stewart would knowingly sell her shares so close to the FDA decision.

The whole affair had the look and feel of insider trading.

But was it really insider trading?

What Martha Stewart did was suspect. "Nobody sells the day before an announcement takes place unless they have inside information," said securities attorney Jake Zamansky. "There are just not that many coincidences like that."

Still, the consensus among legal specialists was that it was not insider trading, which they defined as trading stock on material non-public information.

There was no evidence that Faneuil told Stewart the reason for Waksal's selling; i.e., that the FDA was about to act negatively on Erbitux. That would have constituted insider information for it would have shown that Waksal was trading on the basis of insider knowledge. So no real insider information had been conveyed to Stewart; hence, she could not have known that she had been given insider information.

The feds learned that calls were in fact made during the period from December 20 to 23 between Martha Stewart and ImClone's phones. Here, so it seemed, was actual evidence that Martha Stewart and Sam Waksal were talking to one another while Stewart's ImClone stock was sliding.

If they did talk to one another—and there was no direct evidence that either of them were involved in any of these phone calls (it might have been their staffs), it certainly suggested that Stewart was getting some insider advice on what to do with her ImClone shares. But even these phone calls would not have been enough to prove insider trading.

Sam Waksal, the CEO of ImClone, was found guilty of insider trading for selling his stock after learning that the FDA was about to deny approval of Erbitux—and before the FDA decision was publicly announced. He received a seven-year jail sentence for that crime.

NOT ENOUGH EVIDENCE

As long as the feds could not prove that Stewart spoke with Waksal, the key figure in whatever insider trading may have occurred, on or just before December 27th, they would have a hard time hanging an insider trading charge on her. As noted earlier, she did try to reach him on that day, but could not, and he never returned her phone call.

In those early days of the investigation, the cards all seemed to be in Martha Stewart's hands. For the government to prove that she had engaged in insider trading seemed nearly impossible.

Sure, it seemed too much of a coincidence that she had sold her shares on the eve of the negative Erbitux decision; but strictly speaking that coincidence did not equate with insider trading.

The problem for Stewart, however, was that a federal investigation into the December 27th ImClone stock dealings was going forward.

The feds turned first to Doug Faneuil, interviewing him by phone on January 3, 2002. Once he had been grilled, he contacted Peter Bacanovic to see if he could find out why the SEC was interested in Martha Stewart's stock sale.

Bacanovic cut him off.

"Listen, nothing happened, there's nothing wrong with the sale. This is how it happened, this is how it was, and it's the truth."

"I've spoken to Martha, and everyone's telling the same story. We're all on the same page. It was a stop-loss order at $60, okay? Okay?"

Faneuil would eventually insist that Bacanovic and Stewart had fabricated the $60-a-share agreement; Bacanovic's failure

> *"I've spoken to Martha, and everyone's telling the same story. We're all on the same page."*

to let Faneuil know of the arrangement on the eve of his Miami vacation suggested Faneuil was telling the truth.

The feds then turned to Peter Bacanovic, interviewing him on the phone on January 8th.

He told them that Martha Stewart told him on December 20, 2001 that she had decided to sell her ImClone shares if they fell to $60 per share. He made his pitch to Stewart that she should sell her remaining shares.

"How low does this go before you are prepared to part with this?" he asked, according to his SEC testimony.

"I don't know," he said Stewart responded.

"How about 60 dollars a share?" Bacanovic countered.

"Yes, sure," Stewart said.

In one sense, the entire legal case revolved around the question of whether that conversation actually took place or if Stewart and Bacanovic made it up.

Had there been such an agreement, why was there not one piece of reliable evidence to support its existence?

The evidence that Stewart and Bacanovic fabricated the whole affair is overwhelming: First there were the phone calls back and forth between the two of them: If they were fabricating the $60 a share tale, it certainly was in the interest of Bacanovic and Stewart to coordinate what they were saying to the feds. On January 16th, when the two met for breakfast, the feds believe they discussed just that.

Further evidence existed that Stewart and Bacanovic had created the agreement out of whole cloth: Faneuil had no knowledge of any agreement, and he would have known; indeed he should have known. Further, Faneuil pointed to conversations he held with Bacanovic in which the latter all but acknowledged that he had made up the $60-a-share agreement.

From their conversations with Doug Faneuil and Peter Bacanovic, the feds concluded that they must talk directly with Martha Stewart. They wanted to know all sorts of things from her, but especially whether she knew that the FDA announcement on Erbitux was in the offing when she sold her ImClone shares.

Once she got word that the feds wanted to talk with her, Stewart hired a criminal defense attorney. She chose a firm with which she already had a relationship—one of the most prestigious securities firms in New York: Wachtell, Lipton, Rosen & Katz. Though smaller than many of the better-known law firms, Wachtell, Lipton, Rosen & Katz had the highest profits per partner of any American law firm, averaging over $3 million annually.

INTERVIEWING MARTHA STEWART

Handling Stewart's legal case for Wachtell, Lipton, Rosen & Katz was John Savarese, typical, according to legal analyst Jeffrey Toobin, of the "brilliant and arrogant" attorneys of that law firm. Handsome, socially prominent, a former prosecutor, he helped to convict the bosses of New York's five Mafia families in 1986.

On January 25th, the assistant U.S. Attorney in charge of the Waksal probe, Michael Schacter, contacted Savarese, formally asking for the Stewart interview.

All was not bleak for Martha Stewart; she still had choices.

Her first choice was whether to talk to the feds.

Most attorneys automatically advised their clients not to talk to the authorities, innocent or guilty, even if it meant invoking the Fifth Amendment. No good could come of it. It became all too easy for the prosecutors to find inconsistencies in the person's statements or evidence that was at odds with the person's statements. Had Stewart remained silent, many of her loyal fans might have stood behind her; but she would have had to invoke the Fifth Amendment, and that was treading on dangerous ground.

The interview was set for February 4, 2002.

Stewart was not asked to testify under oath (though Peter Bacanovic was). Normally it was regarded as a good sign for the target of the probe if the government did not want to talk with that person under oath. It suggested a degree of informality and a lower level of interest on the feds' part. Still, few analysts understood the feds' motivation in not forcing Stewart to testify under oath.

Undoubtedly, the feds wanted to lull Stewart into a false sense of security, hoping to give her the impression that the interview would in fact be a walk in the park for her. In short, they wanted her not to take the whole thing seriously. In that way, she might trip herself up in her testimony. They were using guile, something they felt they needed if they were going to nail Martha Stewart.

The media engaged in a shocking amount of misreporting surrounding Stewart's February 4th appearance, simply assuming that Stewart had some choice in whether to talk with the feds.

In fact, she did not. But the media decided that Stewart not only had a choice; but in deciding to talk to the feds, she had made a colossal mistake.

What the media failed to take into account was how damaging it would have been for Stewart to avoid talking to the feds by invoking the Fifth Amendment.

Some in the media even argued that she should not have gone to the February 4th interview, ignoring the likelihood that her non-appearance would surely have trigged a subpoena enforced by U.S. Marshals. Stewart knew better than to duck the feds, not a great way to begin a relationship with them. However grudgingly, most of those summoned to meet with the feds do so. Stewart, in contrast, welcomed the opportunity to come to the session.

Her choice—and her only choice—was whether to invoke the Fifth Amendment or not.

KEEP YOUR MOUTH SHUT

Some top attorneys tried to suggest that Stewart should not have talked to the feds. Among them was Robert Shapiro, the lawyer who successfully defended O.J. Simpson against murder charges. He wrote that:

> *"...and my first instruction to all of them was the same: 'Keep your mouth shut!'"*

'"...long before she was charged with anything, there was her incomprehensible willingness to talk to federal investigators. I have represented clients in dozens of high-profile white-collar criminal cases...and my first instruction to all of them was the same: 'Keep your mouth shut!'"'

"If the SEC wants to talk with someone, they can talk to your lawyers.... Presumably, Ms. Stewart believed she would be able to offer the prosecutors a convincingly innocent explanation of the suspect stock sale. She and her lawyers should have known better."

But Shapiro seems to skip over the damage that would have been done to Stewart had she refused to talk to the feds by invoking the Fifth Amendment.

Enormous risks existed if the CEO of a publicly traded company, as Martha Stewart was, chose to invoke the Fifth.

Her company's board and external auditors, who would have to be apprised of her refusal to talk, might have felt forced to suspend her indefinitely. Far worse, she would surely be admitting to some kind of wrongdoing; the feds assumed that no one took the Fifth without having something to hide.

"We all learn in the third grade that the Fifth Amendment is this wonderful thing protecting our freedom," said one of Stewart's attorneys, "but in the real world, the practical world, it's a Hobson's choice in the extreme. The Government will read invoking the Fifth as a negative. It incentivizes them to say there must be something here that we've got to go after."

Finally, the Securities and Exchange Commission could and surely would use someone's refusal to talk against the person in any civil enforcement proceeding.

Bottom line: Martha Stewart had no choice but to go to the meeting with the federal authorities and, once there, to respond to their questions. Said Marvin Pickholz, attorney for Doug Faneuil, "The reality is that government simply can't function and certainly can't be perceived as being even-handed if people come in and, exercising their constitutional right, don't want to discuss their affairs, don't tell the truth—I think it would probably send a wrong message if we had such a system. We either enforce the law or we don't."

The media assumed—again incorrectly—that Stewart went to the February 4th meeting blind to the trap the federal government was setting for her. But the media failed to appreciate that Stewart desperately wanted to talk to the feds.

To her, the prosecutors were a bunch of young, just-out-of-law-school types who might have been zealous, but were most likely to be overcome with awe at just being in the same room with her. She felt she could handle these "kids." They could not be serious about their probe into her stock sale. If they did not know of her fame and her talents, their mothers surely did, and she was sure some of their mothers' enthusiasm for her would rub off on them.

As long as this investigation into her affairs proceeded, she intended to trivialize it, to attempt to marginalize it. She would simply not take it seriously, and she was sure in time it would go away. She would show her contempt for these "kids" by ignoring them; she would certainly not bring up the probe in the press; she would not discuss the matter with any so-called friends who might then leak the existence of the probe to the press. And she would work behind the scenes to make sure that what she told the feds matched the stories of others to whom they would talk.

Because she could not ignore the February 4th encounter, she decided that she would simply go and mesmerize them—and, like some bad nightmare, she and they would wake up and it would all be over. After all, she was one of America's great communicators. Lanny Davis, the one-time White House counsel to President Bill Clinton, and at one stage a Martha Stewart adviser, had once told her that she was one of the two greatest communicators in America in the modern era; the other had been Ronald Reagan. That was all she had to do on February 4th— communicate. She was sure she could charm the socks off the feds.

Stewart was not overly concerned with the questions the feds might ask her. She assumed, incorrectly, that she would be asked only if she had any contact with Sam Waksal prior to her sale of ImClone stock. She thought she was safe because she knew she had not had contact with him. Once the feds heard that, she assumed they would drop their probe into her stock sale. That was wishful thinking on her part.

Stewart's strategy might have been to make light of the whole affair, but the feds took their probe quite seriously. Nailing her was a top priority. What to her was admirable stubbornness came off as unadulterated arrogance to the feds. What to Stewart was the conviction that she could have done no wrong looked to the feds like the worst kind of snobbish elitism. Rather than deflate their passions, Stewart's belittling of the fed's probe turned the "kids" into very mature attack dogs.

Rather than focusing on the question of whether Martha Stewart should have talked to the feds, a specious issue at best, as noted earlier, the media should have asked the more relevant question: Why did she not seek a deal with the feds at this juncture?

Sure, the feds wanted to hang her out to dry and a public trial would suit them just fine. In fact, their mouths were beginning to water at the thought. But they knew the odds were that her lawyers would be pushing for a quick plea bargain, and under the right conditions they would go for that. After all, getting Martha Stewart to acknowledge that she had committed a crime this early in the game would have counted as a magnificent triumph. It would have also had the virtue of saving months and months of arduous trial preparation and the endurance of the trial itself.

Thus, if Stewart wanted to avoid an indictment and a trial, she had an exit strategy available to her. But she would have to compromise; she would have to veer from her sacred principles. She would have to admit that she *had* done something wrong.

A PERFECT RECORD

Most important, she would have had to begin to take the feds seriously; to acknowledge that the feds were a very formidable force. Everyone else did; everyone else knew that the feds had all the cards in their hands; they had the power to intimidate and all the resources they needed at their command. They had the power to offer deals. But they had one personal advantage as well: "There's something appealing about this young, earnest forthright prosecutor," said one participant in the case, "standing up and being the scolding voice of the community and saying this person did something bad."

Not surprisingly, they had a nearly perfect record, winning all their cases.

But she simply could not make a deal with the feds, however sensible an exit strategy that provided, because to do so was to admit her fallibility. She could no more plea bargain with the feds than she could delete the perfectionism gene from her DNA, the very gene that convinced her that she was flawless.

"Martha Stewart," said Jake Zamansky, the securities attorney who attended the Martha Stewart trial as an outside observer, "is the type of person who is always right. She's known as a perfectionist. To admit that she did something wrong is not in her character. It would have caused some shame to her to admit responsibility but it would have been a two-day story. The cover up is always worse than the crime. She might not even have gotten a fine."

> *"Martha Stewart is the type of person who is always right. She's known as a perfectionist. To admit that she did something wrong is not in her character."*

Even her staunchest supporters recognized that Martha Stewart's belief in her own infallibility was too embedded in her personality to expect her to take rational steps in her own self-interest. "That's just Martha," suggested Andrew Ritchie of SaveMartha.com. "She's fought her whole life for everything she has. And she'll continue to fight, especially where honor is at stake, no matter the risk. I do think she sincerely believed she had done nothing wrong and that she definitely did not believe she would be convicted."

"But this fighting streak in her is very prominent. She once told Oprah Winfrey that she feels as if she can bend steel with her mind. She is probably the most determined person in business. She doesn't relent. She gets her way. In this instance, it was a poor choice not to settle. But that's hindsight. I honestly believe Martha thought she could 'bend steel' in this case and come out smelling like roses."

She would not buckle; she could not. Contrition was out of the question; only the weak and the fallible say they are sorry. Being a perfectionist means never having to say you're sorry.

Her lawyers hoped they could make her see the light. They had been down this road before. Some of them had been federal prosecutors. Perhaps an indictment and trial might have been to their advantage, million-dollar legal fees and the rest, but the sane strategy, they knew, was for Stewart to sit down with the feds and work out a deal.

One day an attorney in the case was talking to a partner at Wachtell, Lipton: "It seems to me," he began, "that Martha would have been well advised for someone at Wachtell, Lipton to say to her: 'All you have to tell the feds is this: I was on an airplane. It landed. I was rushing to the bathroom. Someone told me quickly on the phone that Sam (Waksal) was selling his shares. It just didn't dawn on me what they were saying. It didn't register. I'm a sophisticated person, a stockbroker, and I knew what the rules were, but, talking on the tarmac like that, my antenna were down and I didn't have the same frame of reference that I have in a business setting. I wasn't focused. I admit that. But I want to make up for it. I'll give a half million dollars to charity. I'm really very sorry about it.'"

The Wachtell, Lipton, Rosen & Katz partner offered a facial gesture as if to say, "You think you're the first person to suggest such an idea?" He then commented, "You shouldn't assume that her lawyers were so incompetent that they didn't make that suggestion."

It was a monumental mistake for Martha Stewart to turn down the advice of her lawyers to settle the case. But if she were going to take on the feds in a prolonged legal battle, the last thing she should have done was to provide them with evidence of a consciousness of guilt. Yet that is what she did on January 31st, just five days before she was due to appear before the federal authorities.

Around 5:30 p.m. that day, Stewart asked her secretary, Ann Armstrong, to call up her computer's phone log for December 26th through January 7th.

Perhaps for the first time ever, Stewart sat down at her secretary's desk, and scrolled through the messages.

As Armstrong later recalled, Stewart examined the messages and noted the one from Bacanovic on December 27th, which read, "Peter Bacanovic thinks ImClone is going to start trading downward."

SECOND THOUGHTS

Armstrong explained what Stewart then did:

"Martha saw the message from Peter, and she instantly took the mouse and she put the cursor at the end of the sentence, and she highlighted it back up to the end of Peter's name, and then she started typing over it."

Stewart changed the message to "Peter Bacanovic re ImClone."

Then she had second thoughts, "She instantly stood up," said Armstrong, "and still standing at my desk, she told me to put it back."

'Put it back the way it was.'

Armstrong continued: "Martha then walked back to her office door, and by the time she got to her office door, she asked me to get her son-in-law on the phone."

Alexis's husband, John Cuti, was a litigator who sometimes worked for Stewart and her company. A partner at the law firm of Emery Celli Cuti Brinckerhoff & Abady, he attended the Stewart trial every day.

Once Armstrong got Cuti on the phone, Ann explained to him what was going on. Cuti told Armstrong: "Stop in your tracks." He told her not to change anything else.

The next morning, Stewart left for a quick trip to Germany, which would get her back just before her interview at the U.S. Attorney's Office.

The Government later accused Stewart of deleting the phone message in furtherance of a conspiracy.

It was that momentary second of panic, that decision first to edit a message, and then to restore it, that would doom Martha Stewart. No other act was more damning to her case, no other piece of evidence weighed more heavily against her. Certainly the statement she made to Mariana Pasternak—"Isn't it nice to have brokers who tell you those things?"—was damaging; but, in its vagueness, it offered defense attorneys a chance to try to whittle away at its lethal consequences.

But the actual attempt to delete incriminating language from a computer was bound to resonate far more powerfully with a juror if there were a trial. It was after all a physical act, not something that someone said. It was the legal equivalent of a knockout punch.

No matter how many times Stewart professed her innocence in the coming days, fiddling around with that message ruined any chance she might have had of triumphing in a court of law.

Stewart's attempt to delete the e-mail certainly seemed reason enough for her to invoke the Fifth Amendment when she walked into her session with the feds in five days. But she had no way of knowing that the feds even knew at that stage that she had played around with the e-mail. She was eager to face the feds once and for all—and put an end to all of this.

Stewart did a lot of traveling in late January. It seemed a sign of how nonchalant she was about her legal case. Had she been more concerned, she might have spent the time preparing for what certainly became the most important interview of her life.

John Savarese could have delayed Stewart's appearance before the feds. He could have forced her to test her recollections against the physical evidence. But he did not.

Instead, Savarese sent her into the hands of prosecutors as an under-prepared witness, one who may not have told him the whole story, and who had already tried to doctor evidence in the case.

That morning of February 4th someone placed a call from Martha Stewart's cell phone to Peter Bacanovic's cell phone, further evidence that Stewart and Bacanovic were engaged in a cover up.

Clearly, Stewart was concerned about the probe. She knew that the feds had been talking to Doug Faneuil and Peter Bacanovic. She also knew how vulnerable her company would be if word got out that she was the object of a federal criminal investigation.

She thought carefully about what she would tell the feds—and what she would not.

She needed to have a plausible explanation for the proximity of her stock sale to the FDA announcement. Hence, she would say that she and Peter Bacanovic had agreed to sell ImClone when it hit $60 a share; it was a mere coincidence that it hit that mark when it did.

She must not let on that she knew that Sam Waksal was selling his ImClone shares. Accordingly, she would simply not be able to recall whether she had been told that.

On February 4, 2002, representatives of the SEC, the FBI, and the U.S. Attorney's Office interviewed Martha Stewart at the Manhattan office of the U.S. Attorney's Office. John Savarese accompanied her to the inter-view. Just prior to the meeting, someone on Peter Bacanovic's cell phone called Martha Stewart's cell phone. The feds believed the two were coor-dinating their stories just prior to Stewart's appearance.

It was, to say the least, an odd way for officials from the U.S. Government to conduct a meeting. They were about to interview some-one who in their minds might have been guilty of some very serious crimes. What she had to say to them could and would be used against her—that was for sure. Yet, they brought no audio or video tape recorder, nor a stenographer, and there was no computer in the room for someone to type in precisely what Stewart would say. Instead, an FBI agent had been designated to take hand-written notes and to transcribe those notes into a larger document after the session. The special agent wound up tak-ing only six pages of notes; then turning them into a 30-page document following the meeting. She admitted under oath that at times she relied upon her memory in composing the larger document.

To some involved in the case, the feds seemed at best sloppy and irresponsible in not bringing more sophisticated equipment to transcribe the meeting. But the real cause for the feds' apparent laziness was their eagerness to lull Stewart into believing that she had no reason to hold back. Bringing in high-tech stuff would have been the equivalent, they feared, of walking in the room with Uzis at their sides. They did not want to seem intimidating. They wanted to trick her into thinking they were just a bunch of nice guys who had a few harmless questions to ask.

The effect of their low-tech approach was to put Martha Stewart at a distinct disadvantage from the start. To some who participated in the case, it was astounding that the outcome of Stewart's legal case depended so heavily on the recollections of the FBI agent note-taker. "You bring Martha Stewart in to an interview like that and you don't have a $25 tape recorder that you can buy at a Radio Shack or you don't bring a video tape recorder?" said one participant. "It all seemed deliberate. The 302 (federal parlance for the larger document) became absolutely sacrosanct and that is what you can go to jail on."

For Stewart, the February 4th meeting turned out to be a huge disaster.

She had an answer and an explanation for every question the feds had put to her; but much later, long after the meeting, when the feds had a chance to assess who was telling the truth and who was not, they wound up believing almost nothing Stewart had said to them.

She and Peter Bacanovic, she told the investigators, had decided when ImClone was selling at $74 a share that she would sell her ImClone shares when the stock began trading at $60 per share. Later, the government would say that it did not believe Stewart because there had been no such decision.

She also told the feds that she did not know whether the phone message Peter Bacanovic had left for her on December 27, 2001—"Peter Bacanovic thinks ImClone is going to start trading downward"—was recorded in the phone message log maintained by her assistant. Later, the investigators insisted that this statement was false: Martha Stewart knew, they argued, but concealed the fact that the message was recorded in the phone message log. Stewart, said the feds, had reviewed the message when she temporarily altered it just four days before the interview.

SELLING AT $60 A SHARE

She further told the feds that on December 27, 2001, she had spoken to Peter Bacanovic, who told her that ImClone was trading a little below $60 per share and asked her if she wanted to sell. She stated that she directed Bacanovic to sell her ImClone shares that day because she did not want to be bothered over her vacation. More false statements, the government contended, because, as Stewart knew but covered up, she had spoken to Doug Faneuil, not Peter Bacanovic, on that fateful December 27, 2001, and she had sold her ImClone shares after Faneuil had divulged to her that the Waksals were selling their ImClone shares.

Stewart also volunteered to the feds that she and Bacanovic had on December 27th discussed how the stocks of both Martha Stewart Living Omnimedia and Kmart were doing. This was yet another false statement, the government later said, in that Martha Stewart had spoken to Faneuil, and not to Bacanovic, as she well knew; and that there had been no discussions that day with either of the two stockbrokers regarding MSLO or Kmart.

The prosecutors felt that Stewart and Bacanovic had added these minute details to their purported conversation to lend credibility to their claim that the call took place at all. She needed to show that the call had occurred in order to buttress her claim that she and Bacanovic had agreed to the $60-a-share sell arrangement.

Finally, Stewart insisted to the feds that she and Bacanovic had spoken only once between December 28, 2001, and the day of her appearance; and when they did speak, it was only to talk about publicly disclosed matters. She also argued that Bacanovic had told her nothing of his being questioned by the SEC regarding her account. The investigators did not believe these assertions. They did believe that she was, through these assertions, trying to cover up that she and Bacanovic had agreed to lie to them.

Later, the feds pointed to phone calls placed on February 12th, eight days after Stewart's appearance, between the phones of Stewart and Bacanovic to strengthen their claim that the two were involved in a cover up.

At some point in her testimony to the feds, Martha Stewart decided it was time to put the feds in their place. She wanted to let them know that she did not take them seriously; to make it clear that she had better things to do with her time.

"Can I go now? I have a business to run."

If she had wanted to give the feds a reason to think of her as the proverbial princess from the Hamptons, she could not have done a better job. It was as if she were running the world, and the feds were just irritating little flies buzzing around her head.

Here was all the evidence one would need to argue persuasively that Martha Stewart just didn't get it; she just did not understand that arrogance and hubris would not win her much affection with the feds. It was the opposite. Those ten words drove the feds crazy.

TEN LETHAL WORDS

Their reaction to the ten words was lethal: They would decide when the meeting was over. They resented being reminded that she was this hotshot business leader, rich and famous, for whom federal prosecutors were simply a mild annoyance. They particularly disliked being told in no uncertain terms that theirs was not a serious undertaking—at least not serious to Martha Stewart.

Had they wished to let Stewart off with a mild punishment, hearing her make such a statement ended all discussion of treating her kindly. With those ten words, she had impelled herself closer to an indictment than at any prior point. "That's not the way to approach the government," said securities attorney Jake Zamansky. "You've got to be patient, you've got to be forthcoming, and that's how you show the SEC or the FBI that you really didn't commit any crime. But when you say something like that—I have to run my business—it's sort of like thumbing your nose at the SEC. It's reminiscent of Leona Helmsley saying only the little people pay taxes. It's one of those phrases that people remember. It infuriated the SEC." What brought about Martha Stewart's downfall was not a stock tip; it was her tongue.

In an age of "CNN Breaking News," in an era when the lives and careers of celebrities are sliced and diced 24/7 over the airwaves, not one news story had been written about the Martha Stewart case. It was an extraordinary fact that played deliciously into Stewart's hands. For, she not only needed to keep the feds at bay; she needed to keep the public from finding out about the very existence of the probe.

The probe was nearly three months old, and, as far as the American public was concerned, Martha Stewart remained an icon without blemishes. The probe remained a well-kept secret. Martha Stewart appeared on television and in print, the homemaking hostess pretending that life was just a bowl of cherries. But it was not. On March 22nd, Congressional investigators joined the probe, focusing on ImClone stock trades of company insiders. The investigation was widening; but no one had any interest yet in leaking the news of her potential involvement. For the feds, it was premature to go public; for Stewart, silence was golden. If the public had been in the loop, it seemed unthinkable that Stewart would have been nominated, as she had been on February 22nd, to serve on the board of directors of the New York Stock Exchange.

By the spring the feds were stepping up their assault on Martha Stewart. They had less and less faith in her professions of innocence—all the more reason for her to fall on her sword.

Even after a second "meeting" with the feds over the phone on April 10th, Stewart could have ended the probe by admitting to having made a mistake and by acting contrite. But she stubbornly clung to the tale she had woven.

The striving for perfection, the stubborn streak, the unvarnished ambition—all came from growing up in a family of six children, where achievement was important but financial resources were lacking; where getting the attention of parents was crucial; and where it was easy to develop a competitive streak at a very early age. To win her parents' attention, Martha became interested in gardening. "I remember the first day that I was put out there on the garden path. We had this cobblestone path in our garden, and it had weeds in it, in between—my father gave me a little broken off screwdriver, and he said, take out all the grass. So I sat out there all day, and I became his pet because of that. I was the only one of the six kids that would actually pick out the grass from between the bricks." From that experience and others that would follow, she learned the value of hard work. She saw what it got her. She grew ambitious, excelling in math, hoping to become a teacher; devouring every book she could get her hands on. In her quest to find time to read books, one could see the beginnings of the perfectionist. She had her own favorite reading chair and a favorite tree where she sat and read. "It sounds a little idyllic, sort of Mark Twainish, but it was true. I would find a quiet place. On Sunday mornings, because we had such chaos around our house, everybody running and getting dressed to go to church and everything, I sat in the car and read. I read everything. I read from A to Z in the Stockton Room. I just started on the As and went all the way through. In the adult library, I had to be more choosy because there were so many books. But I would talk to the librarians, I would get suggestions, I would read the book reviews, I would find out what I should be reading." When she set herself a goal, like getting into college, she was steadfast, joining nearly every club she could get into. She was a gym helper, guidance helper, Red Cross representative, member of the art club, and Latin club, all of which her parents knew would look good on her college application. By the end of high school, she had a certain self-confidence that some might call precociousness; others, egotism. "I do what I please," she wrote as her inscription in her high school yearbook, "and I do it with ease."

She was still quite fortunate. A good deal of resources were going into Sam Waksal and ImClone. Martha Stewart remained an enigma for the feds. They wanted to nail her badly, but they were quite far from compiling an indictment. Stewart could not have known any of this, so she grew increasingly concerned. The two meetings with the feds had not put an end to the probe into her stock sale. That alone impelled her to dwell on new strategies and new ways to get this monkey off her back.

CHAPTER

4

I AM INNOCENT

She needed to speak up. She needed to take charge of her own case. She was good at convincing people of her point of view. She had great television skills, terrific communication skills.

But she could not bring herself to speak up on her own behalf. The media had no idea that the feds had her back to the wall. It was better, for the time being, to keep silent. At least so she thought.

She continued to live in a cocoon that sheltered her from the harsh outside realities—the federal probe, the possibility that things could get worse for her legally.

The one thing she didn't want was bad publicity. But unfortunately for her, that was exactly what she got when an unflattering book appeared called *MARTHA Inc.*, authored by Chris Byron.

The review of the Byron book in *BusinessWeek* on April 22, 2002, summed up its venality. Byron, the *BusinessWeek* reviewer wrote, "cast his subject as a coiffed Attila the Hun who will trample on anyone and anything to get to the top. But few would imagine Stewart as an abusive wife, negligent mother, or egocentric tyrant whose path to success is littered with angry former associates and embittered ex-friends."

Byron's portrayal of her as a mean-spirited egotist came backed up with anecdotes.

> *"If you don't know who I am, you don't deserve to be at this table!"*

At a 1995 dinner for Diana, Princess of Wales, he wrote that Stewart screamed at public-relations mogul Robert Dilenschneider: "If you don't know who I am, you don't deserve to be at this table!" During a trip to Colombia in the early 1970s, she allegedly informed her staph-infected husband: "You're not going to ruin my vacation." Stewart hurled obscenities at employees who contradicted the image of her as the kind and sweet domestic diva.

The book placed Stewart in an even greater dilemma. A carefully placed news leak on her part revealing the federal probe against her might have done her some good in the period leading up to the publication of the book. But with the appearance of the book, any revelation of the federal probe could have damaged Stewart seriously. The probe would have buttressed Byron's assertions about Stewart, making what he wrote seem on the mark.

It took a good six months for the federal probe to spill over into the public realm.

The public first learned of the government's six-month probe into Martha Stewart in June 2002. That she had managed to keep the affair out of the media for that long was a distinct triumph for her, but the triumph was about to turn into a public relations disaster.

As part of the ongoing Congressional probe into the matter, ImClone's outside counsel had briefed the powerful Committee on Energy and Commerce staff. In that briefing, the outside counsel disclosed that Martha Stewart had sold all of her ImClone shares on December 27, 2001, the day before ImClone received the FDA's refusal-to-file letter for Erbitux.

On June 5, 2002, Committee staff contacted one of Stewart's attorneys to determine the accuracy of the report of her trade and to provide Stewart with the chance to explain the circumstances of that trade, including her telephone message to Sam Waksal on December 27, 2001.

Stewart's attorneys assured the Committee staff that her trade reflected a preexisting agreement to sell at $60 a share and that she had not received any non-public material information from ImClone.

The following day (June 6th) word got out that the Committee, chaired by Louisiana Republican Billy Tauzin, planned to investigate Stewart's stock sale.

A source close to the congressional investigation had leaked rumors of the House probe. The Associated Press reported for the first time that Stewart had sold her ImClone shares just prior to the Erbitux rejection.

The news leak was further evidence that a plan had been hatched at the highest levels to get Martha Stewart, a plan that included the federal government and Congress.

THE NEXT SCANDAL

For reporters looking for the next scandal, the Stewart probe provided enough juicy material, especially when the AP story noted that Stewart and Waksal had been ex-lovers. "There are allegations that certain people profited handsomely, although illegally, from ImClone stock," the AP wrote. "A source close to the investigation said, on condition of anonymity (that) legal documents given to the committee show that domestic doyenne Martha Stewart also shed 3,000 ImClone shares. Stewart and Waksal have been romantically linked in the past."

Others in the media pounced on the story.

The anchor of Minnesota Public Radio, Cheryl Glaser, broadcast: "It looks like Martha Stewart may have kissed and sold. The doyenne of domesticity has been romantically linked to a man who until two weeks ago was the CEO of a biotech firm named ImClone. ...That's prompted whispers about insider trading."

"It looks like Martha Stewart may have kissed and sold."

Had journalists checked their facts they would have discovered that Stewart and Waksal had never been romantically linked. Waksal once dated Stewart's daughter, Alexis, but not Martha. Furthermore, Waksal did not tip Stewart. But from that moment on, Stewart's reputation as well as that of her company began to suffer.

Media coverage of the investigation was spreading. *The New York Times* ran a front-page story. The public venting of the probe aroused fear on Wall Street and soon her company's stock fell from $19.01 to $11.47.

Stewart became alarmed, and sensed that she had to do something to halt her company stock's downward slide.

She could have escalated her struggle against the feds by taking her story—that the feds were persecuting her—to the public as broadly as possible. She could have gained instant access to the major talk shows,

Larry King, Barbara Walters, etc. But she held back. She decided to pursue a low-key public relations offensive, simply issuing terse public statements defending her sale of ImClone stock without presenting her side in full; without trying to convince the public that she was being intimidated for no good reason.

Why did she choose the low-profile approach?

She still refused to take the federal probe seriously. She still believed that the best way to respond to the federal probe was to display contempt for it, never exhibiting any concern over the harm it might cause her. Appearing over the television airwaves might give the impression that the probe was worrying her.

It was a costly mistake.

The only way she was going to stop the federal probe was to take the initiative, to do what she did best, to appeal to a mass audience, many of whom were her loyal fans; to spell out in the greatest detail possible why and how she was being railroaded by the feds.

She refused to do that, and so her low-profile public relations gambit in June 2002 was doomed from the start. Without her own detailed version of events on the public record, the media ran with one-sided stories that cast her as guilty even before the government brought formal charges against her.

Even worse, by launching her low-key PR offensive, she inadvertently provided the feds with new evidence of her alleged wrongdoing.

By insisting in the scripted public statements of June 2002 that she had done nothing criminally wrong, Martha Stewart—so the feds later argued—was using false and misleading information in order to stop or at least slow the steady erosion of her company's stock price.

Told on June 6th of an upcoming *Wall Street Journal* story about her ImClone shares sale, Stewart had her attorney issue a statement that ran in the story the next day: "The sale was executed because Ms. Stewart had a predetermined price at which she planned to sell the stock. That determination, made more than a month before that trade, was to sell if the stock went less than $60." Prosecutors later called that statement false and misleading.

In an attempt to clear up the confusion surrounding her ImClone trade, Stewart had her attorney, James F. Fitzpatrick, send a letter to Tauzin's committee on June 12, reiterating that she had the $60 a share sale in place well before the Erbitux rejection.

WAKSAL ARRESTED

On that same June 12th, Sam Waksal was arrested and charged with insider trading, accused of advising family members to sell their shares before the FDA announcement, and of trying to dump his own shares. With that news, Martha Stewart Living Omnimedia's stock fell 4.5 percent from $15.90 to $15.

Waksal eventually agreed to plead guilty to the insider-trading charges as well as to obstruction of justice and tax fraud. He began serving a seven-year federal sentence. As part of the bargain, his relatives avoided criminal prosecution. The Waksal prosecution had always been more straightforward than Stewart's. He was clearly an insider who benefited from non-public material information by selling his ImClone shares just prior to the FDA rejection of Erbitux. Stewart was not an insider, making it much more difficult for the feds to prosecute her for insider trading.

A day later (June 13th), the shares in Martha Stewart Living Omnimedia rose 7 percent from $15 to $16.05, bolstering the feds' claim that Stewart had tried to manipulate her stock higher.

Five days later, Stewart's lawyers were again writing to the Congressional Committee, explaining in greater detail Martha Stewart's recollection of events on that fateful December 27th. For the first time, they identified Peter Bacanovic by name as her broker. "After discussion of other business-related matters with her office," her lawyers wrote, "Ms. Stewart was informed that Mr. Peter Bacanovic, her broker at Merrill Lynch, had called and she was connected by her assistant through to Mr. Bacanovic during that same call. While on the phone with Mr. Bacanovic, she was informed that ImClone had traded down below the price of $60 that she and Mr. Bacanovic had previously agreed would be a trigger to sell her remaining position...."

"...Ms. Stewart did not receive any nonpublic information regarding ImClone prior to her sale...."

On June 19th, at a securities analyst and investors conference, she read yet another statement saying much the same thing. Prosecutors later insisted that Stewart had organized the investors' event to bolster her company's ailing stock price. "This was not a meeting with *People* magazine," Karen Seymour, who later prosecuted Stewart, argued.

The feds would only latch on to Martha Stewart's June 2002 public statements as evidence of her alleged involvement in securities fraud a year later when an indictment was handed down against her.

But as of mid-June 2002, investigators had no case against her for insider trading. They were unable to refute her $60 a share agreement tale. Nor did they have sufficient proof that she had lied to them in her two meetings earlier that year.

As for the Congressional piece, the legislators were accumulating a good deal of material, but little that provided a smoking gun that might impel Martha Stewart into court.

Stewart's insistence on her innocence was rejected by the bipartisan leadership of the House Committee on Energy and Commerce; in a letter to Attorney General John Ashcroft, the congressmen said that their investigations "cause us to be deeply skeptical of Ms. Stewart's accounts, and raise a serious question as to whether those accounts were false, misleading, and designed to conceal material facts."

Again the authorities appeared to be ganging up on Stewart. By this time, Congress had precious little evidence that Stewart was guilty of either insider trading or lying to the feds. Yet members of Congress were perfectly willing to announce that they believed she was guilty. By issuing such a statement, Congress sanctioned the Federal Government to pursue Martha Stewart with even greater zeal.

Yet Congress seemed unsure which way to lean. A House Committee spokesperson, for example, issued this ambiguous statement: "As the coincidences pile up, the possibility that no one knew anything goes way down. But it is possible to give the web of seemingly incriminating relationships a more benign interpretation."

LITTLE TEETH

The fact was that the Congressional committee investigating Stewart had very little teeth. With the mounting corporate scandals as background music, legislators felt compelled to give the impression that they were taking the scandals seriously.

And so they gladly focused on Martha Stewart, when the opportunity arose. "It was more of a photo op for Congress as it tried to appear vigorous," said one observer of the Stewart case. "They wanted to look like they were doing something but they really didn't have the authority. All they could do was refer what they found to the Justice Department."

In the end, they treated Stewart with kid gloves. The House Energy and Commerce committee asked her to appear, but it did not subpoena her even though it could have done so. Had she refused to appear after being subpoenaed, she could have been placed in contempt of Congress.

With the feds unable to find sufficient evidence to bring a case against Stewart, however, it seemed possible that the probe might just fizzle.

Stewart could be pleased that the case seemed to be going away. She had worked so hard throughout her childhood and as an adult, attaining great success. She certainly didn't want anything to get in the way of future achievement. She had always managed to accomplish so much. Even as a teenager she was the ultimate multi-tasker. She began modeling at Bonwit Teller at age 13. Modeling afforded her the chance to make large sums of money that would defray the costs of her eventual college education. She made $35 an hour to start, then $50 an hour—a good deal of money in those days. She did a Lifebuoy soap commercial when she was 15; then a Tareyton cigarette commercial. She practiced smoking but when it came time for the shoot, all she had to do was hold the cigarette.

As a 17-year-old in high school, she dreamed of becoming an architect or a chemist. Graduating in the top ten in her high school class, she obtained a partial scholarship to Barnard College in New York. She began Barnard in September 1959, majoring in art history, architecture, and history. She decided to forego the teaching career that she had planned. She continued to work as a model to pay her tuition. One college friend described her as attractive, intelligent, friendly, serious, and funny—and clearly busier than most undergraduates. Hungry for national recognition, she learned in 1961 of Glamour Magazine's contest to find the ten best-dressed college girls. Assuming that winning would get her more modeling work, she was chosen and seemed destined to move up the ladder.

In July 1961, after completing her sophomore year, she married Andy Stewart, a 23 year-old law student at Yale, her first serious boyfriend. She found him warm, intelligent, and quite appealing. They were both very much in love. Friends said he brought out a much more feminine side of Martha. Though her parents were not thrilled, at the age of 19 she married the law student, dropping out of Barnard and moving in to Andy's apartment near Yale; she worked full time as a model to help him get through law school. It was mystifying to her parents and friends that she had given up everything for this young man. Eventually, however, Stewart's family began to like her new husband.

The probe against Martha Stewart suddenly took a new twist. A new break in the case turned matters against Martha Stewart once and for all.

It centered on a young man named Doug Faneuil, the young assistant to Peter Bacanovic.

Ever since December 27, 2001, Faneuil had been torn emotionally by the events of that day. He had serious doubts about Peter Bacanovic's version of events, namely that Bacanovic had an agreement with Stewart to sell when ImClone hit $60. If an agreement had indeed existed, why had Bacanovic gone off on vacation without informing his assistant of the agreement? It just did not make sense.

When the feds had originally interviewed Faneuil, asking him whether there had indeed been a $60-a-share agreement, he manifested complete loyalty to his boss. He knew that if he told the feds about his phone call to Stewart on December 27th, he would cast doubt on the $60-a-share arrangement. Accordingly, he conveniently forgot to mention the phone call to the feds.

If the feds discovered that Faneuil had been withholding valuable information from them, they would have had strong grounds for prosecuting him. Faneuil was a nervous wreck over this prospect.

Hiring an Attorney

When in June, the feds sought out Faneuil again, he had made a fateful decision: He was ready to tell the feds what he knew of the Martha Stewart stock sale; even if it meant that she would be prosecuted; he wanted to avoid going to jail. Of the three principals in the Stewart drama—Stewart, Bacanovic, and Faneuil—Doug knew that the feds were most likely to make a deal with him to turn on Bacanovic and Stewart. He was the smallest fish of the three; the feds had their sights on Stewart, and to a lesser degree, Bacanovic. To help negotiate the deal with the feds, Faneuil hired Marvin Pickholz as his attorney. "Because of the type of person he was," said Marvin Pickholz, "Doug had been going through a period of a great deal of self-introspection and a lot of internal pain. It was troubling to him that what in his mind had started out as just a way of being loyal to his immediate employer, whom he had once described as the best boss he had ever had, had now become something more than a one-to-one loyalty. It really became a question of his own integrity and honesty, and that was weighing way too heavily on him."

Faneuil had not told the literal truth until now and, Pickholz observed, "he really wanted to make things correct. It wasn't a question of vengeance (against Martha Stewart). Nobody was giving him a reward.

He had reached the point in his mind where he just didn't want to do this again (mislead the feds). He just wanted to tell somebody what really happened. He almost didn't care about the consequences." He may well have wanted to tell the truth; but it was hard to believe that Faneuil did not care about the consequences: He was scared out of his mind of going to jail.

At his first meeting with Pickholz, Doug Faneuil wanted to set the record straight with his employers at Merrill Lynch first; but Pickholz suggested that he first tell the prosecutors. "So we did both," said Pickholz. "The lawyer in me told me to go tell the prosecutors first."

During that third week of June 2002, Pickholz alerted Merrill that neither he nor Faneuil would talk with them; on the other hand, Pickholz informed the prosecutors that his client was ready to hold a proffer session.

Merrill Lynch moved quickly to make sure no finger of suspicion could be pointed its way. It suspended both Peter Bacanovic and Doug Faneuil on the grounds of "factual inconsistencies."

Meeting with the feds in the U.S. Attorney's Office in Manhattan, Faneuil revealed that Stewart had sold her shares after he had told her to do so, at the behest of Bacanovic, because Sam Waksal and his family had sold their ImClone stock. Faneuil knew of no client agreement between Martha Stewart and his boss, Bacanovic, he added. Most damaging to Martha Stewart, Faneuil noted that Peter Bacanovic had pressured him to confirm to the feds that the $60-a-share arrangement had been in place.

Faneuil's new testimony, if believed by the feds, meant that Martha Stewart was dead in the water. Until now the feds had been gunning for Stewart, but with precious little ammunition in their arsenal. Now, with Faneuil willing to deal, they had the ammunition they needed against her.

Lisa Marsh was the business reporter for the *New York Post* that summer, covering fashion and retailing. Anything consumer driven fell into her realm of reporting. When the story broke about Martha Stewart's stock sale, "We went on a free-for-all. It was a perfect *New York Post* story, a woman titan of industry fallen because she's done an improper trade."

It was also a perfect story with which to have some fun. How would Martha Stewart decorate her jail cell? "We got a sketch artist. I picked out things we could put in jail. The sketch artist did a pretty fabulous sketch. We got so many e-mails. Some said how could you do this. It's not right. Some said she deserved it. Right away, people loved her or hated her."

A FESTIVAL OF SCHADENFREUDE

Press coverage of Martha Stewart accelerated. Photographers began staking her out. Reporters found out where she was speaking, where she was having lunch. "Things that would never have been covered were now covered to the nth degree," said Lisa Marsh, recalling the heady days.

Stewart felt the mounting pressure.

If she had wanted to keep her legal case a "small personal matter" as she called it, she no longer could do so once the public learned that she was under federal investigation.

She should have joined the public fray, countering the media leaks with major television interviews of her own, laying out in detail why she was innocent.

"There really was this extraordinary festival of Schadenfreude, of joy in her misfortune...."

But just as she had chosen to adopt a low profile after the feds began investigating her, she decided to dive for shelter upon learning how delighted some people were at her legal plight. "...when the news became public that she was under investigation for insider trading," commented Jeffrey Toobin, "there really was this extraordinary festival of *Schadenfreude*, of joy in her misfortune...she is a figure that people love to hate.... She treats people terribly. I mean, simple as that. And that came back to haunt her...."

How did Martha Stewart react to this joy?

One of the few reporters who met with her during her long legal struggle, Toobin noted: "...she's a pretty tough customer and she...can be pretty icy. But I think she was shocked by the degree to which there was this kind of joy in her suffering."

She was so shocked that, instead of seizing the initiative, as she should have done, thus sucking some or all of the oxygen out of the government's offensive, she had to be dragged, kicking and screaming, to discuss her case on television. She went along with her attorneys' advice to keep a low profile and say as little as possible in public. But this was time for her to say: "I am Martha Stewart. I have spent my career communicating my ideas to the public. My public expects to hear from me. You will just have to live with whatever I say to them. "

Accordingly, when she *was* given her first opportunity to speak out over national television, she walked into the wrong forum under the wrong circumstances, and adopted the wrong strategy.

The opportunity presented itself during an appearance on the CBS *The Early Show* on June 25, 2002.

She had agreed to talk about the probe and her reaction to it during her regularly scheduled weekly appearance on CBS' *The Early Show*. Before her morning segment, Stewart was to answer questions posed by CBS News Correspondent Jane Clayson in the show's kitchen area.

Unfortunately for Stewart, her appearance proved one of the most embarrassing moments of her career.

Clayson began with a summary of events surrounding Stewart's sale of ImClone stock. Then came this exchange:

Stewart: I have nothing to say on the matter. I'm really not at liberty to say and I think this will all be resolved in the very near future and I will be exonerated.....

Clayson: I know that.

Stewart: ...of any ridiculousness.

Clayson: I know that image is so important for you and that...

Stewart: When I was a model...and I was all during high school and college...you always wanted to be on the cover of a magazine. That's how your success was judged. The more covers, the better. I am a CEO of a New York Stock Exchange-listed company and I don't want to be on any covers of any newspapers for a long, long time.

In the end, it was not what Martha Stewart said that stood out, but how she said it.

THE CABBAGE CHOPPER

Stewart refused to answer many of the questions, citing the ongoing investigation. She was clearly uncomfortable and eager to get on with her planned presentation, creating a salad. Indeed, all throughout her testy, unnerving segment with Clayson, she never once interrupted her chopping of a cabbage with a large knife. At one point, as the knife sliced through the salad with a great piercing noise, Stewart blurted out: "I want to focus on my salad, because that's why we're here."

The image of a woman under enormous duress could not have been more powerful. In chopping the salad, it was as if she were slicing down the middle of the heads of the prosecutors.

Once the show ended, her attorneys advised her to no longer appear on the CBS morning show and she went along.

The interview caused a media feeding frenzy. Among the more colorful comments on the episode was this one: "In a style more reminiscent of Freddy Krueger than America's Homemaker, Martha angrily chopped cabbage on CBS' *The Early Show*, apparently taken by surprise by questions about the charges. If Scarlett O'Hara didn't get away with 'I'll think about that tomorrow,' Martha's 'Can't we just talk about the salad?' was even more implausible. Suddenly, she publicly confirmed that she was a mean person."

Martha Stewart provided endless jokes for comedians.

To some, her appearance seemed desperate and pathetic; to others, there was a *Saturday Night Live* feeling to it.

Martha Stewart learned little from the cabbage-chopping episode. Rather than draw the self-evident conclusion that she had to present her case better over television, she decided that she had to look to less powerful media channels to get the feds off her back. That strategy proved ineffective.

She created her own new Web site, but could one Web site be expected to combat her increasingly negative press? Not really. It was unimaginable that the feds would grow weak at the knees because of what appeared on the Internet.

Meanwhile, the Martha Stewart Living Omnimedia stock took a beating. On July 24th, the company halved its third-quarter earnings forecast, an acknowledgment that Stewart's legal problems had been taking a toll on the business.

Stewart's advisers, constrained by her attorneys to mount a major television offensive, took the rather feeble step of hiring yet one more public relations firm as if somehow there were new rabbits to pull out of the hat. The Brunswick Group got the nod, but no one noticed any improvement in Stewart's public image.

Unbeknownst to Martha Stewart, Marvin Pickholz was trying to tie down the details of a deal for his client, Doug Faneuil. Pickholz's discussion with the feds that summer did not go smoothly, delaying Stewart's day in court.

When the prosecutors grew distressed upon learning that they had not been told everything, Faneuil sensed that he was "flying without a safety net." Fearing that he might not get a deal at all, he had to convince the feds that he was simply a young kid who had made an honest, but misguided mistake, and not a villain who was trying to game the system to avoid prosecution.

PROVIDING AN OVERVIEW

Pickholz, however, radiated confidence that the feds would ultimately make a deal with his client. To land Stewart, they needed what Faneuil offered, someone who could fill in the details and corroborate most of what he was saying. "They had to have someone who could give them an overview of the case. If they really wanted to look genuine and serious about the case, it would be a little strange to go for the schlemiel at the bottom, the kid who's making $35,000 a year and been in the job for six months, as opposed to the other players."

All of this, however, took time: "You don't just go in there, and say, 'here's my story,' and they say, 'bless you, welcome to the team,'" remarked Pickholz.

Rather, the investigators asked numerous questions of Faneuil, sending agents into the field to seek corroboration of his story.

Finally, "It became clear to them," observed the attorney, "that from the very first, Doug was struggling with this thing and his friends confirmed what he said."

Pickholz hammered home to the feds that he was really a kid, very naïve in many respects. "It was important for me to try to get them to understand that if he had made a mistake, it wasn't a mistake of a malevolent heart, or of an evil person. It wasn't a heinous act, something really evil. He didn't kill anyone. He didn't make any money. He didn't defraud anybody. He didn't steal anything. He was not dealing drugs or arms."

On August 3rd, Stewart celebrated her 61st birthday.

She was coming under further pressure from Congress to offer evidence corroborating her version of events.

The Committee investigating her wanted her to appear for an interview, but she refused. She was in effect challenging Congress to issue a subpoena for her testimony. If she had had no choice about appearing before the feds the previous winter, she now felt she had a choice appearing before Congress. In the interim, she had been battered in the media, virtually declared guilty in many quarters. After the cabbage-slicing episode, she and her attorneys agreed she had better say as little in public as possible.

On August 6th, with little choice but to communicate by mail, House Energy and Commerce Committee Chairman Billy Tauzin and Oversight and Investigations Subcommittee Chairman James Greenwood sent a letter to Martha Stewart's attorney, James F. Fitzpatrick at Arnold & Porter, acknowledging that it now doubted her version of events: "Since the submission of the June 12th letter, the Committee has learned of several developments raising questions about the accuracy of statements made by your legal representatives concerning the circumstances of your December 27, 2001, trade of ImClone stock."

Two days later (August 8th) a federal grand jury indicted Sam Waksal on 13 counts of securities fraud, bank fraud, perjury, obstruction of justice, and other charges after talks toward a possible plea agreement had broken down. He faced a maximum 30-year prison term. The news of Waksal's indictment plunged the Stewart company stock to an all-time low, $6.29 a share. The stock had fallen nearly 60 percent over the summer.

On that same day (August 8th), the *Wall Street Journal* reported that Doug Faneuil might get a deal for testifying against Martha Stewart. According to the newspaper, federal investigators were negotiating an agreement with him in which he could receive immunity from prosecution in exchange for testimony against Martha Stewart.

Behind the scenes, Marvin Pickholz was trying to get prosecutors to give Faneuil what he called a "complete pass" i.e., no punishment whatsoever. The feds were not that generous. In exchange for his testimony against Martha Stewart and Peter Bacanovic, he would be charged with a misdemeanor for withholding information because he received or was promised something of value. At one stage, Bacanovic offered to finance a trip for Faneuil and to obtain tickets for a New York Knicks game. Faneuil was eventually fined the relatively small sum of $2,000 but received no jail time or probation.

Peter Bacanovic was stunned that Faneuil had entered into the bargaining plea. He assumed that, as his assistant, and out of loyalty to his boss, he would go along with the $60-a-share arrangement story. Instead, Faneuil had handed Martha Stewart and Peter Bacanovic on a silver plate to the authorities.

Bacanovic maintained his innocence, insisting that he had no knowledge of what Doug Faneuil had told Martha Stewart on the phone on December 27, 2001. She had sold her stock, Bacanovic kept saying, because the target price of $60 had been reached.

Reports began surfacing that summer that Bacanovic was angry with Martha Stewart for not selling her ImClone shares when he had first advised her to do so. He was spending his summer in five hour conferences with his attorney; taking phone calls from friends, and writing thank-you notes to hundreds of well-wishers. One witty writer noted, of the thank-you note gesture, "Martha Stewart would approve."

On August 9th came more devastating news.

The *Wall Street Journal* revealed that a Stewart friend, Mariana Pasternak, a licensed real-estate agent from Westport, Connecticut, had begun cooperating with the feds. Prosecutors wanted to learn from Pasternak precisely what Martha Stewart knew at the time that she sold the shares. Pasternak was an ideal witness: She had talked with Stewart throughout the day of the stock sale and in the days afterward.

In early September, Congress finally wrapped up its probe of Martha Stewart, asking the Justice Department to begin a criminal investigation into whether she had knowingly lied to lawmakers. Tauzin and Greenwood, writing to Attorney General John Ashcroft on September 10th, noted that while Stewart had insisted that she had an agreement with Peter Bacanovic to sell her ImClone shares when they hit $60, the House Committee simply did not believe her. "Indeed," they wrote, "if there had been such an agreed understanding between Stewart and her broker, the Committee would have expected that Stewart—a former stock broker, New York Stock Exchange board member, and sophisticated businesswoman—would have executed a stop-loss order, obviating any need for her broker to contact her, especially as she was heading to Mexico on vacation."

MORE BAD NEWS

The stream of bad news continued for Martha Stewart.

On October 2nd, Doug Faneuil pleaded guilty to a misdemeanor charge of misleading investigators about the content of his phone call with Stewart, accepting payments to withhold information about why Martha Stewart had suddenly sold ImClone Systems stock.

In his guilty plea, Faneuil noted that Stewart knew that Waksal was unloading his shares of ImClone, thus providing evidence that she had been misleading investigators when she said that she had no memory of being told that anyone in the Waksal family was selling.

But if Faneuil's version was correct—and he had no apparent reason to lie at this point—did that make Stewart guilty of insider trading? Not really.

For her to be guilty of insider trading, she would have had to have known that the broker was doing something wrong in giving her the information; but there was no evidence to suggest that she knew that.

The day after the news of Faneuil's plea, Martha Stewart voluntarily resigned from the board of the New York Stock Exchange. "I did not want the media attention currently surrounding me to distract from the important work of the NYSE and thus felt it was appropriate to resign," she said in a statement.

On October 15th, Sam Waksal finally made his own deal with the authorities. He pled guilty to six counts including securities fraud, bank fraud, conspiracy to obstruct justice, and perjury. He also admitted to tipping his daughter to dump ImClone stock, but significantly he did not implicate Martha Stewart. He knew that the feds were itching for him to blow the whistle on Stewart but he would not do that.

Now that the feds had a strong witness against Martha Stewart, the media began deliberating how the scandal surrounding her might affect her business down the road.

The conclusion was that she was so overly identified with her company that it would inevitably suffer if she took a fall.

Even Ralph Lauren or Tommy Hilfiger were not as closely associated with their companies as Martha Stewart was with hers and that was why advertisers and shareholders, the people who make her company profitable, were increasingly worried over the news involving her legal case.

How many shoppers would buy sheets from an inmate in a federal penitentiary? Not too many, argued the marketing analysts.

Remarkably, her business had not fallen apart on the news of the ImClone scandal. But the enduring nature of the scandal began to scare advertisers.

Perhaps the worst blow to Martha Stewart came on October 22nd when the Securities and Exchange Commission recommended that civil fraud charges be brought against her for insider trading. Stewart had less to fear from the SEC than she did from the federal authorities.

On the surface, it might have seemed that she should have been more concerned. After all, it was easier for the SEC to prove insider-trading charges against her than the feds since the SEC's burden of proof was much lower than it was for the feds.

The SEC had to show only that a preponderance of the evidence indicated Stewart's guilt; the feds had to prove its case beyond a reasonable doubt.

Though most agreed that the SEC charges might be the least of Stewart's troubles, its action almost certainly meant that she could no longer run her business or deal in the stock market. The SEC charges could not lead to jail time for her, but they constituted one more humiliating, image-destroying step; and she did not need that now.

For Martha Stewart, these were troubling, frustrating days. Her lawyers kept telling her not to worry. It would all work out in the end. There would be no indictment; and there would certainly be no trial.

Meanwhile, the media had already pronounced her guilty of insider trading charges.

Perhaps, she thought, she should switch strategies; perhaps it was time to stop trivializing the federal probe. Perhaps it was time to give the public what they seemed to want: to see and hear Martha Stewart and to listen carefully to why she thought she was not guilty.

But her lawyers would quit before they let her go on national television. But perhaps there was another way to get her case before the public—without irritating her attorneys too much. The idea began forming in her head.

CHAPTER

5

THE SECRET PUBLIC RELATIONS CAMPAIGN

With so many forces at work, with so many emotions in play, the public relations campaigns that were being waged in the name of Martha Stewart had a sometimes haphazard, erratic appearance. Even worse, some of those campaigns seemed to have no effect whatsoever.

At first, Susan Magrino took charge of Stewart's public relations; then Stewart turned to the Brunswick Group; then to George Sard of Sard Verbinnen. At times she employed others like Howard Rubenstein and Gershon Kekst on an ad-hoc basis.

Even as all these campaigns were working on her behalf, she was conducting a highly secret public relations operation, details of which have not surfaced until this book.

Her relationship with George Sard was a good example of how she was unable to make much progress on the public relations front. Sard had a tough task: He had to convince one of the world's great communicators that he knew how to conduct a PR campaign better than she did, she who had created one of the nation's most successful personal brands.

To be fair to Sard, he had never handled this kind of mega press event; furthermore, litigation support, which was essentially what he was being asked to do, was really not his specialty—financial communication was.

And now he had one of the hardest clients in the world to handle. "He was listening as much as he was counseling," said someone involved in the case who knew Sard well. Sard wanted Stewart to project a softer side. He wanted her to project a more friendly tone, to be less strident and know-it-all. In short, he wanted her to be more humble.

But Stewart felt she had to sound and act tough. She wanted to stick her chin out and push the theme, "They're trying to take me down but I'm smarter than they are."

When she saw that her way was getting her nowhere, when she realized that it was a losing battle to try to marginalize the feds, she thought she better start tweaking her "I did nothing wrong" strategy.

In her heart, she had always wanted to go public, to issue a delineated defense, but her attorneys had held her back. It bothered her. She thought of herself as a communicator, a fixture in the media, and her legal advisers were keeping her from communicating. She found it terribly frustrating "because you want people to know what you think, what the truth is. You want to tell them everything. And you just can't speak about it. Because anything you say might be held against you."

Unable to convince her attorneys to let her conduct a full-fledged public relations campaign, Stewart went behind their backs, engaging in a secret PR effort to stave off an indictment and trial.

It might have worked had she indeed allowed the people she had engaged to go full throttle; but in the end, she pulled back and only permitted them to operate in a half-hearted way. She produced one more setback to her case. The details are instructive for they show how Stewart propelled herself toward a fall that was certainly avoidable.

It began in the fall of 2002 and its purpose was to get her case before the American public and to stir public opinion in her favor so that no prosecutor would dare bring an indictment against her.

For all the public relations efforts that had preceded this secret one, Stewart's case had barely been presented to the public. She had declared her innocence on a number of occasions and in a variety of formats, including her own Web site, newspaper ads, and public statements issued through her attorneys. But, other than the highly charged, controversial, and supremely embarrassing appearance on CBS—the cabbage-chopping episode—she had said next to nothing in public about her case.

ONLY THE TINIEST OF DETAILS

Having watched how the federal prosecutors had chewed her over at their February 4th meeting with Stewart and their subsequent April 10th phone interview with her, her attorneys decided that she must provide only the tiniest bit of detail about her case in public.

They were concerned that any public appearance she made would damage her case, believing that potential jurors would quickly sense that she had no actual evidence of her innocence.

However often she insisted that she had that $60-a-share agreement, she could provide no evidence of its existence.

Yet, while her attorneys were pressing on her the importance of saying nothing in public, Martha Stewart still wanted to move ahead with a systematic public relations effort that would hopefully set her free.

The man who conducted the secret effort was Lanny Davis, the same Lanny Davis who was counsel to President Bill Clinton and who became a fixture on the talk shows, helping to defend Clinton during the Monica Lewinsky affair.

From 1996 to 1998, Davis served as Special Counsel to the President in the White House and was spokesperson for the President on matters concerning the campaign finance investigations and other legal issues.

Davis has participated in national, state, and local politics for almost 30 years. He served three terms (1980-1992) on the Democratic National Committee representing the State of Maryland.

It was late fall of 2002. The stock of Martha Stewart's company was plummeting. The newspapers had all but convicted her of insider trading and an indictment seemed possible.

Lanny Davis received a phone call from a member of the board of Martha Stewart Living Omnimedia. The board member put a question to Davis.

"What could you do for Martha Stewart if she were to call you?"

"What could you do for Martha Stewart if she were to call you?"

Davis thought a moment. He had never met Martha Stewart but he certainly knew who she was. He, along with millions of others, had read the newspapers, which seemed to have concluded that she was guilty of insider trading. He had no way of knowing whether the media was right.

"She needs to get her story out," Davis told the board member. "If what I'm reading is the truth—and I'd need to know the truth—she ought to be telling the truth." In other words, if what Stewart was saying was true, that she was innocent, she needed to market her innocence far more effectively.

Davis believed that Stewart was being accused of a crime (insider trading) that had not been defined in law very precisely. Hence, the "crime" was widespread; punishing those who engaged in it, he thought, was impractical. To the board member he said: "There aren't enough jails in the United States to contain everyone who has traded on inside information from a broker. And I don't believe that's a crime. Even if someone considers it to be a crime, I don't think Martha Stewart should be prosecuted."

To Davis, it appeared that Stewart was being singled out because of her fame.

"I don't think she should be prosecuted if all she did was trade on a broker's tip since that would be the selection of a celebrity where there are millions of people doing that every day."

Davis likened what Martha Stewart had done "at the very worst" to prohibition in the 1930s. "It was one of those crimes (insider trading) that unless you're a celebrity, it's hard to imagine anyone ever being prosecuted for the amount of money at stake for taking a tip from a broker."

If Davis were going to help her, Stewart would have to be convinced to talk far more candidly in public. "I don't know the facts," he told the MSLO board member. "I need to talk to her and see if she did engage in insider trading."

The board member said he would contact Martha Stewart and pass on Davis' willingness to talk with her. Stewart then phoned Lanny Davis. They chatted for a while and agreed to meet. After his troubleshooting experience in the White House, Davis had set himself up as a kind of strategic problem-solver, an expert on crisis management. Handling Martha Stewart's case fit neatly into his own job description.

But he knew he could not proceed without talking with Martha Stewart's attorneys. They had to be apprised of what he was doing. By this time, Stewart's lead attorney was white-collar defense attorney Bob Morvillo.

Davis phoned Morvillo and introduced himself, hoping to learn the facts of the case from the perspective of Stewart's attorney. As Davis explained later: "I wanted to work with her lawyer, to nail down the facts, to make sure she was telling the truth, or at least that she was credible. Then I would have her on Larry King and Barbara Walters. I would have tried to do all the talk shows. I wanted to saturate all the facts of the story and knock that out of the box."

Do It Anyway

Morvillo refused to speak to Davis, offering no explanation for his refusal. The attorney believed that criminal suspects—and that is precisely what Martha Stewart was at the time—should remain silent. Davis, on the other hand, had no such qualms. He actually thought a criminal suspect could benefit from public exposure.

Taken aback by Morvillo's ice-cold response, Davis had assumed that Stewart had briefed Morvillo about him, which she may well have done. He assumed further that Morvillo would take his call, which Stewart clearly had not convinced her attorney to do.

Davis picked up the phone to Stewart: "Your attorney doesn't want me to do this."

"I want you to do it anyway," Stewart replied.

That was all that Davis had to hear.

Davis was caught in between Stewart's attorney and Martha Stewart herself. It was the only time he had ever been put in the position of taking on a client as a public relations adviser against the wishes of the client's attorneys.

> *Davis picked up the phone to Stewart: "Your attorney doesn't want me to do this."*
> *"I want you to do it anyway," Stewart replied.*

He would try to help Stewart ("The challenge was tempting," he said later) but he was distinctly uncomfortable. Much later Davis acknowledged: "I will never do that again," but noted "under the circumstances I defend myself for making the decision. She was the majority shareholder, the chairman and the CEO, and she was saying she wanted me to help her. So I regarded her as my client."

Next time, he would make sure to have a client's attorney on his side.

In case anyone doubted that Martha Stewart was a tough client for an attorney, here was ample proof. Few clients would dare to override their attorneys on how to handle the case. But Martha Stewart had always run her own show; she had always conducted her own public relations campaigns. She had no desire to let her attorney interfere with her plan to mount a PR campaign that could save her.

Davis was confident he could help Stewart.

After all, in his view, she was one of the best communicators around (second only to Ronald Reagan, in his opinion). But before he put her on display, he had to be certain that what she would say in public would not endanger her case. "I have to have all the facts," he told her. He wanted no surprises watching her on television.

That meant putting together his own team of lawyers; doing his own investigation. As part of his own probe, he interviewed Martha Stewart in person and spoke to her on the phone frequently, asking her help as he sought to verify what she had told him. Davis was pleased with what he heard: "We came up with what we thought was a verifiable story."

In telling the story long after his involvement with Stewart had concluded, Davis still felt uncomfortable explaining what that "verifiable story" was. He blamed attorney-client privilege for not going into more detail. One could safely assume, however, that Stewart had sought to convince Davis that the $60-a-share agreement with Bacanovic was indeed true; she presumably had offered him greater substantiation that it was true than anything she had said before in public or in private. If that was the case, she certainly should have been trumpeting that story to the public at full blast.

Davis told Stewart that the story she told in public would have to be verifiable—and consistent. The authorities would judge her not just on whether she had engaged in insider trading; they would want to know if she had been lying to them. Davis told her, "If you say one word to us that is different from what you said to the prosecutors, you are going to go to jail."

Stewart said she understood the point.

After listening to Stewart and conducting his own investigation, Davis was confident that he could unleash Martha Stewart on to the public. "We corroborated all the important stuff. I was satisfied that she was telling me the truth."

One key point that Davis felt Stewart could stress in her public recitation of the case revolved around the conversation she held on that San Antonio tarmac on December 27th.

She had believed at the time—and still believed—that she had been talking to Peter Bacanovic, when in fact she had been talking to his assistant, Doug Faneuil.

The federal authorities, however, had described her insistence that she had been talking to Bacanovic as an example of her lying to them.

But, Davis believed Stewart had simply made an innocent mistake. It had been unfair of the authorities to try to argue that she had deliberately lied to them. Others, Davis had discovered, had made the same mistake of talking to Doug Faneuil on the phone, misidentifying him as Bacanovic.

MUCH ADO ABOUT NOTHING

A second key point for Stewart to stress if and when she went public was that she had not lied when she told the feds earlier in the year that she could not recall if she had been told on December 27th that the Waksal family was selling its ImClone stock.

Davis grilled Stewart on her recollection of that phone conversation. "She convinced me that she was telling the truth after I did as much checking as I could."

A third critical point that Stewart could sell to the public, Davis was convinced, was her assertion that she and Bacanovic had an agreement to sell ImClone if it dropped to $60 a share. She had already ridden the stock up and down for some time so there was every reason for her to sell the stock when it began dropping in late December 2001, in Davis' view.

Davis felt confident enough in Stewart's descriptions of what had happened to let her go public. "I came to my own conclusion that the story she had to tell would at least strike people as much ado about nothing. That story needed Martha to be out in the public market—to influence the prosecutors not to indict and to turn around the media, which had already convicted her."

> *"I came to my own conclusion that the story she had to tell would at least strike people as much ado about nothing."*

To Davis, the media had been responsible for much of Martha Stewart's woes by misrepresenting vital parts of her legal case.

"She had already been accused of insider trading at a Congressional hearing. There had been headlines that said that she had consistently lied about there being a stop order when in fact she had said there had been no stop order." All that she had ever claimed was that she and Bacanovic had a verbal understanding to sell her ImClone stock when it fell to $60 a share.

The media's conclusion that she was guilty of insider trading before she even went to trial, Davis asserted, started with bungled reporting. "You always saw the 'stop order' reference followed with a 'but'—'but Martha Stewart denied that there was any stop order on ImClone stock....'"

By quoting Stewart as denying the existence of a stop order, the media was insinuating, Davis suggested, that she was demonstrating her own guilt! That bungled reporting, said Davis, was amplified by the Internet echo chamber "that rattles negative information to such a degree that it becomes true."

The media should have quoted Stewart as saying that she had a verbal agreement with Bacanovic to sell the shares at $60 rather than to quote her denial of a stop order. So Davis believed.

However bungled the media's reporting about whether Stewart had a stop order or not, the prosecutors had the advantage for they could show tangible evidence that no stop order existed—all they had to do was to assert that no computer record existed of such a stop order. Stewart, on the other hand, was at a distinct disadvantage in proving that she had a verbal agreement with Bacanovic to sell her ImClone shares at $60. The only person who could directly corroborate her claim, Peter Bacanovic, faced a federal indictment for co-conspiracy with Stewart! How reliable would his testimony be?

A GREAT COMMUNICATOR

Davis was confident that getting Martha Stewart into the public marketplace was a shrewd move because she was "probably the best public communicator, next to Bill Clinton, alive."

He told her: "You are one of the three best communicators of our era (along with Clinton and Ronald Reagan) and you haven't been able to tell your story on Larry King or Barbara Walters and take your chances. What am I missing here?

"My lawyers think I won't be indicted," she replied, "so I shouldn't take the chance of going public."

But Davis adamantly argued that Stewart needed to put her case before the public: "Based on the media, you're guilty. Do you think the prosecutors don't read the papers? Do you think they don't believe you're a liar? You're not explaining it. What we have here is your silence versus these accusations and no one has ever won against such a one-sided argument."

Davis would have loved to go back to Robert Morvillo to make the case personally that Stewart should be allowed to explain herself in public. But Morvillo would still not talk to him. After letting Davis pursue his own plans for a major public relations campaign in secret unbeknownst to Morvillo and against the lawyer's wishes, Stewart simply let Davis dangle in the air. She seemed distinctly uninterested in pleading Davis' case to Morvillo.

Thus, Stewart never went public with any fuller explanations to support her innocence.

Lanny Davis could have quit the Martha Stewart case right there and then.

He certainly would have been justified.

But he still felt he could make a contribution, albeit in a more limited way than he would have liked. He knew that Morvillo had left him with what he later described as a "very limited, very risky strategy."

Unable to put her on the major television talk shows, Davis, going to Plan B, obtained Stewart's approval to find a reporter who would be permitted to carry out his own investigation into her case and hopefully conclude that she was innocent; and then publish an article to that effect. Such an article would have gone a long way to quashing a federal indictment. Stewart would provide the reporter with a full explanation of her side of the story, but she could not be quoted on any of those details.

Davis knew how hard it would be to find just such a reporter who would probably only think it worthwhile interviewing Stewart on the record.

The reporter to whom Davis turned was Jeff Toobin, a onetime attorney and former federal prosecutor, the foremost commentator on the American legal scene. His principal outlet was *New Yorker* magazine, though he appeared frequently as a contributing analyst on CNN and National Public Radio. Toobin had been asking for an interview with Stewart from the time he had learned about the ImClone probe.

Toobin saw in what Davis was offering the makings of a good story, just how good he could not tell until he sat down with Martha Stewart. Listening carefully to the restrictions imposed on him, Toobin tried to see past them, hoping that once he had a chance to meet with her, Stewart might agree to do the interview on the record after all.

On a bitterly cold Sunday afternoon in January 2003, Toobin showed up at Turkey Hill, Stewart's restored 1805 farmhouse in Connecticut.

The two had never met before. Toobin found Stewart nervous at first, and he thought that strange given that she was a public figure, and this was hardly her first interview. But he quickly understood the reason for her anxiety: Stewart had permitted Lanny Davis to arrange the interview without her informing her attorney, Robert Morvillo.

Stewart's attorneys and the federal authorities had more than a passing interest in what Martha Stewart said to Jeff Toobin, on or off the record. A few days before Toobin's article was to appear in the *New Yorker*, according to one account, John Savarese called him and begged him to reveal what Stewart had said to him. When writing about the Savarese overture, Toobin did not say whether he acquiesced, but one has to assume that the reporter said something to the effect that he would have to wait for publication of the article. According to this same account, the Securities and Exchange Commission subpoenaed the tape of his interview with Stewart but Toobin refused to provide it. The SEC chose not to pursue the matter.

A TERRIBLE TIME

When Toobin went to see Stewart, she was going through a terrible time. Almost since the time she had sold her ImClone stock, she had been probed by the Justice Department, by the Securities and Exchange Commission, by the U.S. Attorney's Office, and by Congress. Her business was suffering: Kmart, a critical outlet of her products, had gone bankrupt. Revenues and advertising in her businesses had dropped, as had the value of shares in Martha Stewart Living Omnimedia. Her personal fortune had shriveled and she was no longer a billionaire.

The media had been unkind toward her, worst of all: She had suffered ridicule, abuse, and it didn't stop. A mock magazine cover of *Martha Stewart Living Behind Bars* circulated widely on the Internet. Conan O'Brien quoted Stewart as saying "a subpoena should be served with a nice appetizer." David Letterman said in a monologue that Lizzie Grubman, the publicist who pleaded guilty to running down nightclub customers in her car, had been complaining about the food in jail. "Hang on until Martha Stewart gets there!" Letterman urged.

The criminal investigation was presumably nearing a resolution, and prosecutors in the U.S. Attorney's Office, were, according to media reports, going to decide in the next several weeks whether to indict her.

As soon as Toobin began the interview, he had a sense that Stewart was furious with being probed. She was careful not to say anything against her interrogators. What she did say was that her "public image has been one of trustworthiness, of being a fine, fine editor, a fine purveyor of historic and contemporary information for the homemaker. My business is about homemaking. And that I have been turned into, or vilified openly as, something other than what I really am has been really confusing. I mean, we've produced a lot of good stuff for a lot of good people. And to be maligned for that is kind of weird."

Though Toobin was there to interview Stewart on the legal case, he could not help but inject into the article a significant amount of detail about what it was like to have lunch with the world's most famous homemaker. For instance, he made a point of noting early in the article that Stewart's chef, a woman named Lily, had prepared a "comically elaborate Chinese lunch" for them.

The lunch lasted three hours. Davis, joined by two colleagues from his law firm, joined Stewart and Toobin.

Lanny Davis and his legal team presented Toobin with a summary of the ImClone trade as Stewart described it. "As I later learned," Toobin noted, "that version of the facts had crucial omissions."

From the start of the interview, Toobin was crippled by the rules: Stewart could discuss her feelings about the federal probe and the public reaction; but she would not speak on the record about the facts.

Davis indicated that for a significant part of the lunch, Stewart spoke off the record to Toobin about the facts of the case. (Toobin later called Davis 25 times to clarify aspects of the off-the-record conversation.)

Under Davis' rules, while Toobin could not quote Stewart on what she said about her legal case, he was free to try to corroborate what she said. He sought and received Davis' help on who to contact for that corroboration.

If he could not corroborate matters, Toobin was under no obligation to write a story. Davis knew enough not to ask Toobin for an advance commitment on what he would write. "I just wanted him to hear her story and be a good reporter and a good lawyer."

Unable to dwell on the legal case on the record, as he had hoped to, Toobin was forced to spend much writing space describing what it was like to be at Turkey Hill. Even though he was not that familiar with Stewart's talents, he found the interior familiar, "such is the ubiquity of her style." She gave him a tour of the ground floor. Toobin met her dogs and cats and her song canaries, screeching constantly inside their cages.

For Martha Stewart, dealing with lawyers, journalists, and public relations advisers was not the life she had envisaged as she began her married life to Andy Stewart back in 1961. Two years later, after his graduation from Yale Law School, they took an extended tour of France, Italy, and Greece—all on $5 a day, staying in small country inns, eating simple food made the same old-fashioned way that her parents had taught her. She found a new mission in life: creating the rustic European lifestyle that she had encountered on her trip. Returning to the U.S., she and Andy moved to the Upper West Side where he found a job at a New York City law firm. She returned to Barnard to finish her degree, meanwhile teaching herself how to cook the foods she had tasted in Europe, testing the recipes of television personality Julia Child. Stewart learned how to beautify her apartment by visiting auction houses and purchasing antique furniture. Her mother-in-law was a famous interior designer in her own right. Stewart developed an affinity for interior design, color, and all things to do with homemaking. Friends remembered that everything she did, fixing up the apartment, cooking, hosting parties, had to reach the highest possible quality. Eventually high quality became her trademark.

Economic realties began to intervene. Andy's salary was not earth-shaking; Stewart's modeling career was on hold. She was expecting a baby. In September 1965, Alexis Gilbert Stewart was born. (Mother and daughter had an up and down relationship over the years; but reconciled in time for Alexis to be Martha's constant companion during her legal case.) Martha still had hopes of going to architecture school, but she quickly changed her mind.

Starting in 1965, she began a second career as a stockbroker on Wall Street after seeking advice on how to get started from her stockbroker father-in-law. As a wedding present, Martha and Andy received some stock in a cargo airline enterprise and she became quite interested in the business. She thought it would be interesting to analyze businesses professionally.

She went around Wall Street and interviewed with a few firms. She came upon a young aggressive firm, Perlberg, Monness, Williams and Sidel, which had been looking for new people to instill it with energy. Andrew J. Monness, her future boss, sensed that Stewart would be an instant success. Though her background had been modest, she was highly cultivated, very attractive, "almost a can't miss situation," said

*Monness. She studied hard and passed her broker's exam in August
1968. She began working for Perlberg, Monness, Williams and Sidel.*

*At first she found the job quite tough. Among her clients were men
of the world, book buyers, art collectors, and raconteurs, and they fascinated her. She was one of a handful of women in the stock market.
When most women were just starting to gain access to the work force,
she was a rainmaker for her firm, pulling in a six-figure annual income.
"We did a lot of research on a few companies. Then we would take those
investment ideas and sell the hell out of them. I learned really what
made a good company, what made a good investment, and what made
a lot of money." All that experience would help her when she formed
her own company.*

Jeff Toobin's long piece, "LUNCH AT MARTHA'S: Problems with the
perfect life," appeared in the *New Yorker* magazine in its February 3,
2003 edition.

The first half of the article was about the lunch, not the legal case.
Lanny Davis had been surprised at how much space Toobin devoted to
the lunch though given the restrictions he had imposed on the writer, he
should not have been.

Davis found the first half of the story "colorful and entertaining" but
not particularly helpful because of one thing Toobin mentioned—
Stewart's silver chopsticks!

Toobin had been served quite a lunch, seven courses in all, beginning
with steaming Hunan chicken, crispy beef, and stone crabs. And those
were just the entrees. The lunch was served only the way Martha
Stewart knew how to do. Exquisite, Toobin thought. He noticed silver
chopsticks that she had put out.

BEAUTIFUL CHOPSTICKS

"Wow," he said to her, maybe hoping that a little flattery would loosen
her up a little, "these are really beautiful chopsticks."

"You know," she replied, "in China, the thinner the chopsticks, the
higher the social status. Of course, I had to have the thinnest chopsticks." And then she said, "That's why people hate me."

Lanny Davis could have done without Toobin mentioning the silver
chopsticks. It portrayed her, in his view, as something of an elitist.
"I thought it was unfair because on a personal level she's anything but
an elitist."

The closest that Martha Stewart got to talking about her plight was when Toobin, noting that she looked weary, asked if it was a case of *Schadenfreude*?

"That's the word," she said. "I hear that, like, every day." And she added, in her precise, perfectionist way, "Do you know how to spell it?"

On an unlined white writing pad, which matched her pens, Stewart had written a few notes about topics she wanted to cover, and one, it seemed, was the nature of fame. "It's sort of the American way to go up and down the ladder, maybe several times in a lifetime. And I've had a real long up—along the way my heels being bitten at for various reasons, maybe perfectionism, or maybe exactitude, or something. And now I've had a long way down."

As the lunch progressed, Stewart had kind words for Hillary Clinton for supporting her. ("She's worthy, she's great. You know, that's what I hope I'll be thought of as.") She wanted to convey to Toobin that she was coping despite the pressures: "I'm real lucky, because I am able to sort of compartmentalize, as other people who have been successful compartmentalize. I can be concerned on one hand, and be productive on the other hand. And that's a good trait for me." She felt physically strong. Her work, she said, was her distraction. "I can still sleep. I can still sleep my three or four hours."

She was tolerant of her tormentors: the late night comics, her buddies, she called them. "They have a job to do, they can comment on anybody in a playful way, and I don't think it's at all damaging." What was damaging, she believed, were the photos of her that ran in the *New York Post* that showed her looking haggard and distraught. "The ugliest pictures. And I'm a pretty photogenic person, I mean, and they manage to find the doozies." It bothered her when *Newsweek* wrote next to a photo of her that if she had been nicer to people on the way up, they would have been nicer to her on the way down: "I've never not been nice to anybody."

This was the way Stewart and her public relations advisers had orchestrated the article, with her talking about herself, but not about the specifics. She noted that the investigation had thus far cost her $400 million, mostly in the decline in value of her 30 million plus shares of Martha Stewart Living Omnimedia, but also in legal fees and lost business opportunities. Her stock had traded as low as $5 a share in 2002 but was trading at $9 a share when the Toobin article appeared.

She told Toobin that she had no thoughts of quitting her business.

"Quit a business that is my life?" she said. "Impossible." Indeed, despite the trauma of the last year, she was concentrating on areas where her company could grow. She launched a line of furniture this year and a digest-size magazine—part of a long-range plan, she said, to give the company an identity beyond her own image.

The new magazine was called *Everyday Food*, and it contained only a small reference to Stewart on the cover. "We're not hiding the fact that it's from Martha Stewart Living," she said. "It's just unnecessary to have it that gigantic on the cover."

In this kind of differentiation, Stewart's role model was Ralph Lauren, who created Polo, Purple Label, and other brands less directly tied to his name. "He was able to expand his empire greatly by different brand labels," she said.

ANTICIPATING THE CRISIS

In an almost prescient way, Stewart said, she had virtually anticipated her current crisis, if not its precise form. From the moment that she and her colleagues launched Martha Stewart Living Omnimedia, they had talked about nurturing the company while keeping in mind that one day she might have to leave it.

"We call it 'the bus'—the wayward bus, getting hit by the bus," she said. "You know, those 'D' things—death, dismemberment, dementia, disappearance, whatever they all are. All those 'D' things." As it turned out, though, it wasn't a bus. "It was something else," she said, quickly adding, "But I'm alive. There's the big difference."

When the lunch was over, Davis called his wife to let her know that he was leaving Turkey Hill. His lunch with Martha Stewart was over. "She only wanted to know what were the color of the napkins," Davis recalled.

The Toobin *New Yorker* article was a turning point in the Martha Stewart legal case.

With Stewart's lawyers furious over its publication ("The you-know-what hit the fan," Davis admitted), it became virtually impossible to get Martha Stewart to talk publicly about her legal case from then on. That was what she should have been doing but neither she nor her attorneys wanted to take the chance.

From Davis' point of view, the one redeeming aspect of the article was Toobin's decision to speak on television in favor of Stewart's innocence.

"It was a terrific building block," Davis suggested, for Stewart to take her case public. Had she done so, and had she avoided an indictment, the article would have been viewed as a brilliant gambit.

The article brought little additional sympathy to Stewart.

The quotes that journalists took from the interview did little to help her, focusing as the media did on her confusion over why the public had turned against her.

The true significance of the article was in putting to rest once and for all the hope among Stewart supporters that she would make a deal with the feds. By not using the article as a platform to express public contrition, by not unhinging herself in the article from the "lie" that authorities believed they could indict her on (the $60-a-share tale), she had tacitly acknowledged that she planned to adhere to her strategy to humble the feds on the battlefield. She remained a woman filled with illusions.

Davis was, of course, disappointed that he had been forced to work with his hands tied behind his back.

It can safely be assumed that Davis thought the real culprit in this affair was Robert Morvillo, but he contented himself with saying only that: "You can write that Morvillo declined to talk to me and I followed Martha's instructions and in retrospect I'm sorry I did and will never do it again."

The handing down of the indictment, which came six months later, was for Davis the final disappointment: "The outrage of the indictment was that after all the leaks and headlines about her being involved in insider trading, they didn't indict her for it."

When the case was all over, after Stewart was indicted, after she was tried, and after she was convicted, and after he had a change of mind about Stewart's innocence, Jeff Toobin looked back on the whole affair and felt badly for Lanny Davis. He "believed in getting her story out...Lanny is a very honorable person, and he didn't really know, I believe, the full extent of how guilty she was, or that she was guilty at all...."

CHAPTER

6

FORTY-ONE PAGES TO CHEW OVER

The legal proceedings against Martha Stewart began to take on an inexorable feel. Nothing that Stewart, or her lawyers or her public relations advisers, tried seemed to be working.

A deal still was possible if Stewart would concede some guilt. Yet, while she permitted the lawyers to talk about the possible terms of a deal, she clung to her profession of innocence. Hoping to keep her out of jail, the attorneys proposed that Stewart admit to guilt on a minor charge.

Stewart's attorneys sat down with Manhattan U.S. Attorney Jim Comey, offering an arrangement whereby Stewart would pay a civil fine and escape prison. The attorneys argued that so little money was involved, a criminal prosecution seemed like overkill.

Still gunning for Stewart, the feds wanted Stewart behind bars. It still looked like it would take years to put away Ken Lay, Dennis Koslovsky, and the other antagonists of the less-publicized, but more pernicious, set of corporate scandals rising to the surface in the past few months.

Here was Martha Stewart, neatly wrapped up, with a reliable witness (Doug Faneuil ready to turn against her). If insider charges were not provable, the feds were prepared to charge her with lying to them and with a string of other charges: obstructing justice, securities fraud, and conspiracy.

By April, Stewart's attorneys were desperately searching for a way to end the ordeal. At one point, they had the outlines of a deal that they thought would be agreeable to both the feds and Martha Stewart.

She would plead guilty to making a false statement with a sentencing guideline of zero to six months; in exchange, she would be given probation, but no jail time.

When prosecutors heard the offer, they quickly noted that they could not guarantee that Stewart would avoid jail, giving Stewart little incentive to acquiesce. Had the feds really wanted to help Stewart out of this legal jam, they would have assured her that they would do all in their power to keep her out of jail; but they did not.

> *"You are never going to get a better deal than this. This is a good deal."*

Still, Stewart's lawyers thought the deal too good to refuse.

"Look," one of her lawyers said to her, "you are never going to get a better deal than this. This is a good deal."

She did not think so: "I am not going to take this deal, and the reason I'm not going to take it is because I won't plead guilty to something I didn't do."

"Hey—well, you know," said one of her attorneys, "we're not going to force you to plead guilty to something you say you didn't do."

Martha Stewart did her best to maintain the appearance of keeping up a normal business routine.

On May 3, 2003, she visited Miami and introduced a new furniture line. A predominantly female crowd of several hundred turned out eagerly at Carl's Furniture near the Golden Glades Interchange. She offered her views on decorating, her pets, and her family; she also looked over her new line of Bernhardt-manufactured Martha Stewart Signature Furniture. She was pleased that her legal entanglement had not scared off customers. She previewed for the audience a forthcoming television segment in which she used the new furniture to redecorate her 89-year-old mother's living room as a birthday present.

It was a forgiving crowd.

Said one shopper: "What goes on in a famous person's life doesn't concern me. I just like her products and ideas. Everyone has a scandal in their life."

But Wall Street analysts were less san-
guine. "Even if there is a favorable resolution to Ms. Stewart's legal issues," wrote
Alisa Goldwasser of William Blair &
Company, "we believe that a recovery in
the company's fundamentals will not happen quickly and the company's businesses
may be permanently affected."

> *"What goes on in a famous person's life doesn't concern me. I just like her products and ideas. Everyone has a scandal in their life."*

Plans to Diversify

Still, Stewart and her colleagues at the company were planning to diver-
sify, launching a new magazine to be called *Everyday Food*, among other
projects.

Nothing could disguise the realities: Martha Stewart's legal woes were
a massive burden on the company. "We're in a time of uncertainty, and
what we're trying to do is preserve our assets, even if it means short-
term losses," said Sharon Patrick, president and chief operating officer of
Martha Stewart Omnimedia. "We're managing the company for the long
term."

While she refused to talk about the legal case, journalists in the crowd
that day in Miami still looked for a colorful quote from Stewart on her
troubles. As her handlers tried to whisk her away, one newsperson asked
her when the government probe would end. All she could say was: "Are
you a fortune teller?"

She did speak to one journalist privately, acknowledging how disappointing it had been to have the legal cloud hang over her company for
nearly a year. "I'm sad about that," she admitted, dressed for summer in
white pants and a butter yellow blazer. "It's pretty hard to grasp. I
haven't been accused of anything."

But that could soon change.

It was the first week of June. All indications were that the feds were
about to indict Martha Stewart. Her lawyers decided to enter into plea
negotiations one last time to stave off the indictment.

They offered the same terms that had been on the table in April:
Stewart would plead guilty to a single felony, making a false statement
to federal agents. But again the feds balked at promising her no jail time.

On Sunday, June 1st, Stewart arrived at the Wachtell, Lipton, Rosen & Katz offices, on West 52nd Street. She had to decide whether to accept the deal that John Savarese and his partner Larry Pedowitz had worked out.

During a speakerphone conversation with Stewart, Karen Patton Seymour, the chief of the criminal division of the U.S. Attorney's office in New York, and her colleague Richard Owens, put the matter succinctly:

Would Stewart admit that she had lied to the investigators?

Stewart said that she could not do that. And that ended the meeting.

The next day, reassembling at Robert Morvillo's office, Stewart and her defense team continued to discuss the deal.

Morvillo, at 65, was three years older than his client. For 30 years, he had been one of the top white-collar-criminal-defense attorneys. While his 36-attorney firm had prospered, its offices, on two floors at Fifth Avenue and 46th Street, could not compete with the lavishness of Wachtell, Lipton. Morvillo's private office was cluttered with baseball souvenirs and yellowing files from old cases. Martha Stewart admired him for being self-made, as she was. Thus, they had a kinship.

Savarese and Pedowitz urged Stewart to take the deal. She would never get a better one, they insisted. Going to trial was always a risk. There were no guarantees she would get off. Sure, they acknowledged, were she to plea to a felony, she might not be able to run her company for some time; but the damage would be slight compared to her being indicted, going to trial, and perhaps going to jail.

Stewart listened, thought about it, but argued that she could not agree to a plea bargain. She still believed she was innocent and would be vindicated.

Two days later, her world came crashing down on her.

The moment that Martha Stewart had dreaded for the past 18 months occurred on June 4, 2003, when a federal grand jury in Manhattan indicted her and Peter Bacanovic on nine criminal counts.

She was charged with two counts of making false statements, securities fraud, conspiracy, and obstruction of justice.

Peter Bacanovic's charges were perjury, conspiracy, and obstruction of justice. If Stewart were found guilty on all charges, she faced a maximum sentence of 30 years in prison and a $2 million fine.

Nearly everyone caught the irony: None of the charges included insider trading, the basis for the original probe. Martha Stewart and Peter Bacanovic were being accused of a cover-up for an unspecified crime.

Her attorneys made it clear she would fight the charges.

Still, the indictment was the single worst blow to her image, so carefully manicured, so carefully orchestrated.

Practically speaking, she could not continue to lead her company; she stepped down as Chairman and Chief Executive of Martha Stewart Living Omnimedia. She remained a member of the board.

"I love this company, its people, and everything it stands for," she said with much sadness. "I am stepping aside as Chairman and CEO because it is the right thing to do." Company president Sharon Patrick stepped in as acting CEO and company shareholder Jeffrey Ubben, an investment banker, became acting Chairman. Martha Stewart was named Chief Creative Director of the company.

Sharon Patrick and Martha Stewart had built Martha Stewart Living Omnimedia together. Patrick was the businesswoman, Stewart the creative force and spokesperson. Patrick has been credited with telling Stewart—while they were hiking to Mount Kilimanjaro—that Stewart should purchase Martha Stewart Living from Time Warner and start her own empire. The 1999 IPO was then the culmination of the Stewart-Patrick strategy. "Standing on the stock-exchange podium together was standing on our dreams," Patrick said.

STUNNING BLOW

Stepping down from the leadership of the company was a stunning blow to Stewart. She had built the company from scratch. She and the company were in many ways one and the same. It was not even clear that the company could continue without her in charge. Still, unless and until she was declared innocent, she did the right thing in stepping down as head of the company.

Following the indictment, the Securities and Exchange Commission filed a civil complaint seeking to ban Stewart from ever leading a public company and to limit her activity as an officer of a public company. The complaint was still pending as of October 2005.

Emerging from a black shiny car, she arrived at a federal courthouse in Lower Manhattan on the day that the indictment was handed down, a picture of poise. Shielding her face with a large off-white umbrella, she walked briskly into the courthouse.

She ignored waiting reporters and camera crews.

She was to be formally charged in a few moments.

She looked stern, a bit nervous. Her face was neutral as if she were somewhere else. No one could know how rattled she was over her predicament.

U.S. District Court Judge Miriam Goldman Cedarbaum conducted the brief hearing.

When the judge asked for a plea, Stewart's response of "Not Guilty" was loud and emphatic. Indeed, according to one writer, her response "rang out like a bell, with the first 't' enunciated in the clipped diction familiar to anyone who has ever followed her instructions to plunge blanched green beans into a bowl of 'ice water.'"

The indictment again raised the issue of whether Martha Stewart had been singled out as a celebrity scapegoat for the more egregious crimes of other corporate criminals.

Nonsense, said the prosecutors.

"Martha Stewart is being prosecuted not for who she is but what she did," said James Comey, the U.S. Attorney for the Southern District of New York. Stewart's prosecutors did acknowledge that with the charges against her, they were hoping to send a message to other potentially felonious CEOs.

Robert Morvillo, representing Stewart, took exception to what Comey had said, asking rhetorically: "Is it because she is a woman who has successfully competed in a man's business world by virtue of her talent, hard work, and demanding standards?"

Stewart was released without bail. The next step was to set a date for her trial.

Forgotten in the excitement surrounding Martha Stewart was the indictment of Peter Bacanovic. He also pleaded innocent to all charges against him. Though Bacanovic's attorneys tried to have his case separated from that of Stewart's, he and Martha Stewart would stand trial together.

The 41-page indictment, United States of America v. Martha Stewart and Peter Bacanovic, began by outlining what it alleged happened on December 27, 2001, in minute-by-minute detail.

For example:

"On the morning of December 27, 2001, between 9:00 a.m. and 10:00 a.m. (EST), Douglas Faneuil informed Peter Bacanovic that Sam Waksal and a member of his family (the "Waksal Family Member") were seeking to sell all the ImClone shares they held at Merrill Lynch, then worth over $7.3 million. Faneuil advised Bacanovic that the Waksal Family Member had placed an order to sell all of the Waksal Family Member's ImClone stock."

The indictment then recounted a critical sequence of events, noting that Aliza Waksal's shares had been sold and that Sam Waksal had asked that nearly 80,000 of his shares be sold.

The document explained that Peter Bacanovic had violated Merrill Lynch's policy of keeping client information confidential by directing Doug Faneuil to disclose to Martha Stewart information about the sale of the Waksal shares.

It told of how right after learning that the Waksals were selling their shares, Bacanovic called Stewart and informed her that the ImClone stock was dropping, and ordered Faneuil to tell Stewart about the Waksal transactions.

The indictment then read:

"On Dec. 27, 2001, at approximately 1:39 p.m., EST, Martha Stewart telephoned the office of Peter Bacanovic and spoke to Douglas Faneuil who informed her that Sam Waksal was trying to sell all of the ImClone stock that Waksal held at Merrill Lynch.

Upon hearing this news, Stewart directed Faneuil to sell all of her ImClone stock—3,928 shares. All 3,928 ImClone shares owned by Stewart were sold that day at approximately 1:52 p.m. EST at an average price of $58.43 per share, yielding proceeds of approximately $228,000." The indictment then argued that Martha Stewart had known that the information related to the Waksal shares had been given to her "in violation of the duties of trust and confidence owed to Merrill Lynch and its clients." The federal authorities offered no explanation for how they knew what was in her mind. A key part of Stewart's defense would be that she could not have known that what she had been told violated Merrill Lynch's policies.

The indictment then referred to the ImClone news release announcing the FDA's rejection of Erbitux. It then noted Stewart's savings as a result of her stock sale:

"By selling a total of 3,928 shares of ImClone stock on the same day as the sale and attempted sale of the Waksal shares, Martha Stewart avoided significant trading losses. If Stewart had sold at the price at which ImClone stock opened on Dec. 31, 2001, Stewart would have lost $51,222. If Stewart had sold at the price at which ImClone stock closed on Dec. 31, 2001, Stewart would have lost $45,673."

THE COVER-UP

A second part of the indictment cited statements Martha Stewart had made between January and April 2002 to the authorities to obstruct the official probe that she had concocted with Peter Bacanovic.

The federal authorities made clear in the indictment that they had not bought the Stewart-Bacanovic explanation for her stock sale—the $60-a-share agreement. The two were charged with an attempt to "fabricate and attempt to deceive investigators with a fictitious explanation for her sale...."

The feds were not going to skip lightly over Stewart's attempt to change a Bacanovic phone message.

According to the indictment, upon her being summoned for the February 4, 2002 interview, Stewart had "accessed the phone message log maintained on (the) computer by her assistant and reviewed the phone message that Peter Bacanovic had left for her on Dec. 27, 2001."

"In furtherance of the conspiracy, and knowing that Bacanovic's message for Stewart was based on information regarding the sale and attempted sale of the Waksal shares that Bacanovic subsequently caused to be conveyed to her, Stewart deleted the substance of Bacanovic's phone message, changing the message from 'Peter Bacanovic thinks ImClone is going to start trading downward' to 'Peter Bacanovic re ImClone.' After altering the message, Stewart directed her assistant to return the message to its original wording."

Had they wished, the federal authorities could have cited Stewart's tampering with the phone message as strong evidence of a "consciousness of guilt." They did not, more than likely assuming that the jury would have no trouble interpreting her actions as a sign of her guilt.

MOST CONTROVERSIAL CHARGE

The most controversial charge against her was securities fraud.

In the indictment, the feds focused on a series of public statements Stewart made defending her ImClone sale soon after the disclosure in June 2002 that she was under investigation.

In those public statements, she kept denying that she had received any inside information and said she was simply following the $60-a-share sell arrangement she and Bacanovic had talked about.

The feds, however, felt that she had issued these statements, not only to defend herself against prosecution, but also to stop the erosion of the stock price of Martha Stewart Living Omnimedia. In effect, the feds charged, she was deceiving shareholders who otherwise might have been concerned that insider-trading allegations would hurt the company.

Some securities attorneys felt that the allegation of Stewart's fraud on shareholders was quite novel since it referred to the personal conduct of a corporate officer, rather than company-related conduct.

The fraud charge increased her potential prison time; the maximum sentence for securities fraud was 10 years, twice that of the other charges.

On the day of the indictment, Billy Tauzin and James Greenwood, the two legislators who headed up a 10-month investigation of ImClone, Sam Waksal, and Martha Stewart, issued a remarkable public statement: "This action should send a sobering signal to everyone that insider trading is not a victimless crime—no matter how insignificant the ill-gotten gains—and any attempts to cover it up should be dealt with swiftly and forcefully."

"...While we are making no assumptions as to her innocence or guilt, obstruction of justice—whether it involves Congress or the Justice Department or both—is a very serious charge which must be pursued vigorously and to the fullest extent of the law."

The most significant part of the statement was their mention of insider trading as if Stewart had been charged with that crime. She had not been. But even two members of Congress made the mistake of suggesting that she had been.

Her fall from grace seemed swift and precipitous, nothing like her rise to success and celebrity. That had taken time—years, in fact.

Moving to Westport, Connecticut in 1972, with her husband Andy and her seven-year-old daughter Alexis, Stewart, then 31 years old, decided that she wanted to start her own business, what kind she did not know, only that it would focus on food and entertaining. It was here that she truly began multi-tasking, getting a great deal done. "It was just incredible when you think that she was raising a daughter and cultivating all these hobbies," said Andrew J. Monness, a long-time friend. "She really could do all these things. She could really make a peach pie better than anyone's peach pie, you know what I mean, she could really make a sandwich that was better than anyone's sandwich."

Meanwhile, Andy opened a very successful publishing house.

They found an old (1805) farmhouse that was badly in need of repair. When Stewart's relatives visited, they could not believe that two people with a baby lived in such chaos, such a wreck of a house. But the couple set their minds to creating the perfect life for themselves. The farmhouse was at a place called Turkey Hill.

Every night and weekends they tore down walls, built new rooms and repainted the interior. Martha hand stenciled the floors and presided over the construction of a restaurant-sized kitchen. Meanwhile, they cleared trees, planted gardens, and built a chicken coop. Friends remembered both Stewarts waking at 4:30 a.m. to feed the chickens. They named their six-acre property Turkey Hill.

With her increasingly positive reputation as a great hostess, she decided that she could turn her passion for entertaining into a new career. Placing an ad in the local newspaper in 1975, she offered her services as a caterer. Soon thereafter, the phone rang. The caller asked if she could cater a wedding. Thrilled at the prospect, Stewart enlisted her husband and her mother, who came up from Nutley, New Jersey. That was wise, for it turned out to be a wedding attended by 300 guests. Stewart felt she was ready: She had trained by preparing each recipe from Julia Child's Mastering the Art of French Cooking.

Soon Stewart realized that she had launched a profession on her own and she decided to try to attract upscale Connecticut clients. She began a catering business that would exploit her creative talents in the kitchen, partnering with college friend Norma Collier. They called their business the Uncatered Affair.

(Years later, Collier, by then a financial analyst, acknowledged that "something happened—she gradually lost any consciousness of people as people." Things turned sour for Collier when she walked into the Stewart home holding salmon and puff pastry for 300, overhearing Martha Stewart tell Andy: "I'm more talented, and I deserve to take more money out of the business." Collier soon ended their partnership. Meanwhile, Martha Stewart's catering business thrived.)

Stewart had always believed in herself, and in her innocence; she assumed that made her almost invulnerable. Accordingly, even with an indictment hanging over her head, she would not let this horrible setback get the better of her. The indictment, she assured everyone, would not force her into seclusion.

As the new Chief Creative Director at Martha Stewart Living Omnimedia, she planned to play her usual role in shaping the company's products. She and her colleagues decided that, at least for the time being, the name "Martha Stewart" should appear as prominently as ever in the businesses and in their promotional material.

Branding specialists were shocked that the company would try to carry on with business as usual. There simply had to be less "Martha Stewart" in Martha Stewart's products. But the newly indicted Creative Director had no desire to bury her head in the sand.

THE QUEEN OF COMMUNICATION

She had made her way this far as the Queen of Communication, and she would use the same strategies that she had employed in her business to make her legal case go away.

The day after her indictment, at a cost of $79,000, she took out a full-page ad in *USA Today* proclaiming her innocence.

She seemed determined to keep her business enterprises out of her personal difficulties, or at least try to: "After more than a year, the government has decided to bring charges against me for matters that are personal and entirely unrelated to the business of Martha Stewart Living Omnimedia. I want you all to know that I am innocent—and that I will fight to clear my name."

"I simply returned a call from my stockbroker," Stewart wrote. "Based in large part on prior discussions with my broker about price, I authorized a sale of my remaining shares in a biotech company called ImClone. I later denied any wrongdoing in public statements and voluntary interviews with prosecutors. The government's attempt to criminalize these actions makes no sense to me."

Once again, in professing her innocence, she offered nothing beyond her previous statements that would help clear her name.

Her attitude seemed to be: I am Martha Stewart. It should be good enough that I say I am innocent. You don't need evidence from me.

She also launched a Web site, Marthatalks.com, where she asserted her innocence and asked supporters to send her e-mail messages. The Web site carried messages from her, from her attorneys, and reproduced pro-Stewart articles in the media.

Within two weeks, Marthatalks.com registered 10 million hits and received 55,000 letters of encouragement. (By the following spring, the site had received more than 16 million hits and 81,000 e-mails.)

Praised by public relations specialists for shrewdly trying to influence potential jurors, Stewart relied on the Web site, these specialists said, because she had few other options. In their view, she would have been foolish to appear on national television talk shows where she might put her foot in her mouth and where her arrogance and perfectionism might come through too boldly.

The public relations specialists were wrong.

It was too late for Stewart to appear on the major talk shows to stave off a federal indictment. But there was a pool of potential jurors to influence—and she could have used the television airwaves effectively to plead her case before them. She chose not to.

Her lawyers continued to insist that she remain quiet about the case. All that she could do was issue brief, vague public statements through her Web site and in newspaper advertising, none of which seemed very effective. She hoped that her continuing claims of innocence would rejuvenate her businesses. It seemed a long shot at best.

The damage to Martha Stewart and to her company due to the probe and the indictment had been devastating. Since June 2002, when the probe first became public, Martha Stewart Omnimedia's stock dropped from $19.23 a share to a little over $9 a share, a nearly 50 percent drop over one year.

As for Stewart, she acknowledged that she has lost nearly half her net worth, some $400 million.

On June 10th, Sam Waksal was sentenced to seven years and three months in a federal prison and ordered to pay $3 million in fines and back taxes. He began serving his sentence six weeks later at the Schuylkill Federal Correctional Institute in Minersville, Pennsylvania. He went to jail without saying a word to implicate—or to exonerate— Martha Stewart. (Appearing on *60 Minutes* the following October 5th, he noted: "I got the impression that if they [the investigators] could have Martha, they would be unbelievably happy campers...."

At a brief hearing, attended by both Stewart and Bacanovic, Judge Miriam Goldman Cedarbaum set January 12, 2004, as the date for their trial.

All that Martha Stewart could do was to try to keep her company from suffering more blows. By the end of the summer, she went along with her colleagues' decision to reduce her dependence on her businesses. The company's newest magazine, *Everyday Food*, was to debut in the fall, the first title published by the company that did not feature Stewart's name.

For 13 years, *Martha Stewart Living* carried "Martha's Calendar," a month's worth of information about her activities. Anything Stewart did ("Deadhead roses and perennials") or planned to do ("Wash all cats") was included in the column. Starting September 2003, the column no longer appeared. Gone too was Stewart's "Remembering" column. The words MARTHA STEWART became smaller on *Martha Stewart Living*. Patrick began a new ad campaign: "Take a New Look at Living." All of these "let's-shrink-Martha" changes were startling developments, considering that it had been Stewart who had founded the company and that the company, for all of its existence, had been so Stewart-centric.

It was Sharon Patrick who engineered the downgrading of Martha Stewart at Martha Stewart Living Omnimedia. In one of those "et tu Brute" twists, Patrick, who had long been twinned with Stewart as co-leaders of MSLO, was slicing and dicing Martha Stewart so that her presence was far less visible in the company's products. Patrick had been the key force behind *Everyday Food*; it had been she who had purchased *Body & Soul*, the magazine dealing with yoga and herbs; and she had altered the titles of Stewart's two weekly newspaper columns that had been distributed by the *New York Times* Syndicate. "Ask Martha" became "Living" and "AskMartha Weddings" became "Weddings."

Meanwhile, more bad news came for Stewart as a result of her downward slide: Six CBS television affiliates decided on September 15th to move Stewart's hour-long program from the coveted 9:00 a.m. time slot to a 2:00 a.m. slot due to declining viewership. The new time slot was bound to hurt her ratings even more and thus negatively impact advertising for the show.

THE UNFLAPPABLE MS. STEWART

Despite the blows, Stewart seemed unflappable. In early September, appearing jubilant and energetic, she began a weeklong promotional tour in Canada where her Everyday brand of merchandise was debuting at Sears.

Stewart sought to give the impression that nothing bad was happening to her. She carried on as normally as possible. Once again, she began attending parties; she traveled to Italy; she had business dinners with such people as investment giant Warren Buffett. Her hometown of Nutley, New Jersey, inducted her into its local hall of fame, an effort that was heavily encouraged by Stewart's own public relations handlers.

Her handlers tried a broad array of maneuvers to win her favor with a potential jury pool. They took polls. They kept her Web site running. And they arranged two carefully planned television interviews, one with Barbara Walters, the other with Larry King. Both Stewart and the PR handlers knew that the interviews would have to be tepid—she would agree to the interviews only if her legal case was not discussed.

At most, she could be asked such soft questions as: How do you feel about what is happening to you? Can you imagine what it might be like to be in prison? She could not be asked: What was going through your mind when you agreed to take that controversial stock tip? Or: Did you know that Sam Waksal had just sold his ImClone shares when you decided to sell yours?

The PR handlers wanted her on television, and this watered-down version would have to do. The whole intent was to have Stewart proclaim her innocence over and over again so that anyone who might serve on the jury would have seen and heard her at least once.

> *"I never hold it against a person I am investigating if they want to get their side out and go on TV."*

The Walters interview and a subsequent one with Larry King posed risks for Stewart. Prosecutors loved when a defendant appeared on national television. "I never hold it against a person I am investigating if they want to get their side out and go on TV," said New York Attorney General Eliot Spitzer after Martha Stewart's interview with Barbara Walters. "It locks them further into their story and gives me so much more to work with."

But Stewart was careful not to discuss the details of her legal case except in the same broad generalities she had employed on previous occasions.

On November 7, 2003, she appeared on Walters' *20/20* program, one of the highest-rated shows of the year. The interview had a certain significance: It was the first time that Stewart had talked about her legal plight publicly—however vaguely—since the infamous cabbage-slicing incident in June 2002.

Stewart let viewers know how much she was suffering from her travail. "It hurts a lot, Barbara. I'm hurting."

The criminal prosecution, she told Walters, had been the most difficult part of her life. Prodded by Walters, she skewed her trademark phrase to describe the ordeal: "It is not a good thing."

Walters asked her what had been the most painful part of her legal case.

"I think," said Stewart, "a delay in a good life, a hiatus in a really fine existence. At my age, there's no time for an unexpected, undesirable, unwanted hiatus. None, one that you can't really control. It's difficult."

"Especially," Walters shot back, "for a lady who's used to control?"

"Well," replied Stewart, correcting her, "especially for a lady who has lots more to do."

"Martha," Walters continued, "it is possible that you could be sent to prison for up to 30 years. Are you scared?"

"Who wouldn't be scared? Of course, I'm scared. The last place I would ever want to go is to prison, and I don't think I will be going to prison, though."

In that interview, Stewart seemed alternately subdued and defiant, discussing her humble roots in New Jersey and acknowledging, sort of, that she was not perfect. Stewart said she "sometimes, but not always" had a bad temper and could occasionally be insensitive and driven. But she said she did not know why some of the public did not like her. "Those traits and that behavior, if it were applied to a man, would be admirable. Applied to a woman, you know, she's a 'beetch.'"

There it was again—Martha Stewart behaving as if she was the victim, that she treated everyone just fine.

She insisted that she was innocent and should not be lumped together with massive corporate fraud cases like Enron and WorldCom. Asked whether she ever thought she would be considered a corporate criminal, mentioned in the same breath as Enron and WorldCom, Stewart said: "Absolutely not, and I certainly don't belong in that category. What I did was not against the rules," she asserted.

Stewart also referred to her embarrassing appearance on the CBS morning show. "To tell you the truth, I have not been able to chop a cabbage since," she said, only half-humorously. "No more coleslaw for me. I was making a salad and it got out of hand." It was the first time that she had expressed any remorse over the incident.

She sought to deflect the notion that most people hate her. "I like to think that each and every one of us have people that love us and people that hate us." When Walters noted that not everyone has people who hate them, Stewart snapped: "Well, the people you think hate me don't know me...I don't know why people don't like me. I'm not perfect. The perception that I am perfect, I think got kind of mixed up with the idea that what we're trying to teach is the best possible standard out there. So if we're going to make a cake, Barbara, my cake can't be a flop. People won't watch my show if it's a flop. I'm not a comedy show, I'm a how-to show."

I AM A HUMAN BEING

When the interview was over, Walters believed that Stewart had succeeded in conveying precisely the message that she had felt would go over best with potential jurors: I am a human being. Don't judge me on whether you like me or hate me. That should not be a part of the forthcoming trial.

Walters did think, however, that Stewart missed an opportunity to gain some sympathy at one point in the interview. It occurred when Walters asked her if she thought that people were happy about her legal problems because little miss perfect has fallen on her face. Walters thought Stewart should have said that she was not perfect—but instead she insisted that she had not fallen on her face.

She then granted an interview to Larry King on December 22nd.

In the King interview, she talked briefly about religion and brought along her mother, Martha Kostyra, and several Polish holiday babka they had baked. Stewart tugged at the audiences' heart by asserting that this is "the saddest Christmas ever." She made no other reference to her legal case.

The two interviews fell flat. They had to.

The ground rules barring discussion of her legal case meant that Stewart would not have the chance to bowl over her audience—and potential jurors—through her persuasive skills.

Instead, she whined about people hating her, complained that she was being singled out because she was a woman, and admitted that she was scared of going to prison. As a result, she did very little to shore up support for herself. She continued to give the impression that she was not a very nice person.

Doug Arthur watched the Walters and King interviews and cringed, not because he thought Martha Stewart had spoken too candidly, but that she was giving media interviews while not meeting with him. He was one of the leading Wall Street analysts covering her company. Yet he was being shut out during the greatest crisis that had ever hit Martha Stewart Living Omnimedia. He blamed Stewart's lawyers: "I still cover the company, but I haven't talked to Martha since all of this happened. I used to talk to her a lot. I went to dinners of the company, went to Christmas dinner. I have not actually had a single conversation; her lawyers haven't allowed it."

Pounded by the media for insights in her company, Arthur was annoyed. "It wasn't that I wanted her to explain her legal situation to me; but she could have explained her perspective on her business." When he saw her Walters and King appearances, "I resented it. I told people at her company what I thought. I told them my ass is on the line. My rating is on the line. My company is on the line and I have no access to the company."

It was one more example of the flawed Stewart strategy of not letting the people who could have helped her the most do their thing. The lawyers were keeping Stewart from showing herself off in her best light. And Stewart's company was keeping Doug Arthur from talking regularly about Martha Stewart at a time when the media was eager to hear his thoughts on her.

Stewart had not avoided an indictment. Her trial was due to begin in January. All that she could hope for now was a sympathetic jury and some clever defense attorneys.

The crisis that she had wanted so desperately to prevent now loomed ominously on the horizon.

PART III

SHOWDOWN AT FOLEY SQUARE

CHAPTER

7

OPENING DAYS

Once Martha Stewart was indicted, was a conviction at her trial inevitable?

In retrospect—and everything is always easier to analyze after the fact—it appeared so, even though it was hard to believe she might be found guilty.

After all, she had the best lawyers on her side. She was one of the most famous women in America. Such celebrity surely carried some immunity from a criminal conviction, especially for a minor mistake. The feds could not even charge her with insider trading, the crime she was alleged to have originally committed.

Still, her forthcoming trial should not have been a great surprise. Through her flawed strategies, she had done everything she could do to bring about the trial. Now the only question was: Would she and her attorneys develop a wiser set of strategies to steer her through the perils of the courtroom?

The whole scene at the federal courthouse on Foley Square looked incongruous.

Routinely, one was used to seeing Martha Stewart on television, setting standards for homemaking and home entertainment. That was her venue. Indeed, she owned that particular space.

Now, here she was, like any other alleged criminal, appearing in court, a lawyer at her side, waiting and hoping that the nightmare would soon end.

Who could have imagined that one of the most successful women in America would be brought so low? Who could have believed that she would be huddling with attorneys, attending hearings, getting finger-printed, and preparing for the worst ordeal of her life?

It was indeed surrealistic.

Here she was in a federal courtroom with a jury who would be rendering a verdict affecting her life and career. How could they judge her? She had made her mark over the years by being the one to judge, the one to set standards. If any single event exemplified that, it was the publication of her book, Entertaining, *in 1982, an instant best-seller that sold over a million copies. That book helped to transform her career from caterer to media titan. Ideas on how to entertain with flair had been rolling around in her head in the late 1970s, but it was only when she met one of her catering clients, Allen Mercken of Crown Books, that she had the incentive to write a book. When the book appeared just before Christmas 1982, it sold for $35, making it one of the most expensive cookbooks ever published. She was writing for women who, like herself, had gone to work outside the home, but had too little time to devote to homemaking, gardening, and entertaining. She wanted to help them remain active in the workplace but still be capable of beautifying their home and of entertaining socially. She was confident that* Entertaining *would be a hit because until then no one had packaged a similar idea with great recipes, informative photos, and a readable text. Twelve more books, penned by Stewart, followed. She was proud of their high quality:*

"I don't do anything unless I think it's going to be good, I'm real picky about that. I have set a standard, and I'm going to stick to the standard."

For the woman who set such high standards, January 19, 2004, was truly a nightmare.

It was the first day of her trial.

She would have liked nothing better than to stay away from the proceedings. But her presence was required. Much later, she made it sound as if she had debated whether to appear in court, as if she had a choice. "I wouldn't have missed it. I wanted to see what was going to happen.... You couldn't have kept me away."

These were odd statements—considering that as the defendant she had no choice but to appear at her trial.

Precisely at 9:20 a.m., she emerged at the Manhattan federal courthouse at Foley Square. Reporters and television crews watched from a distance. They had been unable to buttonhole her when she made her other court appearances. The media seemed somehow less aggressive this morning; as if they knew getting Martha Stewart to speak to them was a lost cause. The dozen or so photographers, who had waited impatiently for an hour or so, got their arrival shots, and then began to disperse.

Left with little else to report, they fell back on her attire.

Centre Street was filled with slush but she was wearing high-heeled brown boots to protect herself against the slush. Leaving the car, she pushed her blond hair back. She climbed the steps. Wearing a dark wraparound coat and brown trousers, Martha Stewart held two bags in her right hand. Noticing supporters standing on the icy sidewalks in the numbing cold, she waved to them awkwardly.

The editor of the Web site SaveMartha.com, John Small, was among the supporters. He was wearing a chef's hat and apron and carried a sign that read, "Save Martha! If her stock sale was legit, you must acquit!" It was a play on fabled attorney Johnny Cochran's famous line at the O.J. Simpson trial, and those who remembered the Simpson trial understood the reference.

TWO HOURS ON A BUS

Another Stewart supporter sat two hours on a bus, taking a day off from her job, to brave the cold outside the courthouse. "You go, girl!" she yelled as her heroine strode by. The visitor had learned how to garden by watching Stewart's how-to television show. Martha brought beauty into her life, she told a journalist; that was why she could not stay away. Other Stewart supporters carried silver kitchen utensils such as whisks, slotted spoons, and spatulas. Others held "SAVE MARTHA" placards in pastel colors.

Stewart and her bodyguard approached the front-door metal detector. Others were waiting in line. She was waived to the front. She and the guard passed through the detector. She then went to a fourth-floor war room where her legal team was assembling: Robert Morvillo, her attorney, and three other attorneys, along with a bunch of paralegals from the

Morvillo law firm. Joining them was attorney John Cuti, Martha Stewart's son-in-law.

Five minutes later, the man who was nearly forgotten in all of this, Peter Bacanovic, arrived at the courthouse, emerging from a black GMC Denali sport utility vehicle. He wore a blue tie, charcoal suit, and navy overcoat. Upon entering the courtroom, he approached Martha Stewart, who kissed him on both cheeks. Bacanovic's parents showed up. His mother declared that her son was being railroaded, hardly a surprising thought for the mother of a defendant. She spoke in a loud voice and attracted much attention from the journalists.

Martha Stewart was not the only successful woman in the court. The 74-year-old Brooklyn native named Miriam Goldman Cedarbaum who was to preside over the trial, had been in 1953 only one of eight women to earn her law degree from Columbia University. The U.S. District Court Judge was deemed erudite, businesslike, prudent, refined, no-nonsense, and above all, fair. In 18 years on the bench, she had presided over other highly publicized cases, including some dealing with organized crime, and one regarding a former heavyweight-boxing champion; but the Martha Stewart trial ranked as her highest-profile case.

Cedarbaum and Stewart had both gone to Barnard College (as did Alexis Stewart). Later, when the trial was over, Stewart called Cedarbaum "an elegant lady...an intelligent judge," someone who took the case "entirely seriously. She had great faith in her jurors. She had great faith, again, in the legal system...."

Courtroom 101 over which she would hold sway was known as the ceremonial courtroom for it was where major trials were held. It was the largest courtroom in the courthouse with brown wood-paneled walls; three ten-foot-high windows on one side; and an insignia of the United States, a black-and-gold bronze eagle resting on the wall behind Judge Cedarbaum. The audience sat in two blocs of seats; each with eight rows for some 150 people. In front of the courtroom were desks with five flat-screen computer monitors. To the right of the judge was an American flag and near the flag was a large white screen for projecting documents, etc. To the judge's left was the jury box. Four large chandeliers hung from the ceiling.

Stewart made her way from her war room on the fourth floor to Courtroom 101. Each time that Martha Stewart walked into the courtroom, as she was doing now, it was, Rochelle Steinhaus remembered, something of a grand entrance. Steinhaus covered the trial for Court TV's Web site. In three minutes, the court was due to start. Today and every day, Stewart would walk through the large wood-paneled door at the entrance to the courtroom at precisely that moment. Reporters assumed that she waited until then to enter the courtroom to avoid the questions of journalists waiting to leap at her.

Outside the door sat a court officer at a desk. He had a list of those authorized to enter. When Stewart appeared with her entourage, he said nothing, as if he had no idea who she was. But he knew. Accompanying Stewart were her daughter Alexis and her attorney, Robert Morvillo. Watching Martha Stewart enter, Rochelle Steinhaus was taken with how tall she was. The Court TV reporter had only seen Stewart on television until that moment. "She really does have a very commanding presence," she thought to herself.

A FORCED SMILE

In those first seconds of Stewart's first appearance in court, the reporters were on high alert, waiting to record everything she did, anything she said. It was Stewart's forced smile that Steinhaus remembered. "She'd walk in and kind of nod to people," proceeding to the defense table where she sat down, staring straight ahead. Her daughter sat behind her. "She held her head up high," reported Steinhaus. "Her posture was erect. She didn't look scared at all. She just looked like she would look in a board meeting. She did not let anyone see her sweat, if there was any."

The defense table was stocked with Evian water and bottled green tea from Japan.

Stewart gave the reporters very little to write about. When she spoke, it was in whispers to her attorneys or to her daughter. When she gazed up, it was only to look at witnesses.

The actual trial got under way with Judge Cedarbaum asking Martha Stewart for her plea to the charges. Five times, she repeated her plea of innocence, uttering "not guilty" softly, barely above a whisper, as if she did not want anyone to know that she was in the room.

Next came perhaps the most tedious part of the trial: jury selection.

Quite a few of the jury pool had some connection, however faint, to Martha Stewart: a friendship with daughter Alexis; a job application at Martha Stewart Living Omnimedia. It was intriguing how many people in a random sample of New Yorkers touched Martha Stewart's life in one way or another.

THE JURY IS SET

It took four days to empanel the jury.

The jury eventually comprised mostly women of one minor profession status or another; it had seven whites, four blacks, and a Pakistani among the eight women and four men. This pleased Martha Stewart's attorneys for they planned to point out that it had been Attorney General John Ashcroft's Justice Department that had been prosecuting Stewart. Surely, this jury would want to side with the defendant against the big bad right-wing Republicans in Washington, D.C.

So Morvillo hoped at any rate.

But what was more likely to register with the jury of four blacks and a Pakistani was the issue of just who Martha Stewart was; and she was, as writer Michael Wolff noted, "perhaps the leading symbol of whiteness—Connecticut white, preppy white, cold-fish white, imperious white—in the nation." The real question perplexing the defense team was whether the jury would think of Stewart as an elitist, who exhibited a sense of superiority to the jurors.

It was a jury that came from all walks of life: Adam Sachs, 38, was an information technology specialist; Meg Crane, 64, a graphic designer; Dana D'Alessandro, 42, a stay-at-home mother; Chappell Hartridge, 47, a benefits coordinator with Medicare; Jonathan Laskin, 48, a paralegal and translator; and Rosemary McMahon, 50, foreperson of the jury, a teacher.

The trial continued from Monday through Friday, with weekends off. Morning sessions began at 10:00 a.m. followed by a mid-morning break. By 12:30 or 1 p.m., the court broke for lunch, resuming by 2:00 or 2:30 p.m. The daily sessions ended at 4:30 p.m.

With seats limited and the demand huge, potential attendees had to arrive at court by 8:00 a.m. if they were to have a chance to get a ticket. Reporters were given color-coded file cards; some light orange, some light blue. They also required a special press pass for the entire trial. So large was the crowd that the court provided an unprecedented classroom-like room near the court where a large-screen closed circuit television was set up for the overflow, usually another 100 reporters or so.

The media showed up in force because it was the greatest show in town. Never had a business celebrity of Martha Stewart's stature been compelled to stand trial. She had not been accused of murder; nor did sex play a role in the allegations. But the media was intrigued simply because an icon was standing trial.

Stewart's own demeanor added to the theatrics: She was tight-lipped, secretive, and mysterious. Reporters who had covered other celebrity trials were disappointed to find her standoffish; other white-collar defendants, notably WorldCom's Bernie Ebbers, had been accessible to the media during their trials; but not Stewart.

She was in agony, but she carefully and cleverly kept everyone from peeking in to her psyche, making her even more fascinating. So infrequently did reporters rub shoulders with Stewart in the courtroom that when they did, they remembered every detail. Allen Dodd-Frank of *Bloomberg News* once began walking through the metal detector when suddenly federal Marshals waived Stewart through in front of him. Apologizing, she told Dodd-Frank with a half-smile, "It's a hard way to get preferential treatment, isn't it?"

The media came in droves to the trial, turning an otherwise staid, mundane, often-boring proceeding into high drama. The closest that television cameras could get was just outside the courtroom; about a dozen television trucks with satellite antennas stationed themselves close by.

The Stewart trial attracted all kinds of reporters: general interest ones from *Time* and *Newsweek*; business reporters from the *Wall Street Journal*, *Forbes*, and *BusinessWeek*; celebrity reporters from *People* magazine; and a whole bunch of New York-based television news hounds. It attracted the high-profile celebrity justice reporter, Dominick Dunne of *Vanity Fair*; and an infamous financial analyst named Henry Blodget who covered the proceedings for the online magazine, Slate.com.

Some journalists believed Stewart to be guilty. Dan Ackman of *Forbes* magazine was one of those. Others, like Jeff Toobin of *New Yorker* magazine, thought her innocent. (Later, suggesting that he had been "bamboozled," he would regret his rush to judgment.)

Allen Dodd-Frank of *Bloomberg News* was not going to cover the Stewart trial at first. He was not sure he thought a daily visit to the court was justified.

But the case fascinated him. "This was a celebrity trial that involved a businesswoman whose business was herself. It became apparent that she was a figure of enormous public interest."

LIKE THE SUPER BOWL

The trial attracted some who took on the role of professional observers, people like securities attorney Jake Zamansky, who attended the Stewart trial every day because it was, as he put it, "like going to the Super Bowl."

Zamansky made a point of attending most of the high-profile securities trial: "The Martha Stewart case specifically, and all these other trials are really the most important events that have occurred in the securities field in the last 10 or 20 years. Through these trials, the government is sending a message to Wall Street and corporate America that the type of conduct they engaged in, in the late 1990s and early 2000s, is unacceptable. The government can't go after everybody so they pick out certain high-profile cases like the Stewart one."

Also attending the trial from time to time were Martha Stewart's celebrity friends.

"I'm here for a friend," explained comedian Bill Cosby who sat in the front row. He said he had brought Stewart boxes of Jell-O™ chocolate pudding. Journalists assumed that Cosby's appearance had been orchestrated to tug on the heartstrings of the black jurors.

Rosie O'Donnell, the former daytime television talk show host, showed up and then issued a statement: "I am outraged and beside myself. This is a travesty. Shame on the federal government."

Actor Brian Dennehy appeared, noting that he and Stewart were "old, deep friends."

The strategy of peppering the audience with Stewarts' friends backfired. Jurors found their presence an insulting distraction as well as an unnecessary reminder that Stewart was a member of the rich-and-famous upper crust. When Bill Cosby dressed in a leather jacket, a leather hat, and donned sunglasses in the courtroom, that, according to some jurors, was the last straw.

Handling the government's case was a 42-year-old woman named Karen Seymour, who headed the criminal division of the U.S. Attorney's office. In charge of 150 prosecutors, she was trying her first case since taking the job in 2002. The very fact that Seymour decided to prosecute the case herself provided one more piece of evidence that the federal government wanted to put a Martha Stewart notch on its belt. Some suggested that Seymour was prosecuting Stewart in part at least to deflect any notion that her office was misogynistic, though the logic of the argument seemed fuzzy at best.

Before joining the U.S. Attorney's Office, she had a good deal of courtroom experience: As a federal prosecutor, she had successfully tried an aide to junk bond king Michael Milken and a former AT&T executive. This was her second time in Manhattan's U.S. Attorney's Office. She had left the first time in 1996 for private practice, returning six years later.

Born in Texas, Seymour graduated from Texas Law School and earned a post-graduate degree from the University of London.

The actual trial began, one could say, with opening statements.

Delivering hers, Karen Seymour spoke in a gentle voice. She spoke slowly, carefully. Her language was simple; nothing hysterical or bombastic about her. Frequently smiling, she dressed in a gray suit, gray pearls, a portrait of understatement.

From the government's perspective, she explained, the case was about obstruction, lying, covering up, fabricating evidence, and cheating shareholders. It was, first and foremost, about a secret tip that had given Martha Stewart an advantage over honest investors.

The government needed to show that Stewart had done something wrong in taking that tip in order to show that she had a motive for lying about it to federal authorities. But that presented a dilemma for the government: delving too deeply into that tip took prosecutors into the realm of insider trading, and Stewart was not being charged with that crime.

Judge Cedarbaum refused to let the prosecution bring insider trading into the case; the defense protested that the prosecutors were getting away with just that.

This case, Seymour told the jury, is about someone who is powerful and connected and who got a secret tip that no one else would have been able to get and that act is outside the bounds of the law.

Seymour promised the jury that Mariana Pasternak, a friend of Martha Stewart's, would testify that Stewart had confided that the Waksals were selling their ImClone stock; this was the secret tip that Doug Faneuil had provided to Stewart. Seymour cautioned the jury to scrutinize Doug Faneuil's testimony carefully because he stood to benefit so much from his testimony.

A Tad Condescending

A writer in the courtroom thought Seymour sounded "a tad condescending—the voice of a kindergarten teacher telling her classes a scary story about an evil witch."

Martha Stewart, Seymour told the jury, was a cheater, a liar, and a fabricator (using those precise words). Her motives were selfish; she would screw anyone over, including her shareholders, for profit.

The jurors tried not to stare too much at Martha Stewart, but sometimes they could not help it. She was, after all, Martha Stewart, a television personality, an icon, and it was rare for any of these people to be so close to someone that famous. When some jury members first saw her at the defendant's table, they exhibited more sadness for her than awe. As juror Rosemary McMahon put it after the trial: "I was thinking I was glad I was me, because I felt very strongly at that point, like, better to be sitting here than sitting there." In other words, she was glad not to be rich and famous and on trial. "I was glad. I was glad."

Quite a number of people simply assumed that a jury would never find Martha Stewart guilty. Yet, the case was not a slam-dunk for her, not at all. To do battle against the prosecution, Stewart needed a clever lawyer, the best that money could buy.

She found him in Robert Morvillo.

He was, in many people's opinion, the best white-collar defense attorney in the country. Morvillo had represented such clients as former congressman Robert Garcia and John Zaccaro, husband of former vice presidential candidate Geraldine Ferraro. When "Sopranos" star Robert Iler was charged with robbery, he hired Morvillo.

> *"He has a greasy comb-over, a second chin bigger than his fist, and a stomach that defies expensive tailoring, and he isn't a young sixty-five."*

At age 65, Morvillo was nearing the end of a long, illustrious career. At first glance, he seemed less than iconic. "He is not physically prepossessing," Jeff Toobin wrote. "He has a greasy comb-over, a second chin bigger than his fist, and a stomach that defies expensive tailoring, and he isn't a young sixty-five."

Soon after she had hired Morvillo as her chief defense attorney for her forthcoming trial, Martha Stewart invited him to dinner at a New York restaurant called Café Boulud. She wanted to get to know Morvillo better.

"How many of your clients do you see after a case is done?" she asked him. A few seconds passed before he answered.

"About maybe 5 percent," he answered.

Why was that, she asked.

"'Well, frankly, I represent people at the worst time in their life. And win or lose or draw, people don't want to see me afterward."

She liked the answer—mostly because it was honest. She made it clear that she intended to see him after the case.

Morvillo, it was said, looked like baseball's Don Zimmer but sounded like ex-New York Mayor Ed Koch. Armed with a law degree from Columbia University, Morvillo worked as a federal prosecutor before founding his own law firm in 1973, specializing in white-collar criminal defense work. The firm, Morvillo, Abramowitz, Grand, Iason & Silberberg, grew from three to 36 attorneys.

Morvillo and his founding partners took a moral stance in founding the firm, refusing to take clients involved with organized crime or drugs. Without such clients, he knew that he and his partners could walk into the U.S. Attorney's office representing a defendant and not have anyone say, "Here come those sleazebags again."

To prepare for her defense, Morvillo, who was getting $650 an hour, grilled Stewart over and over in the tenth-floor conference room one flight above his midtown office. He believed it likely that he would want her to testify; hence the grilling. He was, he told a writer, by far the nastiest person in his firm. "I'm rougher on her than any prosecutor will be."

Perhaps significantly, Morvillo made his mark, not in litigation dramas, but in behind-the-scenes maneuvering to keep clients from having to go to trial. That had not worked in the case of Martha Stewart, but that was due to her being stubborn, not to some Morvillo defect. Creating a name for himself in earlier days, before cable television and before the advent of legal commentators on television, had been in some ways easier. Now, Morvillo, like all other attorneys, knew that he and his courtroom work would be scrutinized second by second over national television. He knew he would not like the constant critique; but he vowed to himself that he would not let the commentators get to him.

WAS HE RIGHT FOR STEWART?

A debate of sorts ensued prior to the trial over whether Morvillo was the right attorney for Martha Stewart. No one knew the federal courtrooms or securities law better than he did. That was a plus. So too was his down-to-earth image. That image would soften Martha Stewart's icier image, another plus. But Morvillo had never been involved in the kind of media frenzy that surrounded the Stewart trial; nor had he come up against as tough-minded a judge as Miriam Goldman Cedarbaum.

Clearly, Morvillo was a showman. He played to the jury, but he seemed to play to a wider audience as well despite the lack of television cameras in the courtroom. Unlike any other speaker, his voice boomed through the cavernous courtroom. Yet, on other occasions, he offered only a whisper. He walked up and down the aisle, shouting to make a point; at other times, he simply leaned on the edge of the jury box, folksy as ever. He seemed the consummate actor.

From the moment that Robert Morvillo began his opening statement to the jury, he had a tough sell. His chief argument was that no direct evidence existed against Martha Stewart; and that she had not issued any deliberately false statements.

His best strategy, he apparently believed, was to convince the jury that Stewart had walked into her meeting with federal authorities convinced that all she needed to do was to insist that Sam Waksal had not personally tipped her about the impending FDA announcement rejecting Erbitux.

He also wanted to make insider trading a central focus of the trial. Though Judge Cedarbaum had explicitly said she wanted it off the table, Morvillo wanted the issue to hover over the courtroom so that he could argue that the defense was being crucified for addressing insider trading but was not allowed to defend itself against the charge. The main point he wanted to convey was: Martha Stewart had not been charged with insider trading, so why was the prosecution making it a central issue?

It was a clever strategy. If Morvillo could get the jury to think that Stewart had been charged with insider trading, the jury was likely to find her not guilty—because insider trading was very hard to prove. He felt he could easily tear insider-trading charges apart. Focusing on insider trading had the added advantage of distracting the jury from the feds' main allegation—that Stewart had lied to them.

Morvillo's easy-going style went over well with the jury. He made them feel comfortable—and important. They liked his humor. The jury seemed to respond positively when he called Sam Waksal crazy: "How was Martha possibly to know Waksal would do the craziest, most offensive thing in the world on December 27? She sold her ImClone before even talking to him."

He got big laughs from the jury when he dealt with the conspiracy charge, hoping to show that the feds had them conspiring at a time when they had not even been together:

"How'd that happen? Osmosis? Carrier pigeon? I'm pretty sure there was no pony express in Mexico at the time."

> *"How'd that happen? Osmosis? Carrier pigeon? I'm pretty sure there was no pony express in Mexico at the time."*

Morvillo believed his trump card was Attorney General Ashcroft. If he could get the jury to focus on him as the genuine culprit, angling to bring Martha Stewart down, he could again distract the jury from the feds' accusations that she had lied to them. "You are the protectors of liberty," he said softly to the jurors. He asked them to see through the government's "speculation, surmise, and guesswork" and focus on who the real culprit was here—the Attorney General of the United States of America! "This case is brought to you by the United States Department of Justice under John Ashcroft," he then barked, trying to pronounce Ashcroft's name with as much disgust as he could muster.

The government was accusing Martha Stewart of conspiracy. Morvillo tried to turn that one on its head. It was Congress and Ashcroft's Justice Department that had conspired against this poor innocent woman. "Some government: leak on one side, prosecute on the other. ... George Orwell was about 20 years too early."

BUILT ON SAND

Morvillo argued that the case against Martha Stewart was built on sand. Of December 27, 2001, he said: "This is the day that Sam Waksal decided to go crazy. What he did that day was an act of sheer insanity. ... I submit to you that no one in his right mind would have done this."

> *"This is the day that Sam Waksal decided to go crazy. What he did that day was an act of sheer insanity."*

What Morvillo hoped the jury would conclude was that no one in his right mind would interpret Waksal's selling of his own ImClone shares as a sign that the FDA was going to reject Erbitux. Of course, that was the conclusion that most people drew from the coincidental timing of the sale and the FDA rejection. If Waksal had not sold as a result of learning of the FDA rejection, then what Martha Stewart had been accused of doing—taking that secret tip—was quite harmless.

By far the most damaging piece of evidence that Morvillo had to combat was the Peter Bacanovic phone message that Martha Stewart had altered—and then immediately changed back. For the prosecution, Stewart's alteration of the phone message was virtually an admission of her guilt, solid proof of a consciousness of guilt. Not at all, said Morvillo; it was instead much like the title of the Shakespeare play. "Much Ado About Nothing." "The incident lasted 25 seconds," said Morvillo, as if its brevity proved that it had been harmless.

The day had ended with each side proclaiming victory. Both had scored points. Both had heard the other side expose the weaknesses of their respective cases. What each side thought hardly mattered. Only the jury counted.

Much later, Martha Stewart summarized what it was like being in court. For years, she had run a company, given her opinions on a thousand things, talked to employees who were at her beck and call. Now she had to sit as a defendant in a courtroom dealing with the worst ordeal of her life, and somehow she had to keep her wits. It was a real challenge, she acknowledged, "to set your mind on something else (other than her business). Something else that, oh, is sometimes so mind-boggling. And it was mind-boggling."

By 1986, Martha Stewart had reached a peak in her career: She was a successful caterer, cookbook author, and something new, a lifestyle expert. She was writing articles for magazines and that year she hosted her first television special over CBS, Holiday Entertaining with Martha Stewart. *She stuffed a turkey, and then showed viewers how to roll the entire bird into a puff pastry, decorating it with leaves.*

The following year she surprised many by becoming a spokesperson for the down-market retailer, Kmart, hoping to combat her elitist image. She was becoming a shrewd businesswoman: when Kmart executives demanded that she enter into an exclusive deal with the Lifetime cable channel to promote her new Kmart line, she told them no, she planned to accept the chance to do a segment on NBC's Today Show.

In 1988, her book **Weddings** *appeared, selling 200,000 copies, good news for her career. But her marriage was falling apart, a process that she kept secret for fear of it spoiling her image as the woman with the perfect life. She and Andy had a bitter divorce: He had walked out on her but then insisted in having a share of her earnings. Eventually they came to an agreement. When her fans learned of her divorce, they stuck by her, thinking her as more human, more like them.*

Meanwhile, she was taking steps to turn her multi-tasking into an empire.

By 1990, now 49 years old, Stewart found herself with an empty nest. Newly divorced, she watched her daughter go off to college. She purchased a home in East Hampton, Long Island where her neighbors were Billy Joel and Calvin Klein. She hoped the move would augur a new start in her life.

She searched around for an outlet for the lifestyle ideas she was accumulating, hoping to launch her own magazine, but several publishers turned her down. Finally, Time Warner agreed to test Stewart's drawing power, funding a new magazine with a modest 250,000 print run at first. Though the country was in recession, **Martha Stewart Living***, the new magazine, was an instant hit when it appeared for the first time in July 1991, one of the most profitable launches in magazine history.*

Two years later, in September 1993, she began a syndicated television show with Group W productions. In time, some 97 percent of the American population viewed the 30-minute **Martha Stewart Living***. Soon thereafter, she introduced her own line of home products under the name "The Martha Stewart Everyday Collection."*

She found it hard to keep her private life private.

In 1995, after she had purchased a second home in East Hampton, she got into a tiff with her new neighbor over the landscaping along their boundary line. The media happily covered zoning board hearings, where Martha Stewart's battle was focusing, as if the news coming out of there was urgent and spectacular. In May of that year, she allegedly used her SUV to pin a landscaper up against a fence he was installing for the neighbor. In time, the charges against Stewart were dropped; but the controversy did not help her public image.

Each day Stewart brought a green plastic bottle of tea and placed it on the desk in front of her. At the most painful moments of the trial, she would pick up the bottle. "That was the only way I could tell she was feeling anything, when she threw back a swig from the bottle," said Elizabeth Koch, covering the trial for *Reason* magazine. During opening statements, she displayed no emotion, sitting erect, sometimes leaning forward, sometimes tearing apart a yellow Post-it note, other times scribbling away on a clean white pad. Her face seemed to freeze into a stoical glare. Almost everyone in the room noticed how serious she looked. She rarely looked at the jury. She sat quite still.

No one expected Stewart to be bright and jolly each day while her past was dissected and her future decided. But what impressed so many of the trial's participants was her uniformly cheerless countenance day in and day out. "She would walk by me and everyone else," said Jake Zamansky, the securities attorney, "with a big scowl on her face. I can't remember the lady smiling once."

Alexis, seated behind her mother, bore the same stoical expression as the defendant. She often sat next to attorney Greg Morvillo, son of Martha Stewart's lead attorney.

To Zamansky, Stewart's demeanor did not help her with her most important audience, the eight women and four men of the jury. "If a defendant is relaxed, there's a better perception among the jury that this is a person that may not have a problem." Not that Stewart seemed nervous or fidgety; but she did radiate, as Zamansky recollected, "a self-confidence bordering on arrogance." Worst of all, Stewart's sour disposition conveyed to the jury that she had better things to do with her time. "She gave off a feeling that she was above the proceeding."

STAGE-MANAGED ALOOFNESS

Stewart's aloofness seemed almost stage-managed. She seemed almost trained not to show reactions, not expressing emotion. A lot of defendants roll their eyes or sigh in frustration. Stewart did none of that. Indeed, Kate Hazelwood, who was covering the trial for *BusinessWeek*, found her "immobile, expressionless; I wouldn't even say that it was just aloof, but almost to me consciously checked out. Almost like having a laser-like focus of not being there, as if she had the ability to delineate who she believed herself to be and what was going on in the courtroom. There were two different Marthas. One went along for the ride; the other was on trial."

Clearly, Stewart was under her attorneys' instructions not to say a word to the media. This was frustrating for just about every journalist in the court. Every once in a while a reporter got the chance to toss a question to Stewart but with little result. "We were lined up right next to the elevator bank," recalled Helen Lucaites, who was covering the trial as the legal reporter for WNYW—FOX 5 News. "I asked how the day had gone. Obviously she had had a better day. She looked at me and just smiled. It seemed as though she wanted to talk, but she couldn't because her lawyers had told her not to."

By showing no emotion, by saying nothing that could be picked up by the nearby journalists, Stewart forced the media to look for other things to write. "You looked for anything to report," said Kate Hazelwood, "anything different." And so the reporters began to focus on what Stewart wore to the trial.

To those covering the trial, Stewart's best fashion strategy was to dress in Kmart clothes, to avoid reminding the jury of how wealthy she was. "You can't have a Martha Stewart come to court in sack clothes and ashes," said Marvin Pickholz, attorney for Doug Faneuil, "but you might have wanted to project a human being who is suffering like all of us."

She had a certain latitude in what she wore. After all, the courtroom was not a funeral parlor. No one laid down dress codes. To Stewart, going to court was the equivalent of attending a business meeting. Short pants were out, as were cocktail dresses. She could dress casually, but not too much so. What the media noticed was that Stewart dressed each day as if she were appearing in a fashion show on the latest woman's business attire. Pants suits were her clothes of choice, usually a burgundy red or a light brown. Elizabeth Koch, writing for *Reason* magazine, noted: "We were all waiting for Martha to appear. Everyone wanted to get color about her pashmina. That's all the media talked about, what she is wearing, who did her hair; what the scent of perfume we smelled when she walked by" (something citrusy, Koch thought). The media's interest in Stewart's external appearance seemed to know no limit. "If the press could have figured out what kind of underwear she was wearing, it would have written about that," said Marvin Pickholz.

The $6,000 Birken handbag that Martha Stewart carried to court became a media focus. It was one of the most sought-after handbags in Manhattan, and any juror familiar with that handbag had to be insulted. "Letting her go in with that bag," said television reporter Helen Lucaites, "was a big mistake."

The Birken handbag came to symbolize Martha Stewart, woman of money and success. "While that's not a crime," said Helen Lucaites, "you have to be careful. You want to present an image that will help you." She seemed out of place.

By the first week of the trial, the bag had taken center stage in the media's minds—or so it appeared. No one had ever heard of the bag until *Sex and the City* did an entire episode revolving around it after women in real life had to wait two years to purchase the hard-to-obtain bag. And here was Martha Stewart showing up in court with one of these bags! Ever faithful to Stewart, *Vanity Fair*'s Dominick Dunne dismissed the bag as unworthy of such media comment: it was, after all, 12 years old, he noted.

In a rare comment on the trial, Stewart spoke about the bag when Larry King asked her if in retrospect she thought it had been a mistake to carry an expensive handbag into court.

Stewart: Oh, we're back to the handbag?

King: I've never asked you about the handbag.

Stewart: No, you haven't. I don't mean you. But oh, my gosh, the newspapers and everything. And you know, this case was not about a handbag. It was not about me testifying. The jury was clearly instructed about what the case was about.

Besides dressing less elegantly, Stewart could have found other ways to avoid looking elitist. Instead of having her lunch delivered every day, Marvin Pickholz noted, she could have eaten a hot dog at a corner stand and been photographed with it in her mouth.

But Stewart would not change her habits.

To gain more sympathy with the jury, she could have been more humble, more apologetic, less in your face, but, according to Lou Colasuonno, the public relations man for Peter Bacanovic, she had a longer-term game plan. And to accomplish that, she could not change her stripes. She had to remain the same old Martha Stewart: She had gotten this far behaving one way. She wasn't going to flip flop now. "I think she felt that there will be a whole life after the trial, and I'm not going to grovel now because after this is over, I'm going to have to become the Martha Stewart that I've always been."

Sometimes when the court went into recess, Stewart gazed at the sketches, peeking over the artist's shoulder. "You can make me lovelier than that, can't you?" she chided the artist. It was Stewart the egotist, Stewart the vain. The incident was reminiscent of another time when Martha Stewart saw a pencil drawing of herself in *The Wall Street Journal*, depicting lines on her neck; she contacted the newspaper and asked to have pearls put on her neck to cover up the lines.

HUSTLED OFF TO THE WAR ROOM

When a break in the trial occurred, most of the time Stewart was hustled off to four adjacent rooms on the fourth floor, what the defense team called Martha's war room. It was a place for relaxing, discussing the case, deciding on what to ask witnesses, and coordinating forthcoming trial strategy. Defense attorneys sometimes shot faxes back to their home offices with requests to have written arguments on a certain point quickly drafted.

While in the war room, Stewart talked about what had just happened in court with her attorney, sometimes with Bacanovic.

Lou Colasuonno met with her each day in the war room and not surprisingly found her as serious-minded as she was in the courtroom: "Martha's a pretty private person. She's a little awkward personally. She was friendly and charming in the war room but she was not open, not gregarious. She's personally a little standoffish. She's not outgoing. She didn't make a lot of noise in the room. She was very plugged into the trial, very plugged into her defense."

"She was an integral part of both her legal and public profile strategy. Martha Stewart is a woman with her own mind. She is smart, has always been hands on. There are legendary stories of her walking on to a television set and saying, 'Move this. Get out of my way, I don't like the way this looks.' She's been known to go into stores and see her products and say, 'I don't like the way this is displayed.'" She was no different in the war room, hands on, directing, strategizing, controlling.

None of the journalists had access to the war room with the exception of Dominick Dunne, whose friendship with Stewart trumped his being a member of the media. He showed up for lunch with her four times. It was the one place where Martha Stewart could talk privately with her attorneys and her daughter and know that no one was listening, or trying to listen. Colasuonno added: "I was always amazed how calm she was. The lawyers would be there, they'd be talking, and then she'd go over and talk to her daughter. It was not a social thing, in any way, it wasn't like fun, but it was—it was very quiet and she seemed very together to me all through it."

When the journalists were not trying to describe what Stewart was wearing, they were chatting among themselves, figuring out whether she deserved to be convicted. Most of the journalists thought she was being railroaded. While the general net worth of the reporters was far lower than that of Martha Stewart, many identified far more with her than with the federal authorities.

To the reporters, it was simple: The feds wanted to make an example of Stewart.

Most of the journalists shared the view that hers was a minor offense: She had saved herself far too little money for the feds to be hanging her out to dry like this.

Elizabeth Koch, covering the trial for the Web site of *Reason* magazine, the anti-authoritarian, libertarian journal, at first thought the trial "an egregious example of government overreach. Since the U.S. attorney's office failed to impeach Stewart for insider trading, I believed they'd detained her for being, in a large sense, an insider."

"I went in with a very strong opinion that the government was going after her to make a spectacle of corporate corruption. She would be a fall girl, fall woman. I believed that the government thought she was a prima donna and she was used to getting what she wanted so she would be good to choose because everyone was basically familiar with the fact that she was bitchy. She had this amazing entrepreneurial brilliance, but now she had become too big for everyone."

As the trial progressed, the media split between those who believed she was in fact a liar, yet still believed she would get off; and those who thought, because of her innocence, she would be exonerated. Much was made of the *New Yorker*'s Jeffrey Toobin and his early assessment of Stewart. He had been the only print journalist to interview her during the investigation. While he had never said so in his February 2003 *New Yorker* piece, Toobin apparently felt Stewart had been given a raw deal.

When Koch asked Dominick Dunne whether the people on the dinner party scene thought Stewart innocent or guilty, he replied that people thought she had lied, but that she should get off anyway. Dunne paused and then added, "The punishment should not exceed the crime."

Each day the journalists lunched together in the courtroom cafeteria. Alan Dodd-Frank of *Bloomberg*; Andrea Peyser of the *New York Post*; Charles Gasparino of *Newsweek*; Dominick Dunne, and Henry Blodget, covering for Slate.com. Sometimes Jeff Toobin joined the group. "We were obsessed," said Elizabeth Koch. "We didn't want to leave. It was just so much fun. We wanted to break down our opinions and bounce theories off one another. We wanted to check quotes."

THE AVERAGE PERSON

Eventually, Elizabeth Koch realized that the journalists, by sitting and talking to themselves all the time, were unable to get a solid grasp of what the average person—and hence, the average juror—thought of the trial.

"Out of laziness or conceit—or both—many of us failed to step outside the courthouse and talk to everyday people, to balance our opinions and write more reflective stories. We spent the lunch hour huddled around a single cafeteria table, enriching the day's events with colorful observations: Martha's facial ticks, the swill of her cowlick, the gusto of her green tea swigs...Between our cribbed notes and sorry courtroom psychology, we missed the story: that average Americans believe lying is wrong, even if the culprit is a feminist icon and homemaking pioneer. Even—especially—if she's rich."

Of the journalists covering the trial, by far the most extraordinary was a wiry, blond-haired man who had once been a Wall Street icon before becoming one of its most notorious characters. He was Henry Blodget. At one stage, he was the most famous financial analyst on the Street; but he was now disgraced, accused of misleading middle-class investors with faulty research. He had been fined $4 million and tossed out of the securities industry a year before the Stewart trial. Now he had shown up as a reporter for Slate.com to cover the trial.

He turned out to be the star of the press corps.

His daily reports from the trial were considered must reading not only for the journalists and other observers at the trial; but for a goodly number among the public as well. Dominick Dunne spent morning breaks poring over his dispatches, Michael Wolff cited Blodget's analyses in one of his magazine pieces. Blodget was mentioned in the *Wall Street Journal*'s Bids and Offers section, which provided the latest market gossip.

Providing what he called a "Martha Meter," Blodget rated the likelihood of her conviction in his daily reports. He kept the meter below the 50 percent mark for the entire trial until the closing arguments of the prosecution.

To defend his presence as a reporter at the trial, Blodget noted, "...I find Martha Stewart not only charming but physically attractive. Studies have shown that human beings tend to be favorably disposed toward people they find charming and attractive," he wrote as part of his "full disclosure" statement that appeared with his accounts.

For all the certainty they mustered, the journalists and all those others who believed Stewart innocent were about to come in for a mighty shock.

CHAPTER

8

STAR WITNESS: "BABY" TESTIFIES

To prove its case against Martha Stewart, the government needed someone to testify to all that had happened on December 27, 2001, someone who was in a position to know what Martha Stewart had done on that fateful day.

The government needed to show that Stewart had lied to the federal authorities and then engaged in a cover up to conceal the reason she took the controversial stock tip.

Stewart insisted that she and Peter Bacanovic, her stockbroker, had agreed that she would sell her ImClone shares if and when the stock dropped to $60 a share. That was the lie, the government argued, because there had been no agreement.

Instead what had happened was this: Stewart sold her stock after being given a tip from Doug Faneuil that Sam Waksal had just sold his ImClone shares.

Only three people could testify accurately as to what had happened on that day. One was Martha Stewart, and she had given her version of events; another was Peter Bacanovic, and he had sided with Stewart; the third was Doug Faneuil, who had come under enormous pressure from Bacanovic in the early stage of the case to side with Stewart and him.

Neither Stewart nor Bacanovic were about to say anything that would help the government's case. Neither was about to make a confession, Stewart because she thought she had done nothing wrong; Bacanovic because he cared too much for Stewart.

Only Doug Faneuil was of potential help to the government. And when he, fearing an indictment, eventually decided to cooperate with the authorities and acknowledged his own role in providing the stock tip to Martha Stewart, the feds were able to build a legal case against her.

The feds could not have been thrilled with basing their entire case on Faneuil's testimony. He was testifying in exchange for getting lightly charged. He would not go to jail. So he too had a motive to lie.

The outcome of the case appeared to rest on how credible Doug Faneuil seemed to the jury.

The rest of the evidence against Stewart and Bacanovic was circumstantial. And though Judge Miriam Goldman Cedarbaum had remarked that this circumstantial evidence was "strong," Faneuil's testimony was bound to be stronger.

Doug Faneuil certainly worried whether he would be able to withstand the defense's cross-examination.

But, he worried far more about whether the jury would believe him, in part, because he was gay. No juror should have taken his homosexuality into account—and no juror should have held it against him and punished him by not finding him credible. But still Faneuil worried. According to his attorney, Marvin Pickholz: "When he first sat up on the witness stand, it dawned on him as he looked over all the people: 'What if they don't believe me?' It hit him that they might not believe him and it was the job of two tables of lawyers to try to discredit him and 12 strangers sitting in the jury box to judge him: 12 people who had never met him, who didn't know anything about him."

> "There was no wind in the courtroom, but if there had been, his suit would have flapped."

When he walked to the stand, Doug Faneuil looked like a "beanpole" to Henry Blodget. "There was no wind in the courtroom, but if there had been, his suit would have flapped." As he was sworn in, Faneuil hunched over the guard reminiscent of an athlete leaning over a coach. "My knees are long," he said apologetically to the judge, trying to explain why he could not move the witness chair closer to the microphone.

As he began to speak, defense lawyers listened somberly, realizing that he sounded, unfortunately for them, remarkably credible. He seemed polite. He was always deferential to the judge. To the jury, he came across as likable.

Helping his cause was the deft questioning by Karen Seymour. Standing at the lectern, 15 feet in front of Doug Faneuil, noted one writer in the audience: "Seymour looked like a stern mother helping to rehabilitate her formerly wayward son."

"Did there come a time at Merrill Lynch when you did something illegal?" Seymour asked.

"Yes," said Douglas Faneuil.

"What did you do?" asked Seymour.

"I told one client what another client was doing and then lied about it to cover it up," said Faneuil with a straight face.

The questions and answers flowed so smoothly as to be almost choreographed.

> *"I told one client what another client was doing and then lied about it to cover it up."*

Most gripping was Faneuil's account of what he did on December 27, 2001.

Until then, he had been in the job for just six months. There had been nothing special about his relationship with Martha Stewart—just a few telephone conversations. (On cross, Bacanovic's attorney would try to show that in fact Faneuil had good reason to testify against Stewart.)

Faneuil told jurors of a hectic December morning at Merrill, with Waksal's accountant and Waksal's two daughters barking sell orders at him the very first hour of the day.

He described his call from Aliza Waksal, and how she had she placed an order to sell nearly 40,000 ImClone shares. He then described a call from Waksal's other daughter, Elana, who soon dumped her own shares.

Calls and faxes came as well, he said, from Sam Waksal's accountant, who demanded that Faneuil "ignore all other business" and get Waksal's ImClone shares transferred and sold.

He then gave an account of the call with Peter Bacanovic just after 10:00 a.m., in which Bacanovic asked him to call Martha Stewart.

"We talked initially about [Sam Waksal's accountant] being so pushy," Faneuil noted. "Peter was trying to calm my nerves, saying that [the

> *"Oh my God, get Martha on the phone."*

accountant] was always like that. Then we talked about the morning's events. Suddenly, Peter said, 'Oh my God, get Martha on the phone.'"

This was a clear indication that Bacanovic wanted the stock tip passed to Stewart.

According to Faneuil's testimony, he (Doug) then phoned Martha Stewart, getting her administrative assistant—Ann Armstrong—on the line.

According to Faneuil, Bacanovic, also on the line, did all of the talking. Faneuil did not pay much regard to the conversation, recalling only that he remembered someone saying that Stewart had been on a plane.

When the call was over, Bacanovic called Faneuil back.

"Listen, Martha's going to call. You've got to tell her what's going on."

"Can I tell her about Sam?" Faneuil asked.

"Of course. You must. That's the whole point."

The first sentence was ambiguous: "You've got to tell her what's going on" might have meant: "You've got to tell her about the high volume of ImClone;" or, "you've got to tell her about the price dropping;" or, "you've got to tell her that Erbitux will be rejected."

The second part of the conversation ("Of course. You must. That's the whole point.") was crystal clear.

Bacanovic wanted Stewart to know that there was an urgent reason for her to sell her shares, namely that Sam Waksal was selling his as well. The implication was that Bacanovic knew that something bad was going to happen to ImClone.

In the early afternoon, at Bacanovic's insistence, Faneuil and Martha Stewart spoke. Stewart was on the tarmac of the San Antonio airport where her plane was refueling on its way to Mexico.

"Hi, this is Martha, what's up with Sam?" Faneuil testified that she said.

"'Well,'" he replied, "we have no news on the company, but Peter thought you might like to act on the information that Sam Waksal was trying to sell all of his shares.' At that point, I may have mentioned Waksal's daughters as well, I'm not sure."

"Objection," barked Robert Morvillo. Faneuil, said Stewart's attorney, had no business testifying if he was not sure.

"I'm confident saying with one-hundred-percent surety that I told her that Sam was trying to sell," Faneuil testified. "I'll leave it at that."

Faneuil then testified that Stewart asked if Waksal was selling all of his shares.

"What he does have here, he's trying to sell," Faneuil replied.

Stewart then told him to sell off all her shares at market price—contradicting her story that there was a standing "stop-loss order" to sell the stock if it fell to $60 a share.

Faneuil said Stewart was "extraordinarily upset" and declared, "I want to sell."

Stewart asked for a price quote before selling.

Faneuil asked Stewart if he should e-mail Heidi DeLuca, Stewart's secretary/accountant, about the exchange.

Stewart, Faneuil said, became hysterical. He pitched his voice higher, imitating her, "Absolutely not! You are never allowed to discuss my personal finances with anyone! Under any circumstances!"

The imitation of Stewart went down well with several jurors. A smile crossed their lips and they seemed to say, "Well done."

Faneuil testified that he never heard anything about a stop-loss order—the original cover-up story that Bacanovic tried to weave—until more than a week after the sale. At that point, an agitated Bacanovic insisted that Faneuil adhere to the stop-loss order version.

IMITATING BACANOVIC

Faneuil imitated a breathless Bacanovic insisting the sale was legitimate.

Jumping to the events of December 31, 2001, Faneuil discussed a phone conversation he had with Peter Bacanovic about Doug's forthcoming meeting with Judy Monaghan, the Merrill Lynch administrator.

Monaghan had asked Faneuil "what was going on with these ImClone trades." Faneuil then called Peter Bacanovic and told him that Monaghan was asking questions.

"The reason for Martha Stewart's sale was tax-loss selling," Bacanovic said. "It was tax-loss selling. That's what you tell them. That's Martha's reason for selling, tax-loss."

Faneuil had tried to argue that tax-loss selling was impossible because Stewart had sold at a gain, but Bacanovic would not let him get a word in.

Bacanovic kept saying, "The reason for her sale was tax-loss selling!"

"He completely ignored me and wouldn't let me speak," Faneuil testified.

"OK?" Bacanovic asked, and asked again.

"I said 'OK.'"

When Peter Bacanovic returned from vacation in early January 2002, Faneuil testified, he asked Faneuil to join him at Dean & Deluca, a nearby coffee house.

"He sat me down and told me everything was going to be all right. He told me his history of working at Merrill, how he had worked for a while in a mailroom in Hollywood because he thought he wanted to be an agent, and then he decided to become a broker."

"He told me how after only seven years he had become one of the most successful brokers in the office, how he had never dreamed he would be so successful, and how everyone in his family was proud. Then he told me about his relationship with Martha Stewart. He said she was difficult and frustrating sometimes, but that they were extremely loyal to each other."

"Then I said, 'Let's talk about the 27th. I was there, Peter. I know what happened.' He put his hand on my shoulder and said, 'With all due respect, you don't.'"

Bacanovic then offered Doug a plane ticket to Argentina, Faneuil testified. He said no to that, as well as no to extra time off.

Later, back at Merrill Lynch, Bacanovic called Faneuil into his office and said, "I've spoken to Martha, and I've met with her. Everyone's telling the same story. It was a $60 stop-loss order. We're all on the same page. And it's the truth. It's a true story."

Peter Bacanovic's attorney, David Apfel, cross-examined Faneuil aggressively.

Rather than portray him as marginal to the case, the attorney decided to make Doug Faneuil into the bad guy, not Peter Bacanovic.

He suggested that Faneuil had changed his story; that Faneuil was out for revenge; that he had been the real mastermind of the cover-up, not Bacanovic, and not Stewart.

Apfel came close to accusing Doug Faneuil of being a nutcase, a publicity hound, a moron, and a junkie—all to diminish Faneuil in the eyes of the jury.

The trouble was that Apfel never got very far.

A LION UNDERWATER

Apfel introduced a series of Faneuil's e-mails to his friends to try to suggest that he had ample reason to want revenge against Martha Stewart.

In one e-mail, from October 23, 2001, Faneuil recounted: "I have never, ever been treated so rudely by a stranger on the telephone. She actually hung up on me! And she had the nerve—the NERVE—to mention the layoffs (at Merrill Lynch) in her anger. She said, 'Do you know who the hell is answering your phones? You call and you know what he sounds like? He sounds like this....' And then she made the most ridiculous sound I've heard coming from an adult in quite some time, kind of like a lion roaring underwater. I laughed; I thought she was joking. And then she yelled, 'Merrill Lynch is laying off ten thousand employees because of people like that idiot!' And then she hung up."

Three days later he sent this e-mail: "Martha yelled at me again today, but I snapped in her face and she actually backed down! Baby put Ms. Martha in her place." ("Baby" was Faneuil's nickname.)

Another time, Bacanovic had the temerity to put Stewart on hold, and that led to another Stewart tirade against Faneuil.

"During that conversation," Apfel asked Faneuil, "she told you that she was going to leave Peter Bacanovic and leave Merrill Lynch unless that hold music was changed, is that right?"

"Correct," Faneuil said.

Even Bacanovic had to laugh at the story about Stewart's "hold music" outburst.

The problem for attorney Apfel was that Faneuil's testimony on the e-mails backfired. Rather than illuminate Faneuil's alleged distaste for Stewart, the e-mails cast an enormous spotlight on Martha Stewart's nasty behavior toward employees. Thus, the e-mails hurt Stewart far more than Faneuil. It seemed an easy leap for the jury to make: If Stewart was at heart a nasty woman, she must be guilty of these crimes.

The whole scene seemed so incongruous: a 28-year-old youngster taking on a cultural icon with the battleground a New York courtroom. It was hard to imagine that only a decade earlier, Martha Stewart was sitting on top of the homemaking and entertainment world.

By the mid-1990s, she had become the most famous hostess in America. She was in the words of a People *magazine cover story: "A hypercompetent perfectionist who grew up 'with a sewing needle in one hand and a hammer in the other,' as her sister Laura remembers it.*

Stewart is evangelical about the notion that there is a correct way to plant a tree or plaster a wall—and that anyone with gumption can learn. As The Washington Post *put it recently, "Her vision is not of some impossible paradise where rich people sport among themselves, but a life that might be lived in any American suburb, right now, with the help of a few good recipes and decorating tips."*

In 1995, four years after its launch, Martha Stewart Living *had a circulation of 1.3 million. Her products numbered 14 books, with 5 million copies in print; six videos; signature sheets, paints, and towels; as well as a mail-order lineup that included a $50 cake-decorating kit. Her syndicated TV show reached over 5 million viewers a week; she was also a regular on NBC's* Today *show.*

Millions of Fans

She counted millions of people as fans. But others loathed her and accused her of being a ruthless opportunist; of stealing recipes; and of barking at employees. Such negativism had no visible effect on her businesses, which were booming in 1997. In that year, she repurchased her company, Martha Stewart Enterprises, from Time Warner; Kmart signed her to a new $500 million contract to sell a line of products; and she formed her own company, Martha Stewart Living Omnimedia. Her syndicated television show ran every day and was carried on 177 stations around the U.S. She also wrote a weekly newspaper column, launched a Web site, and hosted a radio show.

She had hit the market at the perfect time when there was a dearth of specific content for television and magazines. Had she reached her peak a decade later, she would have faced far stiffer competition. But she filled a niche beautifully with her holiday television programs, her decorating, home fashion, and entertaining ideas. By appealing to a mass audience, by trying to help everyone—not just the rich—lead a better life, Stewart succeeded where other professional chefs and professional homemakers failed to make breakthroughs.

By this time, Robert Morvillo understood all too well that the jury had fallen in love with the adorable Mr. Faneuil; that it had believed just about every word that he had uttered. It had also found the e-mails largely damaging to Stewart.

Morvillo played down the e-mails, saying it didn't really matter whether Martha Stewart had shouted at an underling. Hey, he said, she's Martha Stewart, and she always yelled at underlings—that was her style!

Taking into account the jury's affection for Faneuil, Morvillo avoided attacking him directly. Instead, he sought to convince the jury that Faneuil had not been encouraged by Stewart to lie to authorities.

In contrast with the belligerent pit-bull approach of Mr. Apfel, Robert Morvillo remained polite, calm, and patient.

He and Judge Cedarbaum squared off against each other at times but the judge held none of the contempt toward him that she felt toward David Apfel.

Once Morvillo asked Faneuil a question that he would not answer directly.

"You were never threatened or asked to lie by Martha, were you?"

"Well, she got angry when I asked whether I should send Heidi DeLuca info about her ImClone trade...."

"Does that answer my question?"

"Well, no."

"But you decided to mention it anyway."

"Is that a question, Mr. Morvillo? Try to stick to questions," Cedarbaum interjected.

When Faneuil talked of being frightened of Bacanovic, of having to lie for him, or of contemplating Bacanovic's possibly going to jail, his voice broke. "As soon as I realized what Bacanovic was asking of me, as soon as I saw what a lie the tax-loss story was, I feared this moment. The thing I've always been most scared of was this moment, right now, being up here on the stand in a position of having to tell the truth when Peter was lying."

CLOSE TO TEARS?

Some in the courtroom thought Doug Faneuil would break into tears. But he did not.

Morvillo asked: "So you felt guilty giving Martha the ImClone info, but your boss told you to do it so you did—putting the ball in his court, right?"

"Right," Faneuil acknowledged.

"Were you attempting to induce Ms. Stewart to trade by giving her the info?"

"That's fair to say."

Morvillo seemed to be getting somewhere. He actually had Doug

Faneuil admitting that he had sort of instigated her ImClone sale—making her a kind of innocent bystander.

Throughout his three days of testimony, Doug Faneuil came across as a likable, sincere young man who had made mistakes but was inherently honest. "He's such an honest, upfront type of person," Faneuil's attorney, Marvin Pickholz suggested. "He's not disingenuous at all. That comes across quickly when he was sitting a few feet from the jury. They could sense that. That's what made him most valuable. You immediately sense that this is not a person who's given to fabricating."

GENUINELY BELIEVABLE

"On Doug's direct," said Pickholz, "I thought he was genuinely believable. His cross started with such a right-out-of-the-box, almost brutal attempt of cross examination, to really come after him. But I noticed the judge. She's so experienced. I noticed that the judge was leaning forward in her chair, and the jurors then sat up in their chairs; it was a sign that I read that they all believed Doug and were kind of offended at this right-out-of-the box attack."

To Kate Hazelwood, the *BusinessWeek* reporter who was there every day, Faneuil had sealed Stewart's fate: "It almost would have required Martha in tears on the stand to counter that."

In post-trial interviews, the jury acknowledged that Faneuil came across as extremely credible. To juror Meg Crane, he "seemed very young and almost vulnerable at first, but as his testimony went on, he became much more confident in what he was saying." Juror Rosemary McMahon found him to be "an intelligent person." When Faneuil's hand shook and his voice cracked, he seemed more credible, not less, jurors suggested.

CHAPTER

9

WITH FRIENDS LIKE THIS...

It seemed only fitting that Martha Stewart's fate at her trial should be determined to a certain degree by two women, both of whom were part of her inner circle. One portrayed Stewart as an executive so desperate that she tried to destroy evidence. The second relayed to the jury a Stewart quote so damaging that it was hard to imagine it had come from a Stewart friend.

The first witness, Martha Stewart's secretary, Ann Armstrong, bore a nervous smile and a haunted look, according to one writer at the trial.

Elizabeth Koch described her as a "dumpy woman in her mid forties with a wispy, dark brown bob and pasty skin. She waves her hands around as if shooing gnats. She giggles and rolls her eyes; lobbing her head from side to side with such force I fear she'll sprain something."

Armstrong's most controversial moment on the stand came when Assistant U.S. Attorney Michael Schacter asked her to describe the events of December 27th.

Bacanovic called in the morning, Armstrong related, and asked her to put him through to Stewart.

She told the caller that Stewart's plane would be touching down in a matter of minutes and she would contact him then.

Armstrong then typed in the now-famous message: "Peter Bacanovic thinks ImClone is going to start trading downward."

Schacter asked what she and Stewart discussed when she called the office after touching down.

"Lots of things," Ann said. "She'd made me plum pudding and…"

Armstrong suddenly began sobbing so grievously she could not speak. She placed both hands over her face, then with one hand reached for a paper towel and started to wipe away the streaming tears, both hands over her face again.

Recovering somewhat, Armstrong continued: "I thanked her for the plum pudding."

A CRYING SPELL

But then she began to sob again.

Male members of the jury widened their eyes; a few women on the jury gasped and covered their mouths.

Trying to be kind, the judge, clearly taken aback by the tears, asked Armstrong if she needed a moment.

Michael Schacter looked confused. He tried to continue his questioning.

Karen Seymour turned in horror, shaking her head at Schacter.

Robert Morvillo stood up twice and requested a recess; all too aware that Armstrong's tears would give her added credibility.

Morvillo stood up and patted Armstrong's shoulder, whispering consolations of some kind.

Armstrong blew her nose and wiped her eyes. After a brief sidebar, Schacter resumed his questioning.

Armstrong began crying all over again.

The judge then ended the session.

The next day, Armstrong was back on the stand. She showed no lingering emotional effects from what one writer at the trial called her "plum-pudding-induced breakdown" on the stand the day before.

Schacter picked up the narrative with Stewart's phone call from the San Antonio airport tarmac to Armstrong.

Did Armstrong have trouble hearing her? Did Armstrong remember Stewart saying she was having trouble hearing her? Was there any background noise on the call?

To these questions, Armstrong's answer was "no."

The prosecution had asked similar questions of every witness who had spoken to Stewart that afternoon—and their answers had also been "no."

The prosecution's questioning of Ann Armstrong then jumped to the events of January 31, 2002.

This was just five days before Stewart was due to sit down with federal authorities who were bound to ask her all sorts of questions about the events of December 27th.

She had to be aware that the feds would want to look at her phone records.

Around 5 o'clock that afternoon, Ann Armstrong testified, Martha Stewart spoke to John Savarese, Stewart's attorney at Wachtell, Lipton, for about half an hour.

After she got off the phone, Armstrong continued, Stewart asked to fax John Savarese the phone messages from Wednesday, December 26 through Monday, January 7.

"Then" testified Armstrong, "she asked if she could see the messages. I brought the message log up on my computer. Martha came over to my computer. ...I scrolled past the messages from the 26th and put up the 27th.

Schacter: What happened after you put up the messages?

Armstrong: Martha saw the message—'Peter Bacanovic thinks ImClone is going to start trading downward'—from Peter; she took the mouse, put the cursor at the end of the sentence, highlighted it back to the end of Peter's name, and then started typing over it.

> *She took the mouse, put the cursor at the end of the sentence, highlighted it back to the end of Peter's name, and then started typing over it.*

"PUT IT BACK. PUT IT BACK."

I was startled. Martha had never sat at my computer before or changed any records.

Schacter: Can you describe where Ms. Stewart and you were?

Armstrong: She was sitting at my desk, and I was standing behind her.

Schacter: What did she replace the message with?

Armstrong: 'Re imclone,' all lowercase. ...

Schacter: What happened after she replaced the message?

> *"Put it back. Put it back to the way it was."*

Armstrong: She instantly stood up and still standing there, said, 'Put it back. Put it back to the way it was.'

(Ann Armstrong asked a staff worker to help her recover the December 27th message log.)

Then she walked over to her door and turned around and asked me to get her son-in-law (Alexis's husband, attorney John Cuti) on the phone. He represented Stewart and her company.

Schacter: When you were back at your computer, what did you do?

Armstrong: I didn't know what to do. I really didn't know what to do. ... Martha was on the phone with her son-in-law for 15 minutes. While she was on the phone, I added punctuation to the message to just reflexively neaten it.

(Specifically, Judge Cedarbaum soon clarified, Armstrong added a colon after "re" and capitalized the "I" and "C" of ImClone.)

"No wonder Stewart sent Armstrong a plum pudding for Christmas," Elizabeth Koch wrote in her trial diary. "We should all have such fanatically detail-oriented assistants."

After Stewart got off the phone with her son-in-law, Armstrong testified, he called Armstrong, told her not to touch anything, to "stop in her tracks," and asked her to meet him later to discuss what had happened.

They met at a restaurant, and Armstrong told Cuti that she was in "a bit of a quandary" about getting the message back because her message-log was not backed up on the server.

Home that evening, Armstrong spoke again to Martha Stewart, who asked her if she had been able to put the message back in its original form.

Armstrong explained that she had not been able to because she could not recall what the original message was.

That evening, Armstrong took a notebook and wrote down everything that happened that day.

Ultimately, Armstrong testified, she discovered a copy of the original message on her computer because her computer had crashed and automatically saved everything.

Upon finding the original, she faxed a copy of it to John Savarese; then sealed a copy for herself in an envelope with a witness watching in the event that she might be asked to testify at a trial.

Armstrong tried to minimize what Stewart had done: After all, she testified, Stewart had told her to change the document back "instantly."

FIDDLING WITH A PHONE LOG

What Ann Armstrong presented, more importantly than the language she employed, was a vivid image of a woman sitting in her secretary's cubicle and fiddling with a phone log on the computer.

"Fiddling with a phone log" amounted to trying to destroy evidence.

Until Ann Armstrong testified, Martha Stewart had put forward the argument that she had absolutely no incentive to lie to the authorities (the central charge against her) because she had done nothing wrong. And yet here for the first time was a vivid illustration of what no defendant wanted to convey to a jury: a consciousness of guilt.

By tampering with evidence, Stewart appeared to be saying: I know I did something wrong—and now I've got to cover it up.

Armstrong's testimony about January 31st struck those at the trial like a lightning bolt. "To me," said securities attorney Jake Zamansky, "that looked pretty damaging. Why would somebody change a phone message and then change it back unless they have something to hide? It's like wiping the fingerprints off of a gun."

It was now Robert Morvillo's turn to cross-examine Ann Armstrong. He had one point he wanted to make:

Morvillo: Did Ms. Stewart ever come to you and ask you to lie?

Armstrong: No.

Morvillo: Did Ms. Stewart ever ask you to conceal the truth about this incident?

Armstrong: No.

Morvillo: After Ms. Stewart learned that the government was going to interview you; did she ever ask you to lie or cover up this incident?

Armstrong: No.

The trouble with Morvillo's questioning was its irrelevance.

Whether Stewart had asked Armstrong to lie was not the issue; what mattered was that Stewart had tampered with evidence; that the incident was indelibly sketched in Armstrong's mind, and that Armstrong had written a contemporaneous version of those events.

Jurors never forgot the image either: "That was so dramatic and so believable," said Rosemary McMahon. "And that was a big piece of what we had to consider in terms of evidence. That hurt Martha Stewart, I think, a lot." Armstrong, said juror Chappell Hartridge "ultimately gave the testimony that was going to bring Martha down. That was a very important piece."

In October 1998, Fortune magazine named Martha Stewart one of the Fifty Most Powerful Women. She was clearly nearing the height of her power. Those who knew her from earlier years cite October 19, 1999, as the most important day of her career. It was on that day that she took her company, Martha Stewart Living Omnimedia, public. By the end of the day, the company's stock had tripled in value. Her company was now worth $1.7 billion. Stewart catered the entire celebration, making homemade pastries. She had begun as a caterer and built a billion-dollar company and empire. She became chief executive officer and chairman of the company, and she owned 61 percent of the equity of the company, 94 percent of the voting power. It was in so many ways her very own enterprise.

The other female witness who on the stand would prove so devastating to Martha Stewart was perhaps her best friend, Mariana Pasternak. The two traveled together. Pasternak was a Westport, Connecticut, real estate broker. She and Stewart spoke every day; saw each other at least once a week.

Pasternak, then 50 years old, was the estranged wife of Westport vascular surgeon Bart Pasternak, who also owned ImClone stock.

Pasternak was well preserved, had high Slavic cheekbones, and her accent sounded Hungarian or at least Middle European. She bore certain similarities to Stewart: Though Pasternak's hair was darker than Stewart's, they had the same expensive coiffure. They shared refined tastes as well. At one stage of her testimony, Robert Morvillo asked

Pasternak, "You were in a chair?" She instantly corrected him: "I was in a chaise."

All the Government wanted from Pasternak in calling her to the stand was to corroborate Doug Faneuil's account of his conversation with Martha Stewart on December 27th.

But Pasternak also provided an intimate glimpse into Martha Stewart's emotional state at a crucial time.

Like other witnesses, Pasternak's testimony became dramatic when she spoke of the events of December 27, 2001.

It was on that day, she testified, that she joined Martha Stewart on a chartered plane to Mexico. Joining them was Kevin Sharkey (an editor at *Martha Stewart Living* and a good friend of both).

When they stopped off in Texas to refuel, the passengers waited in an airport lounge. Pasternak heard Stewart on the phone, speaking in "raised tones," but she could not tell what she was saying.

The three friends were staying at Las Ventanas, a luxurious resort in Los Cabos, Mexico. Prosecutors displayed records showing that the two women ran up tens of thousands of dollars in bills for spa treatments, individual meals, and other services. There was testimony during the trial that Stewart had asked her company to pay for the trip.

On December 30th, the two women had returned to their suite after a guided hike near their resort.

Speaking in a hushed courtroom, Pasternak said she remembered the evening precisely because she and Stewart had been out hiking and were too tired to go down to dinner.

Prosecutors showed a hotel bill for a December 30th guided hike.

The two women were relaxing with soft drinks on their balcony when Pasternak, as she testified, said: "Here we are again, just the two of us on a holiday trip with no male companionship."

They were both divorced, wealthy, and, in romantic terms, alone.

Pasternak turned the conversation to Sam Waksal, who had to be a complicated subject for Stewart. After all, Waksal and Stewart were about the same age, but he had dated her daughter.

"I remember Martha saying Sam was walking funny at the Christmas party, that he was selling or trying to sell his stock, that his daughter was selling or trying to sell her stock," Pasternak testified. "His stock is going down, or went down, and I sold mine," Stewart added.

What Stewart knew about Waksal when she sold her stock went to the heart of the Government's contention that Stewart repeatedly lied to investigators.

Stewart told investigators she never recalled being tipped that Waksal was selling, and that she sold instead because she and her stockbroker had a prearranged agreement to sell Stewart's ImClone shares when they fell below a certain price.

Pasternak had offered crucial testimony, because Stewart had no way of knowing that Waksal and his daughters were selling except from the conversation with Doug Faneuil.

Pasternak's revelation was damaging because Stewart claimed that she sold the stock for an entirely different reason—and not because she knew that the Waksal family was selling their shares.

Schacter kept fishing for more of this female gossip that might provide more damning testimony.

Schacter: Do you have any recollection of speaking with Ms. Stewart on the subject of brokers while you were in Mexico?

> *"Isn't it nice to have brokers who tell you those things."*

Pasternak: I remember one brief statement, which was: "Isn't it nice to have brokers who tell you those things."

Realizing that this was one of the most explosive statements of the trial, and that it had come out of nowhere, the judge immediately dismissed the jury. She knew the attorneys were about to scuffle over this choice sentence.

Journalists in the audience began buzzing.

What was that quote again? When did Martha say that? What was the context?

Those in the courtroom could not have been more stunned if Pasternak had quoted Stewart as saying, "And then Peter Bacanovic and I made up this ridiculous story about a $60 agreement."

The "Isn't it nice" comment blasted Robert Morvillo out of his seat.

Morvillo: Your Honor, I am going to move to strike. There is absolutely no context to that remark. It is obviously not at the same time as the subject—

Judge Cedarbaum: This is said to be a different conversation.

Morvillo: Correct. That conversation is absolutely meaningless. It could mean anything. Therefore, it is not relevant. I move to strike it.

Judge Cedarbaum: Overruled.

With that, she ended the session.

The next day, February 20th, the jury arrived back in the courtroom, anxious to hear more about the juicy Pasternak quote. Pasternak seemed to waver somewhat as she neared the stand. She looked glassy-eyed.

It was Robert Morvillo's turn to question her. He began by leading her moment by moment from the takeoff on December 27th through the next three days and finally to the conversation in question on December 30th.

"When Ms. Stewart first brought up Sam Waksal, you two were relaxing on the terrace in your hotel in Mexico?"

"Yes."

"Were you sitting in chairs?" Morvillo asks.

It was then that Pasternak corrected him by saying, "We were sitting. I was in a chaise."

She reiterated the conversation that centered on family and friends, the events of the day, and the fact that here they were once again on vacation together without male companionship.

Then Pasternak brought up Sam Waksal.

"Martha said he'd disappeared again, that he was walking funny at a dinner party. She told me he'd sold or was trying to sell his stock."

"Did you feel she was telling you inside information?" Morvillo asked.

"No, I felt like she was worried. I said, 'That's so scary, Martha,' because it sounded like he was having financial problems. When she told me she'd sold her ImClone shares, she sounded regretful, or guilty, out of loyalty to a friend."

Morvillo quickly moved on to the second conversation she testified to the day before.

"Do you remember what day this discussion took place, where you were or what time it was?"

"No, I don't recall."

"Do you recall if it was before or after the terrace conversation?"

"No, I don't."

"What do you remember?"

"I remember...I see a scene somewhere on the grounds of the hotel, and...but nothing about why it came up."

"Are you sure the statement—"Isn't it nice to have brokers who tell you those things"—is one Ms. Stewart made? Or was it something you thought?"

"It's fair to say I don't know if it was a statement Martha made or if it was a thought in my mind," she said in rapid prose, so rapid that it caught some in the audience off guard.

Again the journalists turned to each other to ask if they had heard right.

Morvillo had done his homework.

He had looked up her testimony to the SEC where Pasternak had claimed to be uncertain as to the origin of the damning comment. Now, in testimony at the trial, she was conceding, as she had to the SEC, that maybe Stewart had not made that comment after all.

It was no wonder that she appeared in court glassy-eyed. It looked like she had been tossing and turning all night.

Morvillo sat down. Michael Schacter stood up. It was his turn to redirect.

"Do you recall telling the government your best recollection?" he asked Pasternak.

"I recall telling the government that if I had to make my best recollection, I'd say Martha said it."

"Is that still your testimony?"

It was at that precise moment that Martha Stewart took a giant swig from her green tea bottle.

"Yes. My best belief is that Martha said it."

Morvillo got a chance to recross: "But you're not sure Martha said it?"

"I remember, all I remember is looking at Martha, seeing her face, as those words appeared in a stream."

"In a stream?" Morvillo asked.

"Yes."

Morvillo left the words hanging in the air, as if to say to the jury: Perhaps she had a vision.

Although Morvillo was able to raise some doubt as to whether Martha Stewart had made the statement, the jury would take the comment with them into their deliberations, certainly one of the most damning pieces of evidence against Martha Stewart.

An intriguing question arose.

Why did Mariana Pasternak turn on her friend of 20 years?

No one knew for sure.

But there was ample speculation in the media at the time that Pasternak may have turned state's evidence for fear that she might face some charges as well in the probe.

On January 29th, the *New York Post* reported that Pasternak "lives in a tony beach house in Westport" and had been battling her own financial and legal problems. The newspaper said its research into her background included a check of records at the Westport Town Clerk's office.

Apart from the stress of having to testify against her pal, Pasternak was knee-deep in financial problems, according to those records filed at the Westport Town Clerk's office, the newspaper said.

The *Wall Street Journal* reported in August 2002 that Pasternak's ex-husband sold 10,000 shares of ImClone stock shortly before the ImClone news about the FDA's decision was disclosed.

The newspaper provided Pasternak with a motive for testifying against Stewart: namely, that unless she testified, the feds might have gone after her husband just as they had gone after Martha Stewart.

Much later, in July 2004, Larry King asked Martha Stewart what she made of Mariana Pasternak's testimony. What was it like for Stewart to sit and listen to it?

King's guest would not take the bait. "That gets pretty close to the case, so I really am not going to comment on that."

King tried another angle.

"OK, then I'll ask, emotionally, was it difficult to hear a friend talk?"

MY GODCHILDREN

"Let's say," said Martha Stewart, "that her two daughters are my god-children. It's pretty hard to see the whole—the whole thing."

Stewart might as well have said: "With friends like this...."

CHAPTER

10

SITTING IN STONY SILENCE

Stubbornly, Martha Stewart insisted upon her innocence. Her strategy of trying to trivialize the federal investigation into her stock sale had failed miserably. The trial was proof of that. But even though she was being prosecuted, she and her attorneys had the chance to mount a case on her behalf that would convince the jury of her innocence.

She refused to do that, and thus she made another huge mistake.

Why did she remain so passive during the trial? Why did she and her attorneys act as if they had no obligation to show proof of her innocence?

Both the media and the jury wanted to hear from her; they wanted her attorneys to present evidence that would exonerate her. Instead, an unsmiling, sullen Martha Stewart sat through the trial acting as if she had been offended to be in the courtroom.

Why did she not understand what was so self-evident to others? That if she were going to escape legal harm, she had to mount an effective case for herself.

By her behavior and by her demeanor, Stewart gave everyone the answer: She simply believed that, because she was Martha Stewart, because she was an icon, because ultimately the jurors would be too impressed with her celebrity, she would emerge a free woman.

The problem with that kind of thinking was that it bred in the jurors' minds a feeling that Martha Stewart believed she was above us all; that she could behave in any way that she liked, and no one would castigate her for it. But she was wrong.

The jury was comprised of twelve hard-working middle class people, disdainful of haughtiness, resentful of ostentatious signs of wealth. That was why Stewart's expensive handbag in court was like a slap in the face to each juror. As Karen S. Bond, a former federal prisoner and civil litigation attorney, observed: "Stewart's best chance at winning over the jury...was lost when she walked into U.S. District Court in Manhattan carrying the Hermes Birken bag instead of a Kmart Corp. Accessory Works bag. Clearly, if stupidity were a crime...her image consultants would be facing a 20-year prison sentence, too."

Inviting celebrity support to sit in the audience at the trial was as mistaken as carrying the expensive handbag.

She may have thought the jury would be impressed that Martha Stewart had such high-flying friends, but the truth was that the jury resented the celebrity guests as one big intrusion, taking their presence as a deliberate attempt to influence them.

Putting on a feeble defense, flaunting her wealth with that Hermes Birken bag, displaying her celebrity friends, Stewart continued her strategy of trying to trivialize what her adversaries were doing. She was deluding herself if she thought this would score her points with the jury.

Few understood why her attorneys failed to mount a vigorous defense.

The prosecution's case had lasted four weeks; the defense's, just one hour. Clearly her attorneys hoped that the jury would come to its own conclusion that the government's case was weak enough to declare Martha Stewart innocent.

Why had Stewart gone along with such a flawed strategy?

I Don't Take You Seriously

The fact was that she was being utterly consistent. In so many words, she was saying to the federal prosecutors: I don't take you seriously. I don't take your allegations seriously. There's no reason for me to even respond to your charges.

But her attorneys had glaringly erred.

By being heavily circumstantial, the government's case may have appeared weak at least until its chief witness, Doug Faneuil, got on the stand. He shot down Stewart and Bacanovic's main line of defense, the $60-a-share arrangement. Then Ann Armstrong provided the searing evidence that her boss had exhibited a consciousness of guilt. Mariana Pasternak put the icing on the cake, testifying that Stewart had acknowledged to her how nice it was to have friends (stockbrokers) who gave her inside information, dealing another blow to the $60-a-share version.

What Robert Morvillo should have done was to bring witnesses who could have testified to the existence of the $60-a-share agreement between Stewart and Bacanovic. Even if he thought there was no need to do that, the jury was left with the impression that such witnesses simply did not exist.

Morvillo called only one witness for the defense.

Making matters worse, the witness, a junior attorney named Steven Pearl, a former Wachtell, Lipton, Rosen & Katz attorney, seemed at best marginal to the case. Pearl had attended the February 4, 2002, interview the feds had conducted with Stewart. It was the defense team's hope that Pearl, who took notes during the meeting in addition to an FBI agent, would be able to discredit the feds' contention that Stewart had lied to them. But Pearl's testimony was so confusing that it was of little use.

Morvillo could have put numerous others on the stand in defense of Martha Stewart. Instead, he relied on a single unconvincing witness. It was as if the Stewart defense team was snubbing its noses at the jury. Juror Peggy McMahon said after the trial that she and her fellow jurors felt they needed more. "We were waiting. We were hoping." Echoed Juror Jonathan Laskin: "We were hoping they would put up more of a fight...give us more to chew on, but it wasn't there."

To Jake Zamansky, the securities attorney who attended the trial daily, Stewart's lawyers paid a price for the paucity of their defense: "There was arrogance on the part of the lawyers. I think they thought they had done such a great job that they didn't need to put on much of a case. The only witness they called blew up in their face."

> *"There was arrogance on the part of the lawyers. I think they thought they had done such a great job that they didn't need to put on much of a case."*

Even to Stewart supporters, the thinness of the Stewart defense was shocking: "It looked like they had just given up," said Andrew Ritchie, one of the chief writers for SaveMartha.com.

"It was a risky move on Morvillo's part, but I thought it looked sad. Some say Martha left him with no choice because the evidence was so strong against her."

The great symbol of the defense's meager defense was the decision taken by Morvillo and Stewart to keep her off the stand.

It was the worst mistake Stewart made and most likely the one that brought about her conviction.

The single most important reason for her to testify was that by the time she would have been due to get on the stand, she was losing the case. Some argued that she could only do damage to herself by testifying. But, with her back to the wall, she should have taken that risk.

Had she testified, she had a decent shot at winning over the jury simply by virtue of the passion that she could have brought in her presentation.

From the moment that she was indicted and it became clear that there would be a trial, many simply assumed that Stewart would never get convicted and never go to jail. She would be declared innocent.

The reason?

Her attorneys would put her on the stand and, great communicator and charming person that she had been, she would score a personal triumph, winning the jury over to her side.

A COSTLY MISTAKE

But as the trial approached, her attorneys became convinced that she could do more damage to her case by testifying than if she sat silent in her seat throughout the trial even though, at least on television dramas, it was the guilty who always refused to testify.

What Stewart failed to take into account was that the jurors wanted to hear from her. She had no legal obligation to testify—or, for that matter, to mount any kind of defense. But after the prosecution mounted such an effective case, she should have given the jury what it wanted— her on the stand!

The jury had seen her in court every day sit in stony silence. They appeared ready to give her the benefit of the doubt. But first they wanted to hear her version of the events. Even with the strong case the prosecutors had mounted, "The jury was looking for almost any excuse to acquit her," said one participant in the case. "All that she had to do was get on the stand and apologize. All she had to say was that she didn't have the mental intent to violate the law. All she had to do was humanize herself—and she would have gotten off."

Certainly Robert Morvillo had a lot to fear from his client testifying.

Had she indeed lied to the federal authorities, she would have had to lie on the stand to conceal her crime. She would have had to be one great actress to deceive the jury.

Also, how could she explain away the altered e-mail?

After the trial, jurors said that Stewart's fiddling with the e-mail damaged her case severely; they would have loved to hear her explanation of the incident.

How could she explain away her friend's testimony that she had indeed known the Waksals were selling their ImClone shares?

Perhaps worst of all, how could she fend off prosecutors when they brought up past incidents that showed Stewart to be lying to protect her own interests?

Her friends and associates were disappointed that Stewart decided to avoid testifying.

Friend and business associate Donald Trump noted that he had been "devastated that Martha didn't testify. I would have said, 'testify.'" The jury, he felt, expected her to testify. "I think that a jury of 12 people is saying, 'Tell us you didn't do it....'"

A JACLYN SMITH SUIT

Another Stewart friend, Dominick Dunne, covering the trial for *Vanity Fair*, thought, "she could have absolutely charmed that jury, totally and completely." Added legal scholar Karen S. Bond: "Stewart should have put on a Jaclyn Smith suit from Kmart and testified in her own defense. Even

> *"All that she had to do was get on the stand and apologize. All she had to say was that she didn't have the mental intent to violate the law."*

> *"Stewart should have put on a Jaclyn Smith suit from Kmart and testified in her own defense."*

though some would argue that Morvillo was right to keep her off the stand, Martha Stewart clearly knows how to package and sell Martha Stewart to the America that comprises the 'jury of her peers.'"

Lanny Davis, the former White House counsel who had served as Stewart's public relations adviser during her probe, believed that "had she been allowed to tell her full story to the jury, the jury would have liked her and found her credible." She could have even persuaded jurors that her altering the e-mail was not incriminating. "If she wanted to cover up a message that was damaging," said Davis, "she shouldn't have corrected it. The fact is she corrected it."

In post-trial interviews, jurors acknowledged that they were stunned that Stewart had not taken the stand. Juror Amos M. Mellinger concluded that it might have been legitimate for the defense team to claim, as it did, that the defendants—Stewart and Bacanovic—were too smart to have engaged in such a bungled cover-up—but without having the chance to evaluate both of them on the stand, there was no way for the jury to buy into the defense's argument.

The case was beginning to wind down.

Assistant U.S. Attorney Michael Schacter got up from his chair, hesitated for a moment, looking over at the jury as if to say to them, "I have a good story for you"—and then began his closing argument for the prosecution.

Showing the case to be circumstantial, Schacter suggested that no single piece of evidence was on its own sufficient to prove the alleged crimes; but taking all of the evidence together, the government's narrative made sense.

Schacter focused his closing arguments on the testimony of Douglas Faneuil, repeating Faneuil's argument that Bacanovic had forced him into swallowing numerous cover ups with regards to Stewart's dumping her ImClone shares—first to a tax-loss agreement, then a $60 floor agreement. "Use your common sense, ladies and gentlemen," Schacter implored the jury. "Why on earth would anyone make this up?"

The main point of Richard Strassberg, attorney for Bacanovic, was that his client was simply too honest a fellow to have gotten into this trouble. It simply "makes no sense that Peter Bacanovic, who had built his whole life on his integrity, whose entire career depends on his clients' trust, would have told his assistant of six months to betray another client and pass along personal info. Celebrities especially want to guard their stock—if he'd told Martha Stewart about another client's activities, how could she ever trust him again?" Unfortunately for Strassberg and Bacanovic, it was not a very convincing argument.

Robert Morvillo said in his opening statement that the trial was "about (Attorney General) John Ashcroft. John Ashcroft is the one who is bringing this case against Martha Stewart. John Ashcroft. John Ashcroft."

In his closing argument, he said, "I'm not going to talk about John Ashcroft anymore."

Morvillo appeared to believe at the time of his opening that the jury really hated John Ashcroft but by the time he closed, that most jurors had no idea who Ashcroft was. They certainly did not believe, prior to hearing it from Morvillo, that Ashcroft had anything to do with the case. Securities attorney Jake Zamansky thought Morvillo's references to Ashcroft were "almost offensive to the jury."

Morvillo's main point in his closing was that no one could have been so stupid to leave such an obvious trail of evidence: "The government has accused Martha Stewart of participating in a Confederacy of Dunces!"

"If two smart, successful people were to sit down to concoct a story, wouldn't they make sure to match them up? Wouldn't they have made at least certain aspects of it cohere? Look at the gaping inconsistencies! They fall down on the very first element of the case!"

He then went through a whole series of discrepancies that surrounded the $60 arrangement and the eventual sale of ImClone stock—when they made the agreement, where they made it, who else knew about it, and when they were told. "They couldn't even get straight who took down the order and executed the transaction! What kind of conspiracy is this? It's a Conspiracy of Dunces!"

"Martha Stewart was simply too smart to get involved in something so stupid. She was telling the truth when she said she did not recall receiving the tip that Waksal was selling ImClone shares."

But Karen Seymour, in her rebuttal summation, replied that, "Smart people committing stupid crimes or doing stupid things, your common sense tells you that that's what white-collar criminals do every day."

IN YOUR HANDS

At times, Morvillo whispered; at times, he shouted.

"Whatever mistakes she made were good-faith mistakes, not bad-faith mistakes," he said.

One writer said Morvillo "looked like a well-dressed Jackie Gleason."

Morvillo admitted that Martha Stewart did indeed receive a tip that Waksal was trying to dump his and his daughter's stock the day she dumped hers. The admission was a calculated risk on his part.

"Nobody is disputing whether or not Martha Stewart was told the Waksals were selling for the first time. What we are disputing is that it had too much business significance to her that it would have tainted her mind."

Morvillo differed from the other attorneys in his presentation: He was at times downright funny. He had jurors smiling, laughing, and appearing to enjoy themselves. The jury was definitely listening to his every word.

Morvillo excoriated the government for mishandling Stewart's pretrial interviews. The FBI did not tape and then transcribe the tapes. "How can you say whether Martha dodged questions or responded in full when no one bothered to record the questions?" Morvillo asked. "Not recording the interviews allows the government to go after you any way they want."

"How can you accuse Martha of even knowing these were legitimate SEC meetings? The real deal? They didn't hold the interviews in the SEC office, nor did an actual SEC officer conduct the interview—the assistant United States Attorney did. How can you accuse Martha of willfully obstructing justice and lying to officers of the law when they were conducted so informally?"

IT'S A GOOD THING

"Martha Stewart's life is in your hands," Robert Morvillo told the jury "I ask you to acquit Martha Stewart. I ask you to let her return to her life of improving the quality of life for everyone. And if you do that, it will be a good thing."

Some thought Morvillo had just made a huge mistake. Whereas he should have been focusing the jury's attention on what they had in common with Martha Stewart, he was, by referring to her business empire, reminding them of the sharp disparity in wealth between Stewart and the "jury of her peers."

Morvillo's comments were likely to alienate jurors by inferring that even if Stewart had made a mistake, it did not matter because it would benefit all Americans if she could return to her privileged life.

When Morvillo concluded his closing arguments after three hours, a very pleased Martha Stewart hugged him. She seemed elated as she walked out of the courtroom. "We love you, Martha," a crowd of loyalists shouted at her as she emerged from court.

In early March, as the trial was nearing an end, a visitor walked into Martha Stewart's office in New York. He was dressed in a plaid jacket and striped shirt. Others teased him for the odd look—but not Martha Stewart. "Wow! What a fascinating outfit!" she said, giving Mark Burnett a big smile. She reached for her camera to record the outfit for posterity. To Burnett, Stewart's rush for the camera indicated a hidden sense of humor. Perhaps, he thought, he could exploit that humor on television.

Known as the creator of the television reality hit programs, *Survivor* and Donald Trump's *The Apprentice*, Mark Burnett thought it all wrong that Martha Stewart's company should be treating her like a pariah. He thought the company was making a big mistake. "It was," he said somewhat bombastically, "the equivalent of McDonald's taking down the golden arches." No wonder the advertisers were abandoning the ship, even her company no longer displayed confidence in her. Burnett saw a storyline that Americans would go for: Stewart's fall from grace and then her redemption. He thought the idea could be turned into a Stewart-driven television program. He asked her for a meeting. Even if she were found guilty, he thought, she would get a minimal jail sentence. The media will no longer feel it important to knock her. Indeed, the media will want to build her back up again. He wanted to ride that wave as her television partner.

Burnett pitched Stewart two television programs: one would be an hour-long daytime show where she would appear in front of a live audience; the other would be a prime-time reality show. Burnett proposed that both programs be spontaneous so that Stewart's true inner self, humor and all, could be put on display. Everyone knew Stewart's reputation as an icy, cold-hearted business woman, and everyone remembered the witness in her trial who testified that she had threatened to fire her stockbroker if he did not change the hold music on the telephone.

Stewart responded positively and warmly to Burnett and his proposals, simply pleased that anyone at all had believed in her and believed that she had a future after the legal ordeal she was enduring.

Burnett next turned to his co-producer of *The Apprentice*, Donald Trump, and proposed that he and Trump launch a Martha Stewart spin-off. Trump worried at first that it might be too much exposure for the *Apprentice* franchise (ratings for his second and third series indicated that the audience was decreasing). But Burnett pointed out to Trump how successful other spin-offs had been (*CSI*, *Law & Order*). Trump agreed to the idea.

It was March 3, 2004. The case had been going on for five weeks. Now it was nearly over.

One good piece of news for Martha Stewart had occurred five days earlier when Judge Cedarbaum had thrown out the charge of securities fraud against Stewart; it had accused Stewart of trying to prop up the value of Martha Stewart Living Omnimedia by lying to investors about why she dumped ImClone stock in December 2001.

It had been the most serious charge on her indictment with a maximum punishment of 10 years in prison and a $1 million fine. Had she been found guilty of that charge, she would have gone to jail for six years; without the charge, probably no more than 15 to 21 months.

The judge ruled, "No reasonable juror can find beyond a reasonable doubt that the defendant lied for the purpose of influencing the market for the securities of her company."

Without the securities fraud charge, there were still four criminal counts remaining: conspiracy, obstruction of justice, and two counts of lying to investigators—with a maximum sentence of 20 years and a $1 million fine.

Stewart said in a message on her personal Web site that she was pleased with the judge's ruling.

Stock in Martha Stewart Living Omnimedia, which had been heavily hit since her legal troubles began, rose on word of the judge's ruling, up $1.43, or nearly 11 percent to close at $14.53 on the New York Stock Exchange.

Having heard the closing arguments, most of the media, once convinced Stewart would walk free, now believed that she would be found guilty.

Judge Cedarbaum charged the jury that morning. It took two hours. The jury had been waiting for this moment for weeks. They were deeply involved in the case; not one of them had missed a day of the trial. Never did the trial have to be delayed because of juror tardiness, a rarity for New York trials.

Now it was the turn of the jury to deliberate.

All that afternoon the jury discussed the case. Sometimes it asked to see testimony, summary charts, phone records, and other evidence. At first it seemed there might be a verdict in a day or two; then only early the following week.

The next morning, deliberations were delayed after a subway accident stranded four jurors.

In the crowded courtroom, two reporters played chess. One read a novel he had written 20 years earlier.

Some reporters smuggled in newspapers. Others deliberated about the case again. The interest in the case had reached a new peak. One television reporter declared that her network had seven people outside the courtroom along with a "playbook" for reporting.

The moment when the jury would render its verdict was fast approaching.

PART IV

WHAT A WASTE

CHAPTER
11

THE VERDICT IS IN

I t was a moment that was never supposed to happen.

Martha Stewart's attorneys had all but assured her that the moment would never arrive. But then again they had promised her that other moments would not arrive—she would not be indicted; she would not go to trial—and those moments had come.

She was astonished that it had come to this, that a jury was about to begin deliberating her fate. She had not lied to anyone; she had not engaged in conspiracy; she had not obstructed justice. She had, in short, not committed any serious crime. She was innocent.

Nerves were on end and every time the jury sent a signal to the bench—even if it was just to ask a question—it was as if someone had thrown a bomb in the courtroom.

The first signal from the jury was a request for testimony regarding Peter Bacanovic's comments about speaking to Martha Stewart on December 27, 2001. Judge Cedarbaum read the note aloud, then left the courtroom. It was not clear what testimony the jury wanted to see: The two sides bickered over what to show them. That took four hours.

Later that day, the jury asked a technical question regarding a charge against Peter Bacanovic. The judge ruled on the matter the next morning.

Each jury note encouraged more media speculation about how much longer everyone had to wait for a verdict. Some darkly predicted June. It was clear, though, that the jury was taking its time. Both sides tried to take comfort from the absence of a quick verdict.

Elizabeth Koch, the reporter for *Reason* magazine, wandered the corridors and seemed to meet only people who thought Stewart had indeed lied to the feds, but would get off because of a lack of solid evidence.

Meanwhile Charles Gasparino, the *Wall Street Journal* reporter at the trial, reported to his colleagues that he had been barhopping to gauge public opinion on the case. Those he interviewed at bars thought Stewart would get off. They knew Stewart was wealthy, and they had long ago concluded that rich people get away with everything. Gasparino deserved credit for his enthusiasm but his findings did not help understand how the jury would vote.

Finally, word began to spread that the jury had reached a verdict. It was early afternoon, Friday, March 5, 2004.

Having listened to five weeks of testimony, the jury needed less than three days—12 hours of actual deliberation—to decide. It spent much of its time on Bacanovic, far less on Stewart.

A CHINESE LUNCH

As it turned out, a bunch of the journalists who had been covering the trial had been lunching at a restaurant in Chinatown north of the courthouse.

Someone at the table yelled out, "Guys, we have to get back."

Was he pulling their collective legs?

Was a verdict about to be announced?

The journalists sensed that indeed it was time to return to the courtroom. Before they left their seats, they began thinking about how quickly they could get the news to their audiences. "As a TV reporter," said Helen Lucaites, "the first thing you do is put on your make-up."

Outside the courtroom, the media was reinforcing its troops. Extra television crews arrived. Television reporters forced to remain outside the courtroom stood ready to supply bulletins on the verdict.

Slowly, the courtroom was filling up, attorneys, family, friends, reporters, and court officials. Even as the journalists took their seats, they could not be sure that this was indeed the verdict. They did pick up on some telltale signs: After lunching with his wife, the judge's husband hung around the courtroom, not at all routine. Then too there was the presence of the U.S. District Attorney, not at all a courtroom fixture.

Karen Seymour walked in with a smile; Robert Morvillo looked nervous. Seated at the defense table, Martha Stewart looked distraught.

"All rise," the court clerk shouted and everyone stood up.

Judge Cedarbaum walked in. Her face was stiff and gray. She had a look of seriousness to her that the defense team did not like.

"The jury has reached a verdict," she pronounced.

Then the jury walked in.

Often a jury looked exhausted when they arrived in court to deliver a verdict if only because of the emotional toll the trial had taken on them. But the Stewart jury, filing into the courtroom, seemed relaxed. Several jurors smiled. "It was their equanimity that was so startling," wrote Jeff Toobin.

Later, in post-trial interviews, jurors noted that as they walked into the courtroom they were shaking, feeling nervous and sad. Jurors were concerned that they might telegraph their guilty verdict to Stewart as they strode in, as some juries did.

Hence, they turned away from her. "I felt so sad for her," asserted juror Chappell Hartridge. "I didn't want her to read anything from my expression."

A few journalists detected sneers on the faces of some jurors.

"It was just a gut-wrenching atmosphere," recalled Elizabeth Koch. "Everyone was holding in one's breath but you knew what was coming."

Because no television cameras had been allowed at the trial, reporters sitting in the court knew that, upon the announcement of the verdict, they would have to scurry outside—so they could relay the news to their various news organizations. Helen Lucaites was one of those: "We knew it would be a race to get it on the air first."

The judge read the verdict in the case of the United States vs. Martha Stewart.

"Count one: Guilty.

Count two: Guilty.

Count three: Guilty.

Count four: Guilty."

Martha Stewart was found guilty on all four remaining counts against her: conspiracy, obstruction of justice, and two counts of making false statements. Though the maximum she could receive was five years, it appeared likely she would get between 15 and 21 months in prison. Sentencing was set for June 12th.

Then the judge read the verdict for Peter Bacanovic.

He was found guilty on four of the five counts against him.

> "It sounded like hundreds of people were gasping at the same time."

As the Stewart verdict was announced, the courtroom erupted in a huge collective sigh. "It sounded like hundreds of people were gasping at the same time," said Jake Zamansky. "It was like, 'Ahhhh.'"

COMPLETE DISBELIEF

"There was complete disbelief," recalled Zamansky, one of the few courtroom observers to predict that she would be convicted. Henry Blodget whispered to a colleague upon hearing the verdict: "I must have missed something."

The journalists kept their eyes on Martha Stewart. Just before the verdict, she had shown little emotion. She did seem fidgety, blowing her nose, shifting ground. When her verdict was read, she seemed to freeze. "She got stiff as a corpse," said Elizabeth Koch.

There were no tears, no outward sign that she was about to lose her tough-as-nails composure. To the journalists watching her, she showed not the slightest emotion.

Meanwhile, Stewart's daughter Alexis did show emotion.

She dropped her head into her hands and seemed to be shaking for several minutes. Then she began crying. She was shocked at the guilty verdict. She had in fact fainted very briefly. "It might have been a millisecond, but I was dreaming, and then I woke up, and I was unfortunately still there." Most people near her had not realized what had happened to her. She quickly revived, needing no medical assistance.

Martha Stewart's mother, sitting directly in front of her, saw none of this. She stared straight ahead. Most of the journalists saw nothing of what Alexis had gone through either.

To Rochelle Steinhaus, watching the scene right after the verdict, it seemed odd that "her daughter had more of a reaction than Martha did."

Steinhaus's instincts were to run out of the courtroom once she heard the verdict. But she could not. The judge had instructed everyone that they could not leave the courtroom until the entire court proceedings were wrapped up and the judge had called a recess. That took only a few minutes but it was a long few minutes, Steinhaus remembered.

For the journalists, getting the word out would not be easy. Their cell phones had been taken from them before entering court. And yet they would have to convey the verdict to colleagues instantly upon leaving the courtroom. They devised a clever scheme, color-coded scarves. It was archaic, and it turned out to be confusing, as frantic reporters raced to find a spot where they could wave their scarves in full view of their colleagues.

Rochelle Steinhaus headed for the tent that had been set up where Court TV had its camera. A triangular area had been set up on a small patch of grass in the middle of the street facing the courthouse.

The normal cohort of 100 reporters had swollen to three or four times that number on the day of the verdict. Television reporters did their stand-ups practically shoulder to shoulder. While they spoke, they could hear the voices of their colleagues ringing in their ears.

As reporters raced through the corridor, they heard some yelling. It was Peter Bacanovic's mother, jabbing her finger at the *New York Post's* gossipy opinion writer, Andrea Peyser.

"You wanted this all along. You wanted to see Peter in an orange jumpsuit. You made that happen. But he lost his career and his job and he had no motive."

Alexis Stewart reported later how "incredibly saddened, incredibly saddened" her mother was by the verdict, and how saddened her mother was as well "over feeling like her life was wasted."

Then Stewart exited the courtroom, her daughter at her side. Until now, mother and daughter had not embraced. They would leave that presumably for a more private moment. Walking down the steps of the federal court building, Stewart looked over at some supporters and offered them a smile.

To some, Stewart did not seem like the ordinary convicted felon.

"Martha didn't act like the traditional woman who cries after a trial," observed Elaine Lafferty, then the editor-in-chief of *Ms. Magazine.* "In many quarters, a woman is expected to cry to appear like a victim, to talk about their husband and children. But here was this woman, right after her trial and a guilty verdict, pitching her company, being concerned about her company."

Hours after the verdict, she posted a statement on her Web site, marthatalks.com, which said, "I am obviously distressed by the jury's verdict but I continue to take comfort in knowing that I have done nothing wrong and that I have the enduring support of my family and friends. I will appeal the verdict and continue to fight to clear my name. I believe in the fairness of the judicial system and remain confident that I will ultimately prevail."

> "I believe in the fairness of the judicial system and remain confident that I will ultimately prevail."

Within minutes, though, probably at her attorneys' insistence, she had the words "I have done nothing wrong" removed. To leave the sentence on the Web site was to risk angering her sentencing judge.

By continuing to say "I have done nothing wrong," she continued to snub her nose at the judge and jury. She continued to show no remorse.

Elsewhere on the steps of the courthouse, Jake Zamansky was telling CNBC that he had not been surprised by the verdict. "I think it was clear that from Faneuil's testimony and the surrounding circumstances that Martha got a secret tip on December 27th: Waksal was selling. That's very close to securities fraud. She immediately sold (her shares) and then told a different story to the regulators."

To Zamansky, the verdict sent a message to corporate America and to Wall Street: "Don't get anywhere near an insider trade. Don't lie to the government. If you're being investigated for insider trading, you have two choices: keep your mouth shut and take the Fifth, or cooperate with the regulators. Lying to the government is not an option."

The first juror to speak publicly about the verdict was Chappell Hartridge. Reporters stood on tables and chairs so they could see and hear him. "Maybe this is a victory for the little guys who lose money thanks to these kinds of transactions," he famously noted. His "little guys" quote was one of the most widely disseminated of the trial. "Maybe the conviction will give the little guy more confident feelings that I [sic] can invest in markets and get in on the up and up."

What Hartridge did with this controversial statement was to group Martha Stewart in with the Enrons, and Tycos, and WorldComs, and Adelphias, and give her case the same rotten patina of corporate scandal that had been affixed to these more serious cases.

From other post-verdict juror interviews, a portrait of the behind-the-scenes deliberations emerged: Jurors began their deliberations taking note of the various narratives that had been woven at the trial: Stewart's, Bacanovic's, and Faneuil's. They chose to focus on Faneuil first. "We ultimately felt that (Faneuil's testimony) was essentially credible," said juror Jonathan Laskin.

If there was one witness who persuaded the jurors of Stewart's guilt, it was Ann Armstrong. Said Chappell Hartridge: "There had to be a reason Martha was trying to delete that message [that ImClone was selling downward]. I mean, if the message had said, 'the stock is at 60, now it's time to sell as per our agreement,' then that would have been okay. I guess so. These guys are rather, uh, literal."

The jurors had serious doubts as to whether the $60-a-share agreement had existed. Juror Peggy McMahon noted: "We believed that there was a possibility that this agreement existed, but we couldn't find any evidence that that agreement was used on that day. In fact, we found the opposite." Media accounts of the Stewart case overlooked this juror revelation. The fact was that the jury did not convict her for lying about the $60 agreement. It convicted her for another "crime."

The other "crime" had to do with the arrogance that Stewart and her attorneys exhibited during the trial. It was this lethal mixture of hubris and stubbornness that ultimately convicted her. The jurors were reluctant to acknowledge how deeply affected they were by the negative aspects of Stewart's personality. After all, they were supposed to judge her on the evidence. But they could not do so entirely.

NO NEED TO DEFEND MYSELF

"How'd you think Morvillo did defending her?" a journalist shouted to Chappell Hartridge.

"He did the best he could with what he had to work with. It bothered me that they only put one witness on the stand. It's like they were saying, 'I don't need to defend myself. I don't need to persuade the jury. We know we'll get off.' It was kind of...."

"Arrogant?" the *New York Post's* Andrea Peyser asked, hoping he would agree.

"Yeah," Hartridge agreed. "Judging by some of the things they did, I'd say they thought they were special, like they were better than everyone else. I wasn't comfortable with the tone of [Peter Bacanovic's taped SEC testimony]. He sounded kind of...."

"Arrogant?" Peyser again volunteered.

"What about the fact that Martha charges her vacations to the company? Did that play into your decision?"

> *"She takes vacations and doesn't pay for them—it's like she thinks she's better than everyone else."*

"Yeah," Hartridge conceded. "She takes vacations and doesn't pay for them—it's like she thinks she's better than everyone else."

Someone shifted the subject matter.

"What are you thinking of in terms of insider trading?" a reporter asked.

"Well, as I understood it, we weren't supposed to consider insider trading. But as far as not talking to the authorities and not cooperating, yes, she sounded like she thought she was better than everyone else."

The media at large had pronounced Martha Stewart guilty almost from the time that her legal case went public. The journalists in the courtroom thought she was innocent, or that, if guilty, she would still get off. The jury pronounced her guilty, finding the evidence compelling, but convicting her more for being one nasty woman. She herself insisted that she was innocent.

Was she innocent or guilty?

To this author, after combing through the evidence and the testimony, it appeared that there were two separate trials going on, greatly confusing the question of whether Stewart had committed a crime, and just how serious that crime might be.

One trial had to do with the charge of insider trading.

Although the federal prosecutors chose not to prosecute Stewart on this charge, and though the judge insisted that insider trading should not be discussed at the trial, it was a dominant feature of the trial, like Hamlet's ghost, always off to the side, hovering, trying to insinuate itself as much as possible.

The second trial, it seemed to this author, had to do with whether Stewart had lied to the authorities, the actual charge against her in the trial.

The cause of the confusion had to do with which trial was taking place at any given time. Most of the time it seemed like it was a trial about insider trading; a small portion of the time it appeared to be about lying to the authorities.

The federal prosecutors, trying to prove that Stewart lied, spent far more time attempting to show that she had violated some kind of insider trading charge. Presumably they were hoping to show that if she engaged in insider trading, she must have then lied to the authorities—to protect herself against an insider trading charge.

What was so confusing was that the prosecutors never quite successfully showed the linkage between Stewart's involvement in insider trading and her lying to authorities.

That is why much of the time it seemed as if the trial were about insider trading, when it wasn't supposed to be; and why so little of the time, it appeared that the trial was about lying to the authorities, when it was supposed to be about that.

WAS SHE INNOCENT OR GUILTY?

To return to the question: Was Martha Stewart innocent or guilty?

That begs the question: Guilty or innocent of what?

Was she guilty of insider trading, as the feds had at first thought? No. She was not even charged with that crime.

Was she guilty of lying to the authorities? On the strength of the mostly circumstantial evidence, she was.

But a better question to ask is not whether she was innocent or guilty of some crime, but how big a crime was it that she committed.

Here the answer is fairly clear: She committed at best a minor offense.

Whether that minor offense was taking the infamous stock tip from Doug Faneuil or it was lying to the feds, she had done something that countless others were doing every day of the year and getting away with. While that is not usually a good defense, it happens to be true that an enormous number of people spend their careers hunting for inside stock tips, and never get caught. Stewart wasn't searching for a stock tip; but she did get caught.

It's also true that countless numbers tell lies—sometimes more than one a day—but don't get prosecuted.

It is absurd for the feds to have taken Stewart down for lying to them given the shoddy manner in which they made a public record of her pre-trial interviews. It is also absurd for her to have been indicted for "lies" that were at best moments when she simply misidentified someone (Faneuil, thinking it was Bacanovic); or when she could not recall something (that she had been told that Sam Waksal had sold his ImClone shares); or when she insisted that the $60-a-share agreement had been in place (the jury admitted that it could not prove or disprove its existence).

Having said all this, the inevitable conclusion is this: Though Martha Stewart committed no worse than a small offense, she did everything she could to impel her case to an indictment, to a trial, and to prison for her. The feds should not have ganged up on her. But she should not have held them in such contempt. In being contemptuous, she got them angrier, and worsened the prospects that the feds would simply drop the case. She was, in short, her own worst enemy. She was not guilty of a serious crime; but she certainly was guilty of misjudging those who could do her harm.

The verdict, indeed the entire trial, proved devastating to Stewart. It was as she was walking out of the courtroom that she conceded to her daughter that her life had been wasted. It had been the night of the verdict that she felt forced to sleep with her own daughter—to help her get through the nightmares.

"That's not really what moms should do," she acknowledged with some embarrassment, "but sometimes I guess it's nice." She could take little comfort from the end of the trial. It had proven quite costly to her. For one thing, it appeared that she had put on 25 pounds, as all she did in her spare time was devour comfort food, especially brownies she had baked herself.

She gave no interviews on her legal case for the next four months, but then in July, she sat down with Larry King and talked about her reaction to the verdict.

"Well, we were very disappointed, obviously," she began.

Was she surprised?

"I think we were all very surprised. We had sat in the courtroom, all of us, the whole legal team, my daughter, I, my family, my friends, and all of us thought that there would be exoneration. We were so wrong, obviously. And we were very sad."

King noted that Alexis Stewart had taken the verdict worse than her mother.

"Well, when the verdict was passed, she actually fainted and I heard sort of the thump and I thought, 'well, maybe that's just a bang on the bench,' but she had actually fainted. And that's horrible."

The guilty verdict was expected to impact negatively on the Stewart businesses, but how negatively no one could say for certain. Her personal brand had lost its luster, but how much no one could say.

Five years earlier, when Martha Stewart Living Omnimedia went public amid much hopeful anticipation, investors worried privately that if something happened to Stewart, her company, so identified with her, might simply collapse. The image was of Stewart getting hit by a bus; no one imagined this kind of legal predicament.

Would her band of followers remain loyal?

Would they continue to buy her products in great quantities?

Would they turn away from her because she was now a convicted felon?

The betting was that her fans would stay loyal to her over the short run; but it was the long run that had everyone worried.

The impact of the verdict on the company came swiftly: its shares fell 23 percent, from $17 to $10.86 a share, a huge drop in value. Stewart's own personal fortune, based on the 61.2 percent of the company she owned (30 million shares), had dropped from $326 million to $250 million that week.

Three days after the verdict, MSLO announced that the television show that had started the company, *Martha Stewart Living*, was going on hiatus, with no announced date of return.

Months after relegating it to a 2:00 a.m. time slot, WCBS in New York pulled Stewart's syndicated show completely off the air.

Though the Securities and Exchange Commission had not yet compelled her to do so, common sense dictated to Stewart that she step down as a director of her company. She remained "founding editorial director," a title that allowed her to keep creative control over her 550-person company without being officially in charge.

Within a day of the verdict, newspaper articles appeared suggesting that the Stewart conviction might threaten her business empire.

A consumer survey published that week showed that Stewart's "brand negativity" had risen to 33 percent, signifying that one third of all Americans would not buy her products. Potential customers were making a firm statement: Because Martha Stewart had become a convicted felon, they would punish her further by abandoning her products.

According to some analysts, the company might not survive.

But others pointed to its large cash reserves, its lack of debt, and its ability to launch new products successfully as three good reasons why it would in fact make it.

But the company was definitely going to take a further hit. Advertisers would continue to stay away; new products would have to be placed on hold. The whole notion of the Martha Stewart brand would have to be given new thought.

CHAPTER
12

PURGATORY

Her first moments as a convict were chilling and awkward.

Martha Stewart had to face her family first—and her family had to figure out how to deal with her in this new disturbing role.

From the courthouse, Stewart called her sister, Laura Plimpton.

"I'm just so sorry about all of this," she told her sister.

"Yes, we're all so sorry," Laura replied.

Stewart heard genuine sympathy in her sister's voice and she was relieved. She was relieved too to hear from her niece Sophie, Laura's daughter, who assured her aunt, "We're there for you. We can make it through this." Sophie told her aunt how composed she had looked on television when she had emerged from the courtroom.

Former family members felt compelled to offer Stewart their sympathy.

Andy Stewart wrote a letter to his former wife, saying how sorry he was and asking if there was anything he could do to help.

For the first time in five years, Martha Stewart's brother, Frank Kostyra, spoke to his sister. They had met briefly outside the courthouse. He asked her if she had a moment to spare, could she say anything? She was heavily guarded. She did not speak to him other than to give him her phone number.

Stewart's mother was about to turn 90. She was heartbroken over the verdict. To anyone who tried to console her over the phone, she said simply that she had not expected a guilty verdict and she did not want to talk about the subject further. It was too upsetting for her.

Soon after leaving the courthouse, Stewart called her close friend Charles Simonyi, the former Microsoft engineer, in Bellevue, Washington. He found her "very, very sad" over the verdict. While she seemed calm, she was extremely concerned over Alexis, he reported.

For Martha Stewart, the post-verdict period brought new soul-searching.

Her life had become one huge shipwreck. Others faced with her plight routinely retreated from society. In most cases, society would have little or nothing to do with them. But Stewart could not tolerate a situation in which she had to isolate herself from all that she had done in the past. She promised herself that she would try to make a comeback. She did not know how or when or under what circumstances; only that she would try. No decision that she took during her entire legal imbroglio was as enlightened as this one.

The next period would be difficult. Soon she would be sentenced to jail. She would not have to begin serving in jail as long as she appealed her case and that could take years. She would linger in a kind of purgatory—between the past conviction and the uncertain future—until it was decided whether she would have to go to jail.

To plan her comeback, she had to look at the recent past with a new set of eyes. Clearly, something had gone very wrong; but had the federal government simply picked on her unfairly; or were there other factors at play?

WAS I AT FAULT?

She asked herself the hardest question of all: Was I at fault, in part or in full?

The best way to gauge that, she found, was to listen carefully to what the jurors were saying in their post-verdict interviews.

She concluded that they had not liked her very much.

At first they were undoubtedly overwhelmed to be in the same court with such an icon. But, as their post-trial interviews attested, they grew more and more resentful of her elitist airs, her dismissive attitude toward underlings, her cheapness, and her smugness. Certainly they had paid careful attention to the evidence, but, while jurors only hinted at this, it seemed clear that they could have judged the evidence either way; what tipped them to a guilty verdict was Martha Stewart's demeanor.

She had allowed the jurors to think ill of her because she and her attorneys had allowed the government to define her personality. She had simply sat back and done nothing. She added up the mistakes—mounting a flimsy defense; not testifying; appearing in court each day as if it was the last place she wanted to be; packing the audience with her celebrity friends. One mistake after the other—and the result had not been pretty.

She could not have erased the Doug Faneuil e-mails from the jury's minds. She could not have undone Ann Armstrong's tale of the deleted phone log. But she could have tried to convince the jury that she had no malicious or criminal intent when she sold her ImClone stock. She could have acted contrite.

However unfair it had been for the jury to convict her on the basis of not liking her very much, she dared not overlook that fact if she were going to make some repairs in her life.

Slowly she began to understand how she had hurt her cause by consistently misreading the seriousness with which the feds took their legal case against her. She had misread that reality; and now she vowed she would not misread things any more—if she could help it.

Again, she faced a choice.

She could retreat into a shell and continue to proclaim her innocence. She could continue to act as if she had been right all along; and everyone else had been wrong.

At the time of the verdict, when she told her daughter Alexis that she felt her life had been wasted, she might easily have gone into that shell.

But she wanted to make a comeback. She wanted to regain the fame and glory that was once hers. To do that, she realized, she would have to give up her past attitudes; rather than try to trivialize and marginalize anyone or anything that appeared to stand in her way, she decided that she had to learn to deal with these forces in a whole new way. She had to take them seriously.

In the past, by not taking those forces seriously, she had permitted them to define her as highly talented, but mean-spirited. If she were going to make a comeback, she had to define herself; she had to make the world think that she was a nice person. For that she needed a new narrative. She needed the world to think of her in positive terms, heroic if possible. It would not be easy.

Moreover, her attempt at a comeback had to be done in public—otherwise, it would not seem genuine. It had been as a very public Martha Stewart that she had won her early success; and she wanted to replicate that success now. She could not undergo a personality change in private. She had to do it on television, on radio, and in the newspapers. She would have to become a public persona all over again, one that society and the culture accepted back in their arms.

Before she could even begin her personality makeover, she had to get past one more hurdle. She was soon going to be sentenced. She was hoping for a miracle. Perhaps the judge would show real mercy and let her do some form of community service.

Her sentencing was scheduled for July 17, 2004.

Few believed that Martha Stewart would get jail time. Even though she had been found guilty of serious crimes, it still seemed absurd to imagine that an icon like Stewart could actually wind up in jail.

In the courtroom once again before Judge Miriam Goldman Cedarbaum, Stewart stood and, with her voice breaking almost into sobs, told the judge she was afraid that her life would be "completely destroyed." In her shaky voice, she asked the judge to "remember all the good I have done." She flattered Cedarbaum, entrusting her future to her "competent and experienced and merciful hands."

Stewart avoided any admission of guilt—to do that could have put her appeal in jeopardy. But she did make clear to Cedarbaum that she was sorry that others had been hurt by the scandal.

"What was a small personal matter became over the last two and a half years an almost fatal circus event of unprecedented proportions spreading like oil over a vast landscape, even around the world," Stewart said.

It was a rare emotion for Stewart, and Jake Zamansky, the attorney who had sat in on the trial as an observer, noted how rare it was: "I've been in this court for a long time through the trial. This is the first time I've ever seen any emotion out of Martha Stewart."

A MEASURE OF BEAUTY

Robert Morvillo had asked the judge to give Stewart probation and community service, working with poor women. He said Stewart "knows she's not perfect" but deserved mercy. "She has brought a measure of beauty to our everyday world with refined color schemes, floral arrange-ments, and culinary delights," he said. "She has stood for the values of quality and making products as perfect as possible." It was a remarkable assertion: the judge should show leniency because Martha Stewart knew how to make beautiful floral arrangements.

Prosecutors continued to portray the case as a matter of preserving the integrity of government investigations. "Citizens like Ms. Stewart who willingly take the steps to lie to officials when they are under investiga-tion about their own conduct, those citizens should not expect the leniency that Ms. Stewart seeks," prosecutor Karen Seymour told the judge.

The judge noted she had received more than 1,500 letters from Stewart supporters across the country pleading for leniency. The letters talked of how inspirational Stewart had been to people; how philan-thropic. The judge said that she had read every single letter. She had a few read into the record.

Despite the letters, she felt a prison term was appropriate because "lying to government agencies during the course of an investigation is a very serious matter, regardless of the outcome of the investigation."

"I believe that you have suffered, and will continue to suffer, enough," the judge said. She had not, however, lost sight of the seri-ousness of the crime of which she had been convicted. Regulatory agencies simply could not function if there was lying. Nonetheless, the judge said she had decided to be lenient given that Stewart had no record of previous criminal conduct.

> "I believe that you have suffered, and will continue to suffer, enough."

The judge sentenced Stewart to five months in jail to be followed by five months of house arrest. She would have to pay a $30,000 fine as well.

Just as at the time of the verdict, Stewart showed no emotion when the judge handed down the sentence. She stood next to Robert Morvillo, stone-faced. It was almost as if the judge had been talking about some-one else.

Judge Cedarbaum said she would allow Stewart to remain free while her lawyers appealed her conviction to the 2nd U.S. Circuit Court of Appeals.

Cedarbaum agreed with a defense request to recommend to federal prison officials that Stewart serve her time at a minimum-security facility in Danbury, Conn., close to her home in Westport. In that way, Stewart's elderly mother, who lived nearby, could make regular visits.

Peter Bacanovic received the same sentence of five months in prison and five months home confinement. He was fined $4,000.

Stewart admitted later that she was surprised by the sentence. She was pleased that the sentence included five months of house arrest and that the total time in jail was five months, not the expected 16 months. "The judge stayed within the minimum. I'm grateful for that."

Investors reacted positively to the amount of jail time that Stewart received; her company's stock rose 37 percent, or $3.17, to close at $11.81 on the New York Stock Exchange.

By the time Court TV reporter Rochelle Steinhaus walked into the courtroom there were few seats to be had. So she stood behind a pillar, giving her a good view of the proceedings.

When the judge read the sentence, Steinhaus and others in the courtroom were shocked. "If you were surprised that Martha got convicted," she observed, "you were ten times more surprised that she got jail time." Probation had seemed far more likely.

As the judge read the sentence, Steinhaus watched Stewart for a reaction. She had "the same strong chin up. There was no gasp. No visible sign that she was shaking in any way."

Stewart emerged from the federal courthouse, moved to a microphone and, in a rare public appearance, made a statement in front of the cameras. Her comments were carried live across the country. She criticized the prosecution against her as "blown out of all proportion." Then remarkably she made what was essentially a sales pitch for her products.

"Well, I am—you know, I have a company called Martha Stewart Living Omnimedia. Our company makes wonderful products. Our company continues to make wonderful, trusted, terrific products, best quality. And it is my job—one of my jobs is to tell people to buy our products, encourage people to buy our products, hope that people buy our products because they're good. I'm bringing beautiful things to your viewing public. I've done that on our television program for years and years and years. So I'm not—I'm not going to stop and say, you know what, don't buy our products."

"Perhaps all of you out there can continue to show your support by subscribing to our magazine, by buying our products, by encouraging our advertisers to come back in full-force to our magazines," she said. Then she joked that she wasn't trying to make a sales pitch. What was it then?

"And I'll be back," she vowed. "I will be back. Whatever I have to do in the next few months, I hope the months go by quickly. I'm used to all kinds of hard work, as you know, and I'm not afraid. I'm not afraid whatsoever."

> *"I will be back. Whatever I have to do in the next few months, I hope the months go by quickly."*

It was a remarkable performance. Rather than show any sign of contrition, she made a sales pitch! She seemed totally out of synch with the reality staring her in the face. For all of her hopes to stage a quick recovery, for all of her avowals to put the past behind her, she seemed stuck in the past. She still appeared to be thumbing her nose at the prosecutors. She still seemed to trivialize all that had happened to her. She should have been apologizing to her fans; instead she was encouraging them to show their loyalty by buying her products!

She was still mired in the past when she sat down for a post-sentencing interview with Barbara Walters the evening of her sentencing. She came off as defensive, believing that she had been victimized, certainly not a new Martha Stewart at all.

In the interview, she defended herself against charges that she had been arrogant for carrying a $6,000 Hermes Birkin handbag into court.

"Do you know, that is my only handbag?" she said with a look of bemusement. "And I bought it, I think, 12 or 14 years ago. I bought that for myself when I felt successful enough to buy a beautiful handbag. And it did not cost $6,000 12 or 14 years ago."

Asked how she would handle prison food, fellow inmates, and strip searches, Stewart said that she would take her cue from Nelson Mandela's prison experience. The former South African president and anti-apartheid campaigner had spent 27 years in jail. She told Walters: "If it is looming ahead of me, I'm going to have to face it, and take it and do it and get it over with. There's many other good people that have gone to prison. Look at Nelson Mandela." That was an egregious mistake on her part. She was no Nelson Mandela, not even close. He was an international hero, lauded for his stance against apartheid, and for showing great dignity and grace while incarcerated. She was going to prison kicking and screaming. And no one thought she was a heroine for getting caught taking what many thought was an illegal stock tip.

But, as she talked with Barbara Walters, she saw none of this—at least yet. She continued to complain that she had been persecuted. None of it was her fault. The trial, she said, was about making an example of someone "who's built this fantastic business...to bring them down a notch; to scare other people."

TO GOOD THINGS

Later that evening she went out to the Matsuri restaurant in New York with Alexis and some friends, ordering oysters and miso-glazed cod. She made a toast to "good things."

The next night she got together with her brother George Christiansen, for whom she cooked bluestone crabs. She was in good cheer. Friends insisted that she was not in denial. She simply assumed that somehow she would find a way out of the mess.

The next day she spent the afternoon surveying her estate in Bedford, New York; working in the vegetable garden she had planted and at a grove of magnolias that were just taking root. Friends who saw her that day felt she had experienced a true sense of closure from the sentencing; that a good part of the nightmare was over for her; perhaps she might even get a good night's sleep.

She wanted to put the legal case behind her. Only by doing so, she felt, could she truly turn to the public and ask to be taken back into its arms.

But, she was still not prepared to apologize. As she said repeatedly, it was not possible to appeal her case, insist upon her innocence, and offer contrition for what she had done. She still maintained that she had done nothing wrong.

When she appeared on *Larry King* on July 19th, he asked her what she would have done differently if she had her legal case to do all over again.

It was the perfect opportunity for Stewart to express personal regret, but instead she said:

"Well, that's a hard question, because I sold it (her ImClone shares) for a specific reason, it was going down. And I can't imagine, I mean it's just such a conundrum to decide what I could have done, what I should have done, what I should have done afterward. There's so many variables, Larry in a thing like this."

The closest she came to expressing sorrow was an admission of how troubling the case had been for her: "You wake up pretty much every night about 2:00 a.m. saying oh, my gosh, what if I had. What if, what if, what if. And that's pretty terrible for a two and half-year process like this."

Later in the same program, King asked her if she truly regretted what had happened. Again she had the golden opportunity to say that she did indeed feel sorry. But she dodged the question: "You know, I don't know. I don't know if it would have changed the jury's verdict or not. I do not know. I can truthfully say that."

Despite what she was saying in public, she was desperately searching for a quick solution that would help her begin her recovery. To start the recovery, she had to put her legal case behind her, but how could she do that when she might have to go to jail?

She did not want to go to jail. No one wants to go to jail. She had heard such terrible stories about life behind bars that she could not even think of what it might be like. For a long time, she had simply avoided thinking about the subject.

But then it dawned on her. Going to prison at once would give her the opportunity to end her legal case. It had that advantage. Could she simply ask to go to jail at once even as she was appealing her case?

At first, whenever that thought arose, she dismissed it out of hand. Going to jail would be the worst thing that had ever happened to her. She still prayed for a miracle.

But she could not get the thought out of her mind—and she knew why. She desperately wanted to make a comeback. She was eager to show that she could undergo a personality change. Jail seemed the perfect prescription.

If she chose to go to jail right away, she might come across as contrite. The very act of going to jail would seem like an act of contrition—without her having to make any public statement to that effect. She might succeed in getting the public to forgive her. She might turn her businesses around.

She sought opinions from people in the public relations world. She clearly wanted to know whether going to jail would have a positive impact on her reputation. One of those she consulted was Howard

Rubenstein, one of the eminent public relations figures in New York. The two had lunch one day and Stewart asked him what he thought about her going to jail.

Rubenstein was taken aback.

None of his clients had ever asked him such a question and he had certainly never advised a client to go to jail.

This would be a first.

Rubenstein thought long and hard. He had talked with Stewart's lawyers and asked them what were the chances of winning an appeal. Thirty percent was their guess. He doubted that her chances were that high.

He advised her to go to jail. Remaining free pending the appeal would only do further damage to her reputation, he suggested.

Later, Rubenstein acknowledged that it was the most unusual advice he had ever given to someone.

STILL VACILLATING

When Stewart appeared on *Larry King* on July 19th, she was still vacillating.

"I have not made up my mind one way or the other," she noted.

You mean you might go to prison, King asked.

"Well," Stewart replied, "again there's a conundrum. My company needs me. I would like to get back to work. I would like this to be over. This has been a long, drawn-out process. And I would like very much to go back to work. On the one hand, business, Wall Street, advertising, they would like to see finality. They would like to see an end to all of this."

Staying out of jail, allowing the appeals process to work, seemed the more attractive choice for her personally; but she kept coming back to the health of her company: "I, as a person, with rights, with a belief in the judicial system and fairness, think that an appeal is the way to go. So, what do I do, OK. If it weren't wrapped up with my company, and it shouldn't be, but it is, inextricably."

Stewart was perplexed with the media commentators who blithely proposed that she should go to jail. "Do they know what it's like to go to jail? I don't think they know. I don't know what it's like to go to jail."

King mentioned that a lot of people thought she should go to jail just to get it over with.

"Why do they say that?" Stewart asked, again perplexed at the nerve of people who made such proposals when it would be Stewart, and not they, who would have to be in jail. "Would they do it themselves? It's easy to say what somebody else should do. But what to do is the problem here."

At another point in the show, she was asked whether she feared going to jail.

Of course she did.

What did she fear the most?

"I'm not afraid to go to jail. I'm afraid to be incarcerated. I mean, it's a lack of freedom. My freedom is taken away. Anybody in their right mind would fear incarceration. But the thing of going into a jail doesn't—I mean I'm not so afraid of that."

> *"I'm not afraid to go to jail. I'm afraid to be incarcerated. I mean, it's a lack of freedom."*

Stewart mentioned that she had three options, to go, not to go, or to go and appeal.

Understandably, Larry King was puzzled by the thought of Stewart going to jail while her case was still under appeal. What good would winning the appeal do if she had already served jail time?

"What do I get?" she asked King. "I'd have peace of mind. I'm finished. I don't have to go back to another trial, maybe. I don't know if you have to go back to another trial after that or not. No one...."

In other words, if she won her appeal, she might force another trial; but she really did not want that. "It's very, very difficult to go through a trial like this."

She insisted that the decision on whether she would go to jail at once would be hers and hers alone. She would listen to what her lawyers had to say but in the end "I have to weigh it myself. No one can make up my mind."

NO MORE MESS

Another way for Stewart to end her legal case would be a Presidential pardon.

"Wouldn't that be nice," Stewart said.

She was asked if she thought the federal authorities had singled her out.

"Many people have said that it is because I am a woman. Many people have said it is because I am a businessperson, a successful businessperson. But maybe so. I don't know for sure... I think it was a combination, and a coincidence. And I think that even though the government says there's no such thing as coincidence, I think there is coincidence in this world."

She believed that she was prosecuted as part of the nation's eagerness to bring celebrities down: "I've been told during this whole process that oh, in America, we like to build 'em up, we like to break 'em down, we like to see them suffer. We like to see success turn into failure."

King asked her about the accusations that she had been arrogant.

She acknowledged that she could have behaved better, but she had clearly not undergone a complete personality makeover—not yet.

"Yeah, I have been perceived as arrogant. And my explanation was that, you know, I work really, really hard. I'm really hard on myself, Larry. You know that. You know how many hours a day I put in at the job.

"I have sometimes probably forgotten, and I know I have, forgotten to pat the back of someone, or said, thank you, you know, enough times, or even maybe once sometimes. So I—you know, I wish I were perfect. I wish I were just, you know, the nicest, nicest, nicest person on Earth. But I'm a businessperson in addition to a creator of domestic arts. And it's an odd combination. No excuse. But if I were a man, you know, no one would say I was arrogant."

It was slightly jarring to hear Martha Stewart explain why she thought she was not arrogant—as her arrogance oozed through her answer.

Four days after the Stewart interview with Larry King, Doug Faneuil was in Judge Miriam Goldman Cedarbaum's courtroom for a final resolution of his case. She fined him $2,000 for accepting a payoff during the government's probe. It was the equivalent of a slap on the wrist.

Faneuil was filled with remorse. "I want to apologize for my mistakes," he told the judge. "Thankfully I've learned my lesson."

His voice quivered. He admitted that he was afraid his testimony would be discounted, that he would not prevail "against rich and powerful people. I was wrong, and for that I am immensely grateful."

The government had alleged that Peter Bacanovic had plied Doug Faneuil with extra vacation time and airline tickets in exchange for signing off on the story about the $60-a-share stock agreement. Faneuil said that Bacanovic had offered him a week's vacation and a trip to Argentina in early 2002.

Faneuil faced as much as six months in prison after he pleaded guilty to the misdemeanor charge; but the prosecution had recommended no jail time following his testimony that helped convict Martha Stewart.

While Stewart deliberated her future, she inched her way back to the life that she had once led. She went to museums, to New York Yankee games. She tried to get back in shape by going on a reduced-carb diet that included lots of fresh vegetables and salads. She avoided bread and sugar. She worked out every day. She went biking and rollerblading in the Hamptons. Others in her position might have been tempted to hide from view, but not Stewart. She would have none of it.

"For 2 1/2 years? At my time of life? With the things I want to do and the things I want to see and learn? I can't hole myself up. I wouldn't. I wouldn't think of it. It's not—it's not the way I am."

She still had trouble making the decision. But she knew she wanted to get back into the fray.

Even as she neared the age of 63, she did not feel—or look—old. She was certain that, if given the chance, she could resuscitate her embattled company; she could repair her tattered reputation; she could get back into the game, something she desperately wanted to do.

Sadly, she came to realize that going to jail at once, unthinkable as it might be, could allow her to start afresh. She knew that jails existed but they were for other people. Yet now she began to dwell on what life for her might be like behind bars. The very thought became nightmarish.

She was Martha Stewart. How could she suffer such humiliation? What would her fans think? What would happen to her iconic status in America if she entered prison? What might her family and close friends think of her? She knew none of the answers. She knew only that she had no choice, not if she wanted to become that icon again.

Finally, she made a decision.

She would go to jail right away.

Though it was the hardest decision she had made in her life, it was, in retrospect, also her most brilliant. No one could tell just how brilliant it was at the time. No one could guarantee that she would be able to regain her reputation. All that people could say was that Stewart was finally showing some smarts, some courage, and it was going to be a tough haul for her.

The decision was brilliant in part because it was so sophisticated. Here was Martha Stewart finally showing some measure of contrition; here was Martha Stewart in effect offering an apology of sorts. But she would never say the words, "I'm sorry." She would never say the words, "I confess that I am guilty." She was remaining true to her long-standing conviction that she was innocent; but she was bowing to the demands of those who insisted that she show some remorse.

GOING TO JAIL

And so, accompanied by her lawyers and members of the board of directors of Martha Stewart Living Omnimedia, she called a news conference on September 15th at her company's offices in New York on what she called a "beautiful light-filled floor" where among other things, recipes were tested. The first few rows were packed with loyal fans, not journalists. She announced that she had decided to begin serving her sentence as soon as possible. She vowed to continue with her appeal.

"I have labored long and hard to build this company," Stewart began, "and I love the company, my colleagues, and what we create very much. I cannot bear any longer the prolonged suffering while I and my legal team await vindication in the next step of the legal process, the appeal. And although I and my attorneys firmly believe in the strength of that appeal, recent delays and extensions have now made it abundantly clear that my appeal will not be heard until some time next year. So I have decided to serve my sentence now, to put this nightmare behind me and get on with my life and living as soon as possible.

"The only way to reclaim my life and the quality of life of all of those related to me with certainty, now, is to serve my sentence, surrender to the authorities, so that I can quickly return as soon as possible to the life and the work that I love.

"I hope, too, that I will be able to begin serving my sentence in the very near future, because I would like to be back as early in March as possible in order to plant the new spring garden and to truly get things growing again."

She ended her 10-minute appearance with a joke, saying that she had been walking through Manhattan when a man spotted her and said, "Oh, she's out already."

"I hope that my time goes as fast as that," said Stewart. She grew weepy at the end. "I'll see you next year."

Her associates at MSLO Inc. gave her a standing ovation as she left, not taking any questions.

On that day, shares in MS Living rose about 2 percent, or 25 cents to $11.39. The stock had been trading around $19 per share before Stewart's name had been tied to the scandal.

"Her decision brings the matter much closer to the time when she and all of us can truly get back to business as usual," said Thomas Siekman, chairman of the company.

Six days later, Judge Cedarbaum ordered her to surrender on October 8th and to start her sentence.

On September 29th, the Federal Bureau of Prisons announced that she would serve her sentence at the federal prison in Alderson, West Virginia. It denied her request to serve her sentence at the federal prison in Danbury, Connecticut. Alderson was a minimum-security prison, the lowest level of security in the Bureau of Prisons. It had no fences, and inmates were usually able to walk around the compound unescorted.

The decision to go to jail at once was touted as a wise business decision. The media proclaimed her shrewd for sacrificing five months of her life in order to save her businesses. But the media missed the point. Stewart was going to jail not simply to salvage her businesses. She wanted to win the public to her side. She wanted to make a comeback. To do that she needed a personality makeover—and that, she decided, she could only do while in jail.

Lisa Marsh returned to the *New York Post* in January 2004 after taking almost a year off to write a book about Calvin Klein. She began working for the "Page Six" column. As a former business reporter, she thought the new assignment a perfect fit. After all, she believed, all business deals started as gossip. That was her theory. She found that people told her things for her gossip page that they would not tell the business desk.

Marsh began pursuing Stewart, developing excellent sources at the restaurants where power players lunched—Michael's, the Four Seasons, etc.—and she stalked Stewart.

PRE-PRISON WEDDING

The hottest tip was that Stewart's spokesperson of 20 years, Susan Magrino, was getting married in early October in the Bahamas. Magrino and Stewart were close friends; Stewart was organizing the wedding. The press was not invited. It would be Stewart's last public outing before heading for jail. Lisa Marsh thought it a dream assignment for a business/gossip reporter.

Most of the rooms at the tiny, exclusive One & Only Ocean Club had been taken up with the wedding party but Lisa Marsh was able to secure a room. She had attended a few Martha Stewart press conferences, but Marsh was confident that Stewart would not remember her. Magrino, however, knew Marsh, who simply planned to hide when she saw the spokesperson coming. "I didn't want to have a confrontation with Susan," Marsh explained. "It was, after all, her wedding."

Joined by a photographer also working for the *Post*, Marsh planned to corner Stewart and pepper her with questions only at the very tail end of the weekend. "I didn't want to tip my hand or blow my cover until she was leaving." Meanwhile, she and her photographer (holding nothing more fancy than a point-and-shoot camera) passed themselves off as tourists.

Early Saturday morning Marsh had great luck, running into Stewart by herself on the beach. Off at a distance, Marsh saw the Bahamian track team training. Though tempted to approach Stewart, Marsh restrained herself, figuring it was better to wait until Sunday.

Later in the morning, Marsh and her photographer headed for the hotel pool in search of Stewart. They found *New York Daily News* photographers in the bushes, relying on long lenses. "We freaked out," recalled Marsh, ignoring the fact that she and her photographer were lurking around, just not in bushes. Innocently, Marsh approached a security guard and noted that strangers "who didn't look like they belonged" were sheltered in the foliage, as if she was the hotel manager. "Maybe they're paparazzi," she offered, and then gleefully stood by as the guard hastily escorted the *Daily News* team off the premises. To the security guard, Marsh was just another tourist, or a wedding guest.

Later in the day, with Marsh and her photographer watching Stewart on the phone in a restaurant near the pool, it began raining.

"Can't you do something about the weather?" Stewart asked the person on the other end of the line.

She sounded as if she meant every word: It was the day of the wedding. Martha Stewart wanted sunshine.

The rain came down harder. Everyone moved inside. Marsh and her photographer sidled up to the bar, seating themselves next to two Stewart employees. On their other side was—Martha Stewart!

Lisa Marsh was thrilled. She saw what Stewart was eating; and heard every word that Stewart was saying.

THE GAMBLER

Recounting her entire evening a day earlier, including the rehearsal dinner, Stewart recounted how she and one of the fellows at the bar had gone to a place called Atlantis to gamble at blackjack that same evening—and she had won several thousand dollars. The fellow had lost $600.

Sharon Patrick, CEO of Martha Stewart Living Omnimedia, showed up. Stewart told her about her gambling.

"It's really funny that you lost," Sharon said to the fellow at which point Stewart chimed in, "Don't worry. It's OK," indicating that she planned to reimburse the poor fellow.

Marsh was sitting close enough for Stewart to ask who she was; but she never asked. Before leaving Stewart peaked at Marsh's $32 order of salmon, telling her that the food looked "beautiful." It was not quite the interview that Marsh had planned. But "we were golden," she had her story, she had kicked out her rivals, and she still had one full day to go.

As sunset approached, wedding guests arrived for the ceremony in the hotel's garden. Sipping drinks on the veranda while watching the guests approach, Marsh learned to her chagrin that her drinking companions were from *In Touch*, *People* magazine, and *Splash News!*

The next morning—Sunday—Marsh received a tip that Stewart was leaving at the crack of dawn. Rising at 6 a.m., the reporter staked out the front of the hotel, hoping to buttonhole the prison-bound Stewart. But the crafty Martha was on the beach. Marsh ran after her but even after she located Stewart, she was too bemused to ask questions. Marsh was still pleased. She had enough material for a great behind-the-scenes look at Martha Stewart five days before she went off to jail.

PART V

THE UNLIKELY PRISONER

CHAPTER

13

OTHERWISE
OCCUPIED AT YALE

The prison was nicknamed "Camp Cupcake," meant to imply that it was a relatively painless place to spend prison time. The inmates scoffed at the term because they knew that a prison is a prison, and Alderson was no picnic.

She told her friends and family that she would be all right; that the five months would pass quickly; that she realized that taking her medicine was in her interest. It was her ticket to getting back on her feet in the shortest possible time.

She wanted those closest to her not to worry; but she personally was terrified. She had heard all the stories of what women prisoners were like. She knew that from the first moment that she stepped into the prison she would be the center of attention among the inmates. She would not be able to disguise the fact that she was Martha Stewart.

How would the inmates treat her? What if things got nasty? Who would be there to protect her?

During her entire career, she had been in charge; she had exerted control over her environment. Once in jail, she would be told what to do and how to do it 24 hours a day, 7 days a week. How would she endure such servitude?

She arrived at the jail in a state of numbness. She promised herself she would never look back; she would not allow herself the pain and agony of second-guessing what she might have done to avoid such a fate. Plenty of others were doing that for her. Let them carry on with their instant analyses; she would deal with the here and now. She knew that she would be better off thinking only of what was happening in her life at present.

Still, the whole experience of getting processed into prison life ate at her. She felt her freedom being taken from her inch by inch. She had the feeling that every eye was on her—the eyes of the inmates, the eyes of the wardens, the eyes of the country. She could not tell what all these people who were staring at her were thinking. She decided not to look them squarely in the eye. She vowed that she would do whatever was asked of her, nothing less. She would try to blend in, knowing how impossible that would be. But she was conscious of how crucial it was for her to be seen as just another inmate. The less attention she drew, the better off she would be. So she thought.

She vowed not to seek special privileges or exemptions from the drudgery of prison life. It would be natural for the prison authorities and the inmates to extend courtesies to her because of who she was. But nothing good could come of her seeming to curry favor.

Prison came at just the right time for Martha Stewart.

She had decided to go to prison to get the experience over with.

That was the reason she gave in public. But she had another reason, one that she kept to herself, and did not share with anyone else. She could not share it with anyone because she had not really been able to articulate it in her own mind.

PERSONALITY CHANGE

The best that she could come up with was that she wanted to make a personality change. She wanted to show a nicer side and she wanted to exhibit a greater degree of humility. Simply by announcing that she had decided upon prison right away looked humble enough; with that decision, she was showing that she was willing to take her punishment— that she was not too good to do jail time.

Whether she could show a nicer side to her personality while confined at Alderson was not certain at all. For, she had no idea what prison life would be like. She had no way of knowing whether she would be able to get along with the other prisoners. Nor could she know how the prisoners would react to her. It almost seemed at first as if she were asking too much of herself. Perhaps her goal should have been just surviving the five months. She could have waited until her release to start her personality makeover.

But she did not want to lose any time.

She knew that time was one of her greatest enemies. She was 63 years old; her reputation was near ruin. She was going to jail. If things were going to change for her, they would have to change at once.

To improve her reputation, she had to change what people thought of her. Prison was a very private, secretive place and getting information out was hard to do. But that worked in her favor. She could control what the public learned about her prison stay. Most of her fans had stayed loyal, but they had put her on a kind of probation. They wanted to see how she would emerge from her legal nightmare. If she became a nicer person, they would stick with her. If she did not, they would abandon her once and for all.

She understood all that and by that understanding, she was already starting her personality makeover. In the past, she had not taken her rivals—or even her friends—very seriously. She lorded over them, not particularly caring what they thought of her; but shocked to find that some genuinely hated her. She could not figure out why.

This time, she took the outside world with a new seriousness.

In the past, when she encountered people who disliked her or wanted to go after her, she sought to marginalize them. This time, she decided to take everyone seriously. Taking them seriously meant asking what it was they wanted from her. And what they wanted was for her to do good things and be a nice person. She promised herself she would do that at Alderson.

And so everything she did and said while she was in jail—and everything that was leaked to the media—was aimed at winning back her loyal fan base; at showing them that she was a different, kinder person; that she wanted to make a comeback.

Stewart began orchestrating her image with her entry into the prison. She did not want her photograph splashed all over the world's newspapers on the day that she went to prison. She did not want to ram it down people's throats that Martha Stewart was becoming a prisoner. And so it was arranged that she could arrive without the media knowing the exact time or the precise circumstances.

The only communication she had that day, October 8, 2004, with the public was a statement she issued:

> "Today marks the beginning of the end of a terrible experience, and I am now one step closer to getting this awful time behind me. I deeply appreciate all of the support I have received throughout this ordeal from those people closest to me and from many thousands of well wishers around the world.

"Today marks the beginning of the end of a terrible experience, and I am now one step closer to getting this awful time behind me."

"While I am serving my sentence, my attorneys will continue to pursue my appeal. They believe it is a strong appeal that presents very serious legal issues, and the brief will be filed shortly with the court.

"Over the next five months, Martha Stewart Living Omnimedia will be in the good hands of its talented management team and creative staff, and every day I am away, I will look forward to rejoining them to pursue my life's work. That work is all about creating beautiful, practical, and educational magazines and television programs as well as inspiring and useful products for the home.

"I'll see you again in March."

The first thing Martha Stewart did upon arriving at the all-women federal prison facility at Alderson was to go through "R and D"— receive and discharge.

She began by filling out paperwork so that the clothes she wore into the prison could be sent home. She then had to appear naked in front of a female correction officer who searched her without actually touching her body.

The officer told her to run her fingers through her hair, to open her mouth and lift her tongue, to place her hands against the walls to balance herself so the officer could see the bottom of her feet. She was told to lift one foot at a time. Then she was to told to squat and cough.

This "strip search" was meant to detect whether Stewart was bringing any contraband items into the prison. The whole process took a few minutes.

She was then photographed. The photo was attached to a credit-card size ID card that she had to carry on her person at all times. It also carried Stewart's prison number. The prisoner used the card to obtain items from vending machines and to do laundry.

Prison medical personnel then interviewed Stewart, asking what medications, if any, she was taking, determining whether the medicine was necessary. Someone addicted to a drug would not be given that drug; but a prisoner would be allowed to use heart or blood pressure medicine.

On a prisoner's second day at Alderson, she went to the laundry department at 7:30 a.m. to be given a complete set of clothes. But Stewart's second day fell on a Saturday, and so she had to wait until Monday for that. She was given four uniforms; four pairs of pants; four pairs of shorts; five pairs of socks; five pairs of underwear; five bras; and one nightgown. She was also given a coat for outside; and shoes for inside, basic black oxfords. For kitchen work, she was issued steel-toed shoes to comply with federal safety regulations.

As day one turned into day two, she felt a sense of relief. She put the nightmarish thoughts of what prison life would be like on a mental shelf, always conscious that she might suddenly experience such nightmares. But as each moment passed without incident, as prisoners went beyond a quick smile and hello to engage her in conversation, she felt that she could do this, she could survive the five months.

When Stewart completed her time in receive and discharge, she went to the admission and orientation building; there she was assigned to the admissions and orientation cottage, where new prisoners ("commits" in Alderson vernacular) were sent for two weeks.

When the first week passed, Stewart began to sense the rhythms of prison life: in many ways, life was so much more regimented and so much less fast-paced than on the outside.

She never fully came to terms with being in prison; for her it was a surrealistic experience. She referred to Alderson as Yale so that she would never have to utter the word jail. (Presumably she chose Yale because it rhymed with jail.) Even after she was out of jail six months, she found it nearly impossible to mention the "j" word. When Donald Trump mentioned to her on her daytime television program *Martha* on September 21, 2005 that he had wanted her to attend his wedding the previous January, Stewart replied, "I wanted to be there too but I was otherwise occupied."

> "I wanted to be there too but I was otherwise occupied."

Suddenly she had time on her hands. That had never been the case on the outside.

> *"The camp is like an old-fashioned college campus—without the freedom, of course."*

In her first "letter" to her fans, she posted a statement on her Web site, reporting that "The best news—everyone is nice—both the officials and my fellow inmates. I have adjusted and am very busy. The camp is like an old-fashioned college campus—without the freedom, of course."

A COLLEGE CAMPUS

Never once did she mention that she was in a prison. By calling it a camp and comparing it to a college campus, she was hoping to suggest that she was just off on a vacation, however enforced.

Five days a week—Monday through Friday—Stewart attended class, from 7:30 a.m. to 3:00 p.m. Representatives from the various prison departments spoke to the inmates: from psychology services, education, food service, commissary, laundry, and recreation. She learned, among other things, what educational opportunities existed on the premises; how the commissary worked; how to have money sent to her; how to make phone calls. She was given a PIN number so that she could access her commissary account and transfer money to her telephone account (enabling her to make calls direct instead of calling collect).

Depending upon what was available from the laundry, she wore either a khaki-colored jump suit or a khaki-colored two-piece uniform that included a button-down shirt.

Following the two weeks of orientation, she was given a test—not considered difficult—to assure her familiarity with prison procedures.

Alderson was considered a work camp and everyone held a job; but before she could work, she had to pass a medical exam.

Stewart could look for a job or be assigned to one. She was assigned one.

She was assigned a job working in the administration building, con-sidered one of the better jobs at Alderson: vacuuming, dusting, mopping, cleaning the bathroom, including scrubbing the toilets; and raking leaves. A new prisoner normally pulled kitchen duty for the first 90 days; but not Stewart, she kept her job for her entire incarceration. No one quite knows why she did not pull the usual 90-day kitchen duty. But she was considered an excellent worker.

Stewart rose whenever she wished but had to be at work by 7:30 a.m. After rising, she took a shower, applied cosmetics, and arranged her hair. Breakfast, served between 6:00 a.m. and 7:00 a.m., was optional. Lunch was from 11:00 a.m. to 12:30 p.m. Her workday ended at 3:45 p.m. At each change of location, she had to go through a roll call.

The 4:00 p.m. stand-up count was a daily ritual, mandatory at all federal prison facilities. To miss it was to incur the wrath of correction officers. Dinner was from 4:30 p.m. to 5:00 p.m. or as long as there were inmates to serve it.

Evenings were up to each prisoner.

Stewart and her fellow inmates could walk around the compound; visit the recreation building with its library containing a television and video tape recorder, and its CD room containing 10 CD players in small booths. The recreation building dispensed video games, and held classes in bible, religious studies, and yoga, it also had a fitness room replete with treadmills. If Stewart wished, she could have remained in her housing unit and watched television.

Prisoners had to be by their beds at 10:00 p.m. for a final roll call with lights out a half hour later. With special permission, however, Stewart could watch TV until 1:00 a.m. on weeknights; or all night on Fridays and Saturdays.

As high as 1,300 inmates, the prison population at Alderson was 980 during Stewart's stay. In some cases, entire families were inmates; a certain number of the prisoners were elderly.

To many people, Alderson had the look and feel of a college campus, with its old buildings, beautifully kept grounds, and low security. "It's not a scary place in any way," said Chrisa Gonzales, a former inmate. "Driving into the prison, you would say to yourself, 'This may not be so bad.'" There are no fences, no barbed wire. No gun towers. To Gonzales, "It's a very pretty place."

Chrisa Gonzales, 36, served in four women's facilities, including Alderson. She is now a sentencing consultant and some of her clients are in Alderson. She received a five-year sentence for conspiracy to distribute marijuana, serving four years. She was at Alderson from September 2001 to April 2002.

Compared to other prison environments, Alderson had its advantages: "Before I went to prison," said one inmate, "I thought I was going to a place like Alcatraz. You'd get beat up or raped but it was nothing like that."

NO CAPPUCCINOS

For someone like Martha Stewart, confinement in jail meant missing certain things that she was used to. One was having a cappuccino.

"We asked the guards every day for a cappuccino—you know, just as a joke. And they'd come in with their cups of coffee and stuff. ... I didn't miss the cappuccino at all. It's the idea I missed."

For those prisoners who had done the rounds of federal prison facilities, Alderson was at its best during the holidays. "At Alderson, we were treated better," said one such Alderson inmate. "At holidays, they seem to take you into consideration. They realize you are away from your family and that's not easy."

The Alderson prison facility, known as a camp, had the lowest level security among federal bureau of prisons. Prisoners did not require barbed wire or excessive confinement since none had been violent. Theoretically, prisoners could simply walk out with a great deal more ease than Clint Eastwood dug himself out of Alcatraz. "It's pretty easy to walk away," said Gonzales. "You probably wouldn't be stopped." But few took the risk. Reaching the town of Alderson in prison khaki, the person would be instantly recognized. If Martha Stewart had tried to escape, she would have been given another 18 months to 5 years. Imagine: Martha on the lam! It's not any more surrealistic than the rest of her legal tale.

The Alderson cottages held 70 to 90 inmates. Within them were rooms that contained 2 inmates; and much larger rooms, called bus stops, that housed 8 to 15. A newly arrived inmate normally went into the bus stop but Stewart remained in the two-person units her entire stay, a perk that was rare. The waiting list for the two-inmate rooms was three to six months.

Because of her age, Stewart slept on the bottom bunk but she lacked a good reading light. She would have gladly swapped places and slept above where the reading light was better.

The framing of Martha Stewart's image while she was in jail began with stories that she was getting friendly with prisoners; that she was empathizing with their plight. The public was fed tidbits of Stewart's prison life, suggesting that she was changing into someone who actually got along with others.

The Stewart image-makers focused in their news leaks on how well she was doing in jail, how many friends she had made, how she had become a kind of counselor to some inmates. In their portrayal of her, she seemed less like an inmate and more like a guidance counselor who showed up periodically for visits and chats with the prisoners. She shared books with other inmates. She read to them from letters she received. She advised them about their post-prison lives.

None of that happened at first, of course.

When Stewart arrived at Alderson, the public was told through leaks from friends who had visited her that she spent a lot of time alone, walking the grounds, keeping to herself. Inmates naturally kept aloof from her, waiting to see how eager she was for companionship.

It was only natural for prisoners to be mistrusting of her. They knew that she would feel superior to them. She faced a huge challenge fitting in.

But in time, the public was told, she established contact with her fellow inmates, and they responded, not with mistrust, but with warmth.

THE MAYOR OF IRVINGTON

Former Irvington, New Jersey, Mayor Sara Bost, 57, an inmate at Alderson at the same time as Stewart, recalled that some inmates were concerned about Stewart's arrival; they feared that she would get special treatment. But they quickly befriended her, offering to carry her bags and make her bed, and calling her "Miss Martha." Stewart said she would handle such chores herself.

The two-term mayor of the northern New Jersey town became friendly with Stewart at the end of her ten-month term at Alderson; she was jailed for witness tampering. Bost found no sign of a depressed Martha Stewart. "It was more of a toughness I saw about her. She more or less had an attitude of 'Let me do this and get on with it.'"

It was important to Stewart that she not seem down in the dumps. She wanted to present an image of someone ready to bounce back. One leak to that effect came from Margaret Roach, the editor of *Martha Stewart Living* who, after visiting the nation's most famous inmate, made sure to pass on that Stewart was "never idle or distracted or down."

Indeed she was passing the time by making to-do lists; decorating the prison's chapel for a memorial service with objects from nature; mastering microwave cooking. She was reading Bob Dylan's *Chronicles: Volume One*; crocheting holiday gifts for her dogs; teaching yoga to inmates. To hear Margaret Roach tell it, Stewart was so busy she did not have time to get depressed.

Steve Gerard, a long-time friend of Stewart's, and his wife Jane, visited Stewart frequently in prison: Steve four times, Jane six times. Steve spoke to Stewart on the phone frequently as well. He was chairman and CEO of Century Business Services.

Gerard went on *Larry King* to let everyone know that he had never found Stewart down or depressed. "Every time I talked to her, she was positive. She was trying to find the best in each day and then capitalize on it. She certainly had concerns for others. She's made her concerns about the food known and about some of the health conditions known. But that was more a compassionate view for her fellow inmates than it was for her. I think she did all of the tasks they assigned her in a bright, aggressive, positive way. And I never saw any—I never saw her being upset or any great despair in her voice."

In short, Stewart was doing fine—and in no time at all, she would be launching her return to the glory that once was.

It was important to Stewart to show that she had developed an empathy with her fellow inmates. Hence, stories were leaked that displayed her developing a fresh understanding of the plight of women prisoners. When she learned that some of the women were at Alderson for six or seven years for first-time nonviolent drug offenses, she winced, according to these news reports. It was supposedly to her credit that she was now getting along and showing sympathy for a whole class of people who had been strangers to her in her previous life. The public learned, for instance, of a 33-year-old woman named Kimberly Renee Bennett who was serving 50 months for conspiracy to distribute cocaine.

She was Stewart's roommate and the two got along from the first instant. (It was not easy being Stewart's roommate, for she slept with a light on.)

Stewart found that the women responded to kind gestures on her part and there were plenty she could make—if she tried. In the past, she had never tried.

A correction officer died of a heart attack in November. A memorial service was held for him in the inmates' chapel. Stewart came upon flowers on the grounds; officials gave her some material to work with, and she made flower arrangements for the memorial service. That small, but powerful gesture helped to solidify her relations with inmates. And Stewart made sure that the public learned of that incident.

News leaks also told of how Stewart had became a kind of liaison between the other prisoners and prison authorities. Learning that an inmate's family had disowned her, Stewart helped the inmate compose a letter to the woman's sister. Writing movingly of the isolation of prison life, Stewart begged the woman to reach out to her incarcerated sister. The letter had an effect and the family came together.

It was crucial to show Stewart's munificence, and so there were stories of how she distributed farewell care packages (containing toiletries and other necessities purchased with her $290 balance at the commissary) to some of the more needy inmates; of how she offered to cook Christmas dinner and bake pies. Though much of what she had offered was against prison rules, the stories made sure to point out that she had won over the prisoners with her gestures.

NICE SPICE RACK

Even when she incurred a minor infraction of the rules, smuggling seasonings out of the kitchen in her bra, the newspaper disclosures made her seem more endearing somehow (the infraction became a *New York Post* headline: "Nice Spice Rack"). Correction officers, making a routine check of Stewart's locker, had found pilfered cinnamon. Given an "incident report" she pulled extra duty cleaning and picking up trash. She was equally endearing when she complained of prison food; inmates sharing her views grew even closer to her—and all of that found its way into the media.

Some of the more light-hearted news reports made it sound as if Stewart had gone away to a vacation spa rather than to jail. Margaret Roach, the editor of *Martha Stewart Living*, visited her one day and then reported that they had both leaned against the visiting room wall and did a modified version of the yoga pose called "downward-facing dog"—"from which she seamlessly moved into a headstand."

The image of the prison-as-spa seeped into the accounts of Stewart's daily exercise routines. Ironically, she had more time for personal fitness inside prison than out. She took daily power walks around the prison grounds; after dinner she used the treadmill and weight machine. She and other inmates did yoga together. By January, it was reported that she had lost ten pounds in jail. The message was clear. Martha Stewart was getting ready for a comeback.

She was also, according to the word disseminated from prison, a kind of recreational director, inviting inmates to her room for a small New Year's Eve party, organizing board games, sorting the Scrabble pieces to make sure each set had the right number of letters.

Much of the image-making had to do with conveying the impression that Stewart was going through a true self-help program, becoming a better person, learning how to get along with people, exploiting her leadership and homemaking talents.

The more comfortable she became in the shaping of her new image, the more Stewart issued public pronouncements from her cell, talking of her post-prison plans and leaving the impression that she planned a monumental comeback in March 2005.

The public pronouncements were indeed unique.

None of the other white-collar criminals of the past decade had the temerity or the strength of character to organize a comeback while in prison. Once the judge had given each one of them a prison sentence, that was the last the public heard of them. When other celebrity women went to jail, whether it was Heidi Fleiss, Susan McDougall, or Leona Helmsley, they were mum during their time in jail.

For Martha Stewart to plan a post-prison renaissance of her career took enormous courage on her part. She risked being humiliated and excoriated all over again. She had no idea whether those who controlled the resources of the American media culture—television, radio, print— would feel that she was worth a fresh investment. Certainly she was a curiosity—a fallen icon that the feds had victimized and who had brashly refused to admit any fault—but would the public want to sanction her comeback?

No one knew.

By all normal standards, she should not have been contemplating a comeback from inside the Alderson facility. She should have been contemplating a post-prison period of quiet and reflection while she waited to see which way the wind was blowing; whether the public would ever accept her back as one of its cherished celebrities.

But Stewart felt she could not wait for that to happen. She had to mount a comeback that was as in-your-face as it was grandiose; it had to involve television, radio, and print. One day she was in a prison uniform; the next she would be in everyone's living rooms, or at least she hoped to be.

In getting the comeback off the ground, she had to be careful; she had to gauge public opinion after each step; she could not seem to be rushing, though that is precisely what she would be doing.

She began her public pronouncements on something of a low-key, promoting prison reform. She knew that she would make some news with whatever she had to say on the subject. Prison reform was a safe way to start. It was only natural that she would take up the cause of her new friends. And no one would fault her for siding with women prisoners. Their plight resonated with large segments of the nation.

CHRISTMAS MESSAGE

Posting a Christmas message on her Web site, she wrote about the poor, uneducated women in her jail, who needed drug rehabilitation instead of incarceration:

"When one is incarcerated with other inmates, it is hard to be selfish at Christmas—hard to think of Christmases past and Christmases future—that I know will be as they always were for me—beautiful! So many of the women here in Alderson will never have the joy and wellbeing that you and I experience. Many of them have been here for years—devoid of care, devoid of love, devoid of family.

"I beseech you all to think about these women—to encourage the American people to ask for reforms, both in sentencing guidelines, in length of incarceration for nonviolent first-time offenders, and for those involved in drug-taking. They would be much better served in a true rehabilitation center than in prison where there is no real help, no real programs to rehabilitate, no programs to educate, no way to be prepared for life 'out there' where each person will ultimately find herself, many with no skills and no preparation for living.

"I am fine, really. I look forward to being home, to getting back to my valuable work, to creating, cooking, and making television. I have had time to think, time to write, time to exercise, time to not eat the bad food, and time to walk and contemplate the future. I've had my work here too. Cleaning has been my job—washing, scrubbing, sweeping, vacuuming, raking leaves, and much more. But like everyone else here, I would rather be doing all of this in my own home, and not here—away from family and friends.

Happy holidays,

Martha Stewart

"P.S. I thought you might be interested in the brief my lawyers filed with the Court this afternoon."

Before going into prison she had planted the seeds for her comeback, agreeing to work with television producer Mark Burnett on a pair of television shows, one in prime time, the other in the day.

To get across the message that a new Martha Stewart was springing to life even in prison, she arranged for a series of announcements during her five-month stay at Alderson that made it clear that she planned an elaborate public comeback. Each announcement told of another post-prison project that Martha Stewart planned—two television shows, returning to the writing of her column at *Martha Stewart Living*, etc.

On December 8th, Mark Burnett announced that Stewart would be doing her version of *The Apprentice* to be co-produced by him and Donald Trump. Expressing huge admiration for Stewart, Trump thought it ridiculous that she should have gone to jail and O.J. Simpson was playing golf in Florida; he suggested that others in her situation would have been unable to handle what she went through with grace and dignity.

Much debate swirled in the coming months over what kind of hostess Martha Stewart would be, the Donald Trump kind saying "You're fired" each week; or a more benign business leader, refusing to fire the losers in whatever competition the program drums up around the kitchen. One thing was clear: Stewart had a great advantage over Trump when it came to product placements on her new show. He had to make deals with all sorts of companies; she, however, could call upon Martha Stewart paints, pots and pans, furniture, etc.

VISITING HOURS

Stewart may well have used visiting hours to calibrate her public pronouncements such as the one telling of the Martha Stewart *Apprentice* show.

Transacting business during visiting hours, 8:00 a.m. to 8:00 p.m. on Saturdays, Sundays, and federal holidays, was forbidden. But prison officials hardly monitored the conversations the inmates had with visitors. The lone correction officer in the visiting room could not possibly hear what each prisoner was discussing with a visitor. When she was at Alderson, Chrisa Gonzales never saw an officer warn an inmate about talking with a visitor about business.

Then too Stewart could walk with a visitor into an area that was fenced in with slides and picnic tables and there would be no correction officer present. It was the perfect opportunity to talk business.

The only time an officer might issue a warning would be to prevent inmates from having too much physical contact with visitors though holding hands was fine as was hugging upon arrival.

Plenty of opportunity existed for Stewart to chat about business with outsiders. Inmates were permitted five adult visitors who could spend the entire day.

While in jail, she had been busy recasting her company's board with allies who could help her return to the spotlight. According to the media reports, Stewart had grown dismayed at Sharon Patrick, the company CEO, for minimizing Stewart's role within the organization. Stewart replaced Sharon Patrick in November 2004 with Susan Lyne, a senior entertainment executive, who had just left Disney.

Lyne was known as the woman who pushed the TV smash hit, *Desperate Housewives*. The most interesting character on the show— Bree Van De Kamp, recently separated, emotionally challenged, was modeled after Stewart. Bree made basil puree and brought muffins to a grieving family.

Lyne was president of ABC Entertainment, the managing editor of New York's *The Village Voice* from 1978 to 1982, as well as founder of *Premier* magazine.

While in jail, Stewart met frequently with Susan Lyne, and with Mark Burnett, the television reality show producer who was organizing her new show modeled after Donald Trump's *The Apprentice* that was due to air in the fall of 2005. Stewart, Burnett, and Lyne all gave the impression that they were just having friendly chats—with no business transacted. "I'm sure Mark Burnett and Martha were not chatting about the weather," said Chrisa Gonzales.

All of the news leaks, all of the calibrated public pronouncements, all of the efforts to reshape Martha Stewart's image worked, and by the spring of 2005, as she prepared to depart Alderson, she seemed a changed person. She had managed her image deftly. She had the public and the media eating out of her hand. In five short months, the personality makeover was complete.

Inside and outside of prison, she was a heroine.

Who could have imagined that female prisoners at the bottom of society's food chain would proudly claim her as one of their own; that inmates she had once feared would serenade her with a song in the chapel to say farewell?

Who would have thought that the public would exhibit a warm and fuzzy affection for the new Martha Stewart? Illustrative of that was the sharp rise of her company's stock during her prison term. In early 2004, her stock had fallen to $8.30; yet on February 23, 2005, it had reached $37.45.

On March 3rd, two days short of a year after her guilty conviction at Foley Square, she spent her last evening in prison.

An inmate styled her hair. Then she was guest of honor at a farewell party where she and 20 inmates watched a *Larry King Live* program about her. She then put on the gray hand-knit poncho that a prison friend had made for her. In a few minutes, she would be free.

CHAPTER

14

THE ELECTRONIC ANKLET LADY

M arch 4, 2005.

The trace of a smile crossed her lips as Martha Stewart boarded the plane that was taking her to her freedom.

She once fretted over whether she could tolerate prison life. Now she felt a certain satisfaction. She had gotten through it. She had, so she liked to think, put her time inside to good use. Still, the time passed slowly, and she missed her work, her friends, her family, and she missed being in the spotlight, she missed being Martha Stewart.

She emerged into freedom on a soft cushion. Most of the other 600,000 prisoners who would end their prison stays in 2005 in America had a much harder time. Friends shunned them. Potential employers suddenly declared that an advertised opening had been filled. Making an honest day's wage became a severe challenge. The ex-con label haunted and burdened the newly freed prisoners like a boulder around their necks. None of them thought in terms of a comeback that would return them to the status they had before going to jail. For them survival was the goal.

Martha Stewart had no trouble finding a job.

Though she was still unable to take back the reins of Martha Stewart Living Omnimedia, she would serve as creative director, allowing her to do much of what she was doing before. She remained the company's majority shareholder though no longer Chairman and CEO.

She would not starve. She planned to write a monthly column for the company's flagship magazine, *Martha Stewart Living*, for which she would be paid $75,000 per column. She was to host two television shows in the fall—one in the daytime; the other in prime time evenings—as well as host segments of an around-the-clock radio channel. And, with her stock having risen sharply in value, she was once again a billionaire.

PRIVATE JETS AND MANSIONS

For Stewart, the transition from prison to freedom was almost seamless, as if she were merely ending a vacation and returning to work.

Within a half hour of gaining her freedom, she had boarded a private jet lent to her by her good friend, Charles Simonyi, the legendary software programmer who gave the world Microsoft Word and Excel. She then flew three hours to Bedford, New York, where she began five months of house arrest at her 153-acre, $16 million mansion.

What was so remarkable about the commentary of the news analysts on this day—and it carried on for the entire news cycle—was the almost universal admiration, sometimes spilling over into downright adulation, in their voices.

Most significant about the news coverage of Stewart's impending prison release was its upbeat nature. The same television analysts who, before she had even been indicted, relished pronouncing her guilty, the same analysts who pronounced her career over on the day of her conviction, those same people were now proclaiming her a new heroine.

The public was coming around as well, but not as speedily or as warmly as the media. A *USA Today*/CNN Gallup poll of 1008 adults, taken between February 25th and 27th, a week before her release, found 57 percent of the women polled sympathetic toward Stewart, up from 35 percent when Stewart was indicted in June 2003. Only 37 percent of the men were sympathetic toward her.

More than half of the women said they hoped Martha Stewart would succeed in her comeback; while more than half of the men said they did not care.

Her fame—and her infamy—pushed all other news aside for the moment. On the day of her release, millions of people were trying to recover from a deadly tsunami, one of the worst natural disasters of the era; a beloved and venerated Pope was dying in Rome, affecting at least one billion people on the planet; a 45-year-old singer and dancer, the most popular figure in popular music of his day, was on trial for alleged sexual abuse of children. But on this day in early March 2005, Martha Stewart's prison release was the top story of the day.

Fully aware that the media was all over the airport, Stewart said nothing to journalists. She simply smiled and waved.

She was wearing jeans, high-heeled boots, and a floppy gray-knit poncho over a green long-sleeved top, civilian garb that felt good after five months of khaki prison attire. She had no cloak over her head. She did not try to shield her face from the cameras. Exhibiting none of the shame or ignominy that other white-collar executives felt upon leaving prison, Stewart looked more like a political candidate after a weary day of campaigning than an ex-con just released from jail.

Nancy Grace, commenting from CNN's studios, looked Stewart over, noticed that she was dressed in a shawl and jeans, and commented: "She was stylish. She was radiant. She had a huge smile." Deborah Feyerick, the CNN reporter on the scene, could not have agreed more: "She looked happy. She looked rested and she looked young."

And, considering where she had been, she looked pretty darn good. "I got to say," purred Nancy Grace, "she looked fantastic. She's a lean, mean fighting machine." One could almost hear Stewart loyalists burst into collective applause; one could almost hear the cynics cringing, uttering, "Give me a break!"

CNN panelist Keith Naughton of *Newsweek* joined the pro-Stewart hurrahs: "She just looked much more casual than we've seen her before. She just looked very relaxed and really started waving and smiling and looked warm. Even throughout her whole trial, she never looked sort of warm and comfortable as she did right now. Maybe that's just part of the image makeover or maybe that indicates a real change."

A second CNN panelist, the same Henry Blodget who attended the trial every day, chimed in: "That looks perky. That is a perky wave. She looks upbeat and perky."

Naughton: "She looks fabulous."

Nancy Grace: "OK, you know what, they said she was down but she's not down and out. Martha Stewart making a comeback. There she goes everybody. We've waited up all night. She's free. She's back. We're going to see what happens now.... (The plane) is slowly disappearing. Martha Stewart taking off for another chapter in her life."

> *"She's going to be leaving," the reporter told anchor Nancy Grace, "and she's going to be leaving in victory."*

A little later Feyerick was no longer reporting neutrally. She had become all but a Martha Stewart groupie. "She's going to be leaving," the reporter told anchor Nancy Grace, "and she's going to be leaving in victory. We're here waiting...to see a smile, to see a wave, to see some sort of acknowledgment that she's heading off to a very bright future."

Stepping into the private Falcon 50 jet, Stewart provided the perfect public relations moment: the freshly-minted Martha Stewart, eager to get started with her revival, beautifully orchestrating her bid for a comeback, a 63-year-old woman with the same blond mane and a few blond strands hanging over her eyes.

FIRING UP HER COMPUTER

Upon arriving inside the plane, she fired up her computer, went to her Web site, marthastewart.com, and composed a statement, noting that her prison experience "has been life altering and life affirming. Someday, I hope to have the chance to talk more about all that has happened, the extraordinary people I have met here and all that I have learned. Right now, as you can imagine, I am thrilled to be returning to my more familiar life. My heart is filled with joy at the prospect of the warm embraces of my family, friends, and colleagues. Certainly, there is no place like home."

The statement was significant as much for what it did not say as for what it did. No longer was Martha Stewart professing her innocence of the charges brought against her. No longer was she railing at the "ridiculousness" of those chargers. No longer did she sound as if she wanted to pick a fight with anyone connected to the FBI, SEC, Congress, or the United States Attorney's Office.

Once the plane was on the ground three hours later, Martha Stewart was driven 30 more minutes to her estate in Bedford, New York where she would in the next few days begin five months of house arrest.

She was home—but under house arrest.

While she would be severely restricted in her movements, she would not be in jail. That was the good part. She could leave home for 48 hours a week, 6 days a week to work, to go to medical or dental appointments, to attend religious services, and to do food shopping. (Stewart hired a chef to work out of her home; no visits to the local super-market for her.) She was not permitted to roam her Bedford estate. She was under home confinement—it meant just that. While she could spend six days away from home, Stewart had to spend one day a week confined to home for 24 hours straight.

Most humiliating of all, she had to wear an electronic ankle bracelet so that her movements could be monitored. The electronic anklet was an absurd, almost comical attempt on the part of the authorities to hover over Martha Stewart. If the idea was to make sure that Stewart did not slip out of the country, or even sneak away from the location she was visiting, it was a cruel joke.

As one of the most recognizable women in America, Martha Stewart could not slip away anywhere without hundreds of people recognizing her at once. She would have had to mount a perfect disguise to escape, and why should she even want to mislead the authorities? The judge had done her a huge favor by putting her under home arrest; Stewart had no incentive to violate the rules—she would have gone back to jail instantly.

She had once boasted that she had learned how to remove the transmitter while browsing the Internet, but that comment led probation officials to deny that she had ever done so. She had probably found something on the Internet akin to what she had said; but her probation officials could never admit that it was that easy to learn how to dismantle the thing.

As most people would, she found the anklet irritating—both to her personally and physically. It played havoc with her skin, and when she sought to put some padding between her skin and the device, the authorities said no. "I am not allowed to take it off at any time, and I am not allowed, while in my home, to have any padding under the strap," she explained to supporters during one Internet chat. "I hope none of you ever has to wear one."

> *"I am not allowed to take it off at any time, and I am not allowed, while in my home, to have any padding under the strap."*

The judge could have ordered periodic drug testing of Stewart, but that was waived as unnecessary in her case.

Soon after she arrived at her Bedford home, there was some confusion over whether she had already violated the rules of her home confinement by coming outside and chatting with reporters. She had not violated the rules. The probation office had given her a 72-hour grace period before she would be fitted with the electronic anklet and confined to her home.

In the early morning hours of a Friday, she woke up to her first full day of freedom. She had the weekend to relax, visit with relatives and friends, enjoy being at home and free.

She was frustrated by the prospect of house arrest. She wanted to get out into the public realm at once; to begin her real comeback. She knew that to truly regain her reputation, she needed to become visible; but she could not thrust herself into the spotlight given the restrictions that would soon be placed on her.

No Less the Worse

She was eager to show the media that she was no less the worse after her prison experience, that her mind was still functioning at full throttle. And she wanted to exhibit a touch of the new Martha Stewart.

Concerned about the risks, she decided not to hold a news conference. She did not want journalists parsing her every word, dissecting her every thought. She did not want them searching for the old Martha Stewart— and deciding that they had found her! She let the story of her prison release play itself out in pictures, not words. The media had embraced her in the past few days as a heroine making a triumphant return. It could not get any better than that.

Shrewdly, she chose not to coop herself up in her mansion as if she had considered her house arrest shameful. Instead, she made several early permitted forays around her estate, knowing that media helicopters over-head would get footage of her every act. She gave sugar to her horses, offered freezing journalists hot chocolate, walking around the estate, and chatted briefly with reporters but at a distance.

The next morning, she released a brief video of her in the kitchen with her mother and others, with her mother distributing cake. The video was significant: It was important for Stewart to show the world that, immediately upon her release, she was back in the kitchen, back to homemaking. She looked relaxed and at peace with herself, as if a great burden had been lifted from her; which indeed it had. The video carried another carefully scripted, subtle message: I told you I would be back, and I am. I plan to remain in the public spotlight. I plan to get my life back. And I want it to happen as soon as possible.

A little over a month after Martha Stewart's release from prison, *Time* magazine published its annual list of the world's 100 most influential people. By all rational standards, Stewart should never have made the list. She might have been one of the most influential Americans in the past before her legal troubles; but fighting an indictment, engaging in a court battle, and spending time in jail certainly had to have cut down on her once-vaunted influence. Still, *Time* magazine in its April 11, 2005 edition saw fit to include her on its list along with George Bush, Michael Moore, Jamie Foxx, and Condoleezza Rice.

However odd Stewart's selection seemed, *Time* magazine had, however unwittingly, played a major role in her comeback. By putting her on the list, the most prestigious news magazine in America had all but said: "We forgive you, Martha, for all you have done. We see you, as do many others, as a heroine for going to jail and surviving the experience. We want you back. Welcome back, Martha."

In keeping with Stewart's decision to mount a broad-based public offensive to launch her comeback, she adopted a multi-platform strategy—television, radio, and print. She wanted to be seen and heard in as many places and as often as possible. She did not want to put all of her comeback eggs in one basket. There would be no Martha Stewart road show, testing out whether the public wanted to have her stage a comeback. She would put herself before the public in the most grandiose way possible—with the opening episode of *The Apprentice: Martha Stewart* on prime time television over the NBC television network.

She would not show up unannounced at some fancy restaurant and in the presence of a few handpicked journalists, and announce in a soft voice, "I'm back." She was going to do it across the nation's airwaves. It had been national television that had made her an icon. She was going to rely upon TV to do the same thing for her all over again.

The response to overtures put out by Stewart allies, especially Mark Burnett, was heartwarming for her. The same medium that at the time of her conviction was relegating her television program to the early morning hours now wanted her back in prime time. She was, as her staunch ally Donald Trump, pronounced, "hot."

Just as she needed refurbishing, Martha Stewart Living Omnimedia needed a facelift as well.

Stewart's legal troubles put the company on the spot. For the first time, senior executives, once completely dependent on Martha Stewart to make the business a success, had to figure out how to get along without her. Given that she had become a distinct liability throughout her legal case, they also had to figure out how to give the businesses less of a "Martha Stewart" look. It would not be easy.

The company was caught between two contradictory goals: one was to continue to exploit all the good that had come from being a company that was Martha Stewart-centric; the other was moving beyond Stewart, diversifying, creating products that were company-centric.

Its executives always knew that being so closely identified with Martha Stewart was potentially problematic. When it went public in 1999, the company cited the fact that "Martha Stewart remains the personification of our brands" as a large risk factor. At the same time, the executives could not escape reality: People bought the company's products because of Martha Stewart.

A LONG CLIMB

The company had a long climb uphill to recuperate fully. On February 23, 2005, MSLO reported a net loss of $59.6 million on sales of $187.4 million; it was the second consecutive year the company had lost money. Significantly, the only part of the company that showed even slight growth was merchandising, which happened to be the one business least associated with Martha Stewart.

The one barometer that showed how the company was doing was advertising, and the ad revenues for the flagship *Martha Stewart Living* magazine had declined to $71.7 million in 2004; that was less than one-third of what the advertising had been for the magazine in 2002. Its average circulation fell as well from 2.4 million to 1.9 million. (Remember Stewart's courthouse step pleas for her fans to subscribe to the magazine as a way of showing support for her.) The publication accounted for one third of the company's revenues in 2004.

The stock of Martha Stewart Living Omnimedia has fluctuated wildly throughout Stewart's legal travails, dropping when it appeared that she was getting into more trouble; rising when it appeared that she might get through her legal predicament without too much pain. As speculation mounted on whether Stewart's comeback would succeed, the stock's daily volume rose to more than .5 million shares even though the public float of 20.7 million shares was limited.

While Stewart was in jail, the company toyed with the idea of purchasing or developing non-Stewart brands; but with it becoming increasingly clear that she was about to ride a great wave of success, executives returned to the "let's-bank-on-Martha" strategy. Executives toyed with the idea of trying to elevate other MSLO personalities into Stewart-like celebrity status—one was pet expert Marc Morrone—but the failure of that strategy only pointed out how dependent the company was on the real Martha Stewart.

Stewart's planned comeback posed a major risk for the company. So much of what Stewart hoped to do—the television programs, the radio segments, etc.—had little or nothing to do with her company. MSLO could only hope to bask in the warm glow of her triumphant return, and hope that some of the Martha magic rubbed off on the businesses. Sadly for MSLO, it will get zero revenues from Stewart's *The Apprentice*. MSLO executives were also concerned that Stewart might cast too strong an image as the tough female boss, putting a dent in her long-standing image as Ms. Perfect Homemaker.

The future of MSLO rested squarely on the shoulders of Susan Lyne. Her strategy seemed to be to try to have the best of both worlds: exploit Stewart's return and at the same time build new partnerships and franchises. To help her with this gigantic task, she hired Charles A. Koppelman, who was a veteran of the music industry (he had advised Michael Jackson and shoe entrepreneur Steve Madden). Koppelman had become a MLSO board member in July 2004; and vice chairman of the board since December 2004. Koppelman was given a one-year $450,000 contract. His job was to analyze possible new media and merchandising deals. In 2005, he became chairman of the board of Stewart's company.

Susan Lyne was working overtime to exploit Stewart's return. She wanted to leverage the library of recipes, articles, television programs, and other content and turn much if not all of it into cash-producing operations. She planned to build up *Everyday Food*, a relatively new brand that is not Stewart-centric; it has a magazine and television program; she wanted to do the same with a natural-lifestyle magazine called *Body & Soul* that the company purchased in 2004 and was relaunched in April 2005.

Precisely how Stewart wanted to reintegrate herself into the company was not entirely known to Lyne and other senior executives. She was the company's largest shareholder with more than 29 million shares. She automatically had the most influence of anyone in the company.

Meanwhile, Stewart made clear that hers would be a powerful voice within the company.

On Monday, March 7th, just a few days after getting out of jail, Stewart addressed MSLO staff members in New York, announcing a new mission for the company. In the past, the company had appealed largely to the upscale homemaker. Now, Stewart wanted the company to embrace a broader slice of viewers and readers. She wanted MSLO to be less alienating to ordinary people.

Marketing specialists saw her new mission as a great challenge: She would have to reach out to new viewers and readers without alienating her loyal fan base. She would have to make sure that her magazine and television shows retained their uniqueness. She had aimed for high standards and for a level of perfection in all that she did; she could not sacrifice that now. She would not be Martha Stewart anymore.

In her speech to MSLO staff, she promised that the company would concentrate not just on the technical aspects of entertaining and cooking, but also on why such activities were important in nurturing relationships in an uncertain world. The diverse group of people she had met in prison had inspired her, she said, and she hoped to "make life better" for one and all.

Recasting the MSLO message came as her company had shed millions of dollars, lost myriad advertisers, and had required sizeable cutbacks in personnel—all since her legal troubles began in 2002. To be sure, the MSLO stock had surged while Stewart was in prison, but her brand had suffered from such negative publicity that the company had a long way to go to rebound.

The increasing competitiveness of the home decorating magazines and products added extra pressure on MSLO.

A BILLIONAIRE BEHIND BARS

Four days after her speech, *Forbes* magazine published its list of the world's billionaires, and Martha Stewart made the list for the first time. Estimating her net worth at $1 billion, the magazine put her in last place, 620th, tied with 39 others. "A run-up in shares of her Martha Stewart Living Omnimedia made her a billionaire behind bars," said

Forbes (Microsoft's Bill Gates headed the list with $46.5 billion in net worth).

With April came the news that Martha Stewart planned to host segments of an around-the-clock radio channel for Sirius Satellite Radio later in 2005. Stewart's company had reached a deal with Sirius to create a 24-hour channel featuring cooking, gardening, and entertaining programming for women. It was to be called Martha Stewart Living Radio. "This will be the first 'around the clock' channel devoted entirely to areas of interest for women," Stewart said in a statement.

In early May, Martha Stewart showed off her new talk show to a select group of 400 ad executives. She did not show them her famous ankle accessory.

During an hour-long presentation at the New York Public Library, she pitched her daytime how to program. She propped her leg on a chair and lifted up the cuff of her white pantsuit just a bit, revealing a gold shoe. "There's something under here that I'm not going to show," Stewart said, toying with the audience. She was referring to the ankle bracelet that monitored her movements. "Whoever is watching me knows exactly where I am. This is an approved event."

Stewart showed off a clip from *Martha*, the new syndicated talk show set to debut on NBC in September. The show was to be broadcast often live before a studio audience, and was to feature her domestic tips as well as surprise appearances by celebrities.

One segment shown to the executives had Stewart unexpectedly showing up at the home of a woman who declared herself the "Jewish Martha Stewart." She peered into the woman's spice cabinet and poked at her entrée to see if it was done. Stewart acknowledged that, what with all the fuss about her temper in recent years, Mark Burnett hoped to show off her sense of humor somewhat more.

The good news for Stewart was the enthusiastic response that NBC had been getting early on to the show. Already it had sold the syndicated show in 85 percent of the nation, including every top-20 television market. Stations were engaged in bidding wars for the show, driving the price of the show three times above what was normal in certain markets. Television executives who bought the show believed that Stewart had been chastened, that she still had her special style, and, the latest thing, she had a new dose of humility. She seemed human and the television executives believed that audiences would respond positively to that.

Stewart announced to 130 shareholders on May 14th that she was targeting her official comeback for September. It was then that she would begin her Donald Trump spin-off, *The Apprentice: Martha Stewart*, which was to air starting September 21st, and run for 13 weeks. The winner will receive a job in Martha Stewart's company. She also announced *Martha*, her revised daily homemaking show, that was set to air September 12th, and her radio programming, due to begin in the fall. (In the summer, Stewart announced that she had written a book called *Martha's Rules* that would be published in October. The book is supposed to be drawn from her various business experiences. "My goal with this book," she said in a press release, "is to help people turn their passions into successful businesses, as I did myself through many of the things I learned over the years." It was, however, absurd, for anyone to think that in reading the book, they would become another Martha Stewart, any more than someone reading a book about Michael Jordan could learn how to play basketball the way he did.)

IT WON'T HAPPEN OVERNIGHT

To the shareholders, Susan Lyne, the President and CEO of Martha Stewart Living Omnimedia, sounded a cautiously optimistic note about returning the company to profitability.

"It won't happen overnight, but we are encouraged." Stewart was delighted to declare: "The hard times are pretty much over."

Stewart used the time of her home arrest to adopt a low profile toward the media—she gave a relatively small number of print interviews and one television interview during that time—concentrating on the planning of the September launch of her comeback. All of the interviews added little to what the public knew of the period before and during her trial and of her time in prison.

She gave one interview to *People* magazine, published on May 9th. Although the headline suggested that she spoke candidly about surviving Alderson, the article dealt almost entirely with her post-prison routine. The reporter asked such tough questions as: "You look fabulous—what are you doing?" "What's your workout routine?" and "Your skin is amazing. What's your secret?"

She gave an interview to *Vanity Fair* in August. The magazine had promoted the piece as the first behind-the-scenes look at Stewart while in jail. But when it was published, it was evident that Stewart had been very circumspect toward reporter Matt Tyrnauer about her incarceration. While Stewart aides suggested that Stewart was reluctant to conduct these interviews because at some point she planned to write her own book, it made sense for her to be tight-lipped about her period in jail for other reasons as well. If she were going to convince the public that she had indeed gone through a personality makeover, she had to treat the less attractive parts of her recent past as if they did not exist. The orchestrating of her comeback required that she emphasize how much she resembled Martha Stewart the icon, not Martha Stewart the felon.

When she did address her prison experience, she cleverly portrayed it in idyllic terms. If she had to talk about it, she made sure to cast the federal facility as not a bad place at all. To do otherwise would have served as a reminder that she had committed a terrible crime and had been punished by being sent to a very bad place.

GOING ON VACATION

To the *New York Times*, she declared that she felt "that I could go and have a vacation." She made quotation marks with her fingers in the air to acknowledge that Alderson was not exactly a five-star hotel. "This was a time to think about the future. I pretty much thought about a lot of serious good things."

To the *Vanity Fair* reporter, she suggested that Alderson paradoxically offered an escape from her jammed daily schedule in civilian life; and therefore was far more pleasant that being under house arrest. "It was," she was quoted as saying, "by far the least bad part of the last three years. At Alderson, I could go out every morning at 6:30 and be back only for one count at 4 o'clock, and then out until 10 every night." Compared to being under house arrest, it was the essence of freedom. She found her house arrest by comparison "confining."

> *"It was," she was quoted as saying, "by far the least bad part of the last three years."*

She restricted the number of interviews she gave during house arrest in part because she did not want reporters dredging up the past over and over again. If she were going to convince the public that she was a changed woman, contrite without ever having to mouth the words, she had to avoid encounters with journalists. So she believed. The *Vanity Fair* interview was a case in point. She must have known that Matt

Tyrnauer would ask her, as he did, if she felt she owed anyone an apology for what had happened since she had been criticized for not having made such a public statement.

Stewart was clearly rattled by the question.

Even if she had wanted to sound contrite, there was the matter of her appeal. She could not argue to the court that she had done nothing wrong, but apologize for it in a national magazine interview.

So she had to dance around the question, and it was an artful dance she performed: "You can't be sorry for something that—let's see, how can I say this? I'm on appeal. You don't appeal if you think that you should be sorry but I am sorry for the chaos, the damage, and the problems that the situation created. It hurt a lot of people. But I didn't hurt a lot of people—the situation hurt a lot of people. People lost their jobs, businesses were hurt, revenues were lost, stock prices went down."

But, for the most part, the media was dancing to Stewart's tune. CBS planned to air an unauthorized, made-for-television movie about Stewart's rise and fall in April 2005; but put it off until the fall so that it would air closer to the time of her official comeback.

Cybil Shepherd, who also played Stewart in a previous unauthorized television movie, was to portray Stewart from the day her company went public in October 1999 to her release from prison in March. The CBS press release announcing the movie, *Martha Behind Bars*, offered a fascinating illustration of how the media was playing the unwitting role of both spectator and participant in the Martha Stewart comeback story. "Prison proves to be a life-altering experience for Stewart, and when she is released, the nation embraces a new Martha—ready to put the past behind her and start a fresh chapter in her intriguing, remarkable life." The Stewart public relations machine could have not have scripted the press release more to its liking.

The media had gotten on board in such a big way because its decision-makers knew that Americans loved a comeback story. "They like that Martha made it rich from scratch," commented Andrew Ritchie, one of her loyal fans writing for savemartha.com, "that she got into trouble and that she had to pay a price for it. They like that she did the time with grace and dignity (going in early was genius) and that now she has EARNED a second chance. People needed to see her earn something again. They loved her when she was earning her way up the ladder."

Once at the top, she bought mansions and started to sink into the celebrity world of glamour. People liked that for a while, but the image of Martha as a domineering boss and a control freak smelled much more rancid when she was surrounded by lavish homes and an extravagant lifestyle. The media loved to take her down every chance they could. Byron's book, *MARTHA Inc.*, is a prime example of that.

SECOND CHANCE

Now that she's been through the wringer, they are giving her a second chance and actually giving some tailwind to her cause! The shift has been amazing.

One of Stewart's attorneys expressed delight at her comeback: "Martha's comeback has been truly extraordinary. It is a tribute to her entrepreneurship, drive and talent. It also is a reminder of how she built her company from scratch. No one handed anything to her and now she is once again drawing upon her amazing personality and determination to revive her business. You have to be very happy for her and for her company and its employees."

August 10, 2005 was set to be the big day. That was when her five months of house arrest was to come to an end. She would then be free to pursue her career and her life without being confined to her Bedford home for all but those 48 precious hours.

But then something happened.

Her home arrest did not come to an end on that day. It was extended by another three weeks. The actual reason for the delay has been only murkily discussed in public. Stewart's attorney, Walter Dellinger, issued a one-sentence letter stating that Stewart "has agreed to an extension of the terms of her home confinement until Aug. 31." A fine bit of rewriting of history, that terse statement was. He made it sound as if her parole officer had asked her to please remain under home confinement for another three weeks, and she had gone along with his proposal. That sounded preposterous. Yet no one came forth with the real reason for the extension.

All that had happened was that Martha Stewart's comeback was delayed a bit longer. But there was no doubt that it was about to happen.

Late in August, Stewart held a news conference in New York to provide details of her two new television series. She showed off the set of *Martha*, the syndicated weekday lifestyle show featuring a loft that had a fully functioning kitchen, and a garden for growing houseplants.

"It's a how-to-show with entertainment and a live audience," she said. "It's not a talk show—I don't see a couch anywhere."

Reporters asked questions about *The Apprentice: Martha Stewart* but she ducked most of them, including what catch phrase she intended to use that would be the equivalent of Donald Trump's famous "You're fired."

The program would focus not on business as Trump's *The Apprentice* did; but on fun and getting more out of life. The show would have 10 women and 6 men, ranging in age from 22 to 42, compete for 13 weeks on tasks related to Martha Stewart's areas of expertise, including publishing, apparel, branding, and entertainment. Alexis Stewart and Charles Koppelman, the company's chairman, would appear on the program with Stewart.

On August 31st, Stewart told an Associated Press reporter that at five minutes after midnight she was going to take off the electronic anklet and gain one more aspect of her freedom.

At a news conference in New York that week she sat next to Mark Burnett and Susan Lyne, and at one point thrust her leg up in the air showing off the anklet. The look on her face said, "You want to know what they did to me?"

She admitted to feeling "nervous excitement" at the thought of getting rid of the device. The probation authorities had advised her that unless she heard from them otherwise, she could cut the anklet off at 12:01 am, Thursday, September 1st; with that all monitoring of her would cease. The Associated Press noted that she would still have to endure the constant monitoring of reporters and photographers.

Stewart continued to be on probation for another 18 months; this meant that she could not get drunk, own a gun, or leave the federal court district and travel to other homes in Connecticut, Maine, and the Hamptons on Long Island, without permission. She had to meet with her probation office whenever requested and she had to submit to monthly reports on her activities. One was tempted to say to the probation officers: Just watch television, folks!

Perhaps the most remarkable announcement of all was the one that week announcing that Stewart would resume working full-time August 31st. Had she not been working full-time even while wearing that anklet and being under house arrest?

Meanwhile, Wall Street, along with the rest of the country, awaited Stewart's return in September with much excitement. Her stock rose 10 percent on August 29ᵗʰ as the time for the debut of her two television shows neared, hitting $33.59, the highest it had been since the previous March. The stock had climbed over 20 percent the past week.

While the stock had reached $34 in March at the time of Stewart's release from prison, it fell back over the next few months, especially when in July the company posted a quarterly loss of $44.5 million and forecast a loss for the third and fourth quarters.

Everything was set, for what many were billing as one of the most remarkable comebacks of the era. She had done it swiftly; she had done it in public; and she had been as full-throated and broad-gauged in her approach as possible. She wanted no one to make a mistake: She was back.

PART
VI

THE COMEBACK

CHAPTER

15

HEROINE BEFORE THE CAMERAS

Martha Stewart's probation officer had told her that unless she heard otherwise, she was free to cut the electronic ankle bracelet off as soon as the month of August ended.

She heard nothing from the probation officer, and so at 12:05 a.m., September 1st, Martha Stewart removed the bracelet.

It was easy enough to cut off. At that point, all monitoring ceased. Soon thereafter, she went to sleep. She was too tired to celebrate.

The cutting off of the ankle bracelet marked the end of the most difficult and shameful period in her life. She was thrilled that the time had finally come when she was rid of the equivalent of a ball and chain. The casting off of the bracelet marked a new beginning for her as well; for now it was truly time for her comeback to begin.

Later that morning, Stewart got out of town, something she had not been able to do for the past year. She emerged from her Westchester County estate at 8 a.m. and headed for a private plane at the county's airport, flying off to Mount Desert Island in Maine, where she had a home.

Martha Stewart's return to public life and celebrity in the fall of 2005 was all the more astonishing because she had just ended five months in jail and five months of house arrest; and she had to continue on probation for the next 18 months. She had to report regularly to a probation officer. She had to ask and receive permission to travel outside a certain area. And she had to be careful not to consort with ex-felons ("which," she told *Time* magazine in its September 11, 2005 edition, "is kind of scary because there are quite a few people who have been to jail, and you would never know who they are.").

But she was determined not to let 18 months of probation keep her from making a big, splashy comeback.

That was the difference between other ex-cons and Martha Stewart. "Splashy" was not a word that other ex-cons typically want associated with their period right after jail. They want their return to society to be as low key as possible. They want to see how quickly and whether society would welcome them back as citizens equal to those who had not gone to jail.

Low key was not part of Martha Stewart's vocabulary. She had thought long and hard about the kind of comeback she wanted to make. She spent little time trying to figure out how the public would react to her efforts. She devoted most of her time to deciding what venues were right for her, and what venues were wrong. Television definitely seemed to be right.

The strategy of making that comeback in September 2005 was put in place long before that. It was a strategy that was big and bold and risky—for no prisoner had ever sought to relaunch a career with quite the audacity, quite the in-your-face brazenness that Martha Stewart displayed. No prisoner had ever sought to make her rehabilitation a public event—or rather, a series of public events.

SHE HAD WILLING ALLIES

Martha Stewart decided as early as the spring of 2005 that she could and would regain the fame and popularity that once was hers. Fortunately for her, she had willing allies, especially Mark Burnett and Donald Trump, who were eager to sponsor her return to national television, not just on one daytime program, but on a primetime evening version of Trump's *The Apprentice* as well.

She read the public opinion polls that showed that the public was coming around to support her, and she took heart from that support. She seemed more famous in jail and just out of jail than in earlier periods. A Gallup poll noted that 52 percent of Americans had a favorable impression of her, which was higher than before she went to prison.

Stewart had no interest in postponing her comeback. She could have used the five months of house arrest from March to August 2005 as the start of a much longer retreat into a private life that she had never really known. She could have turned down not just the television programs, but the national radio program, the how-to business book, and the magazine columns. She could have chosen to hold off on returning as the spokesperson for all of her businesses.

But she wanted a comeback that would happen sooner rather than later, that would put her very much in the public eye, and that would occur along a broad front of media and cultural outlets. She wanted no one to miss the point she wanted to make: She planned to treat her legal difficulties as if they had never happened; she intended to win back her fence-sitting fans and all those "Martha-is-guilty" media critics by appearing in front of a whole variety of audiences, just as she had done in her earlier years.

She wanted the old Martha to shine through, the one who had captivated millions of people on television before her legal difficulties began. Many may have wanted Stewart to display arrogance and mean-spiritedness in her new television programs—and such behavior might have garnered her top ratings—but she rejected such tactics. That was not the Martha Stewart she wanted to project before the public in the fall of 2005.

As she planned her comeback, no one asked whether it was a good idea for her to saturate the airwaves with her television and radio programs. No one was there to ask what would happen if the public did not respond enthusiastically to her programs. It was simply assumed that all would go well, that the television and radio programs would be a huge success, and that her comeback would seem like the most natural of phenomena.

September 2005 became the month for Martha Stewart's comeback. It made extraordinary sense for her to launch the comeback that month. The vacation-filled summer was over. People were returning to work. The nation was getting ready to watch a whole new batch of television programs. And she was able to create a certain buzz that summer over her new television programs. Reporters wrote enough stories speculating on what her new shows would look like to keep her in the news. But essentially all through the summer, she appeared little in public, preparing for the big splash that would come in the fall.

Her own magazine, *Martha Stewart Living*, became a key vehicle for her return to public life. The September issue featured Stewart prominently on the cover, standing in a living room, a wide smile on her face. Except for the "welcome-back-Martha" April 2005 edition, she had not graced the cover of her own magazine since January 2001. Inside the September issue were three large ads for her television and radio shows, replete with Stewart photos. The contrast with the magazine a year earlier, when Stewart hardly appeared on its pages, was striking.

Stewart's return to celebrity may have seemed to carry a sense of inevitability to it, but it was not automatic that she would gain backers for her plan to rehabilitate herself on national television. Indeed, it turned out that, at first, Donald Trump had not been thinking at all of Martha Stewart as the person he would choose to create an alternative version of his highly successful *The Apprentice*.

Only later would he reveal that he had seriously considered two other choices before selecting Stewart for a new version of *The Apprentice*: British mogul Richard Branson and Dallas Mavericks owner Mark Cuban. Trump dropped them as candidates when the two men hosted their own short-lived reality shows.

RIGHT NOW SHE'S HOT

Trump told the author: "Branson and Cuban did the market research for us, because frankly if I had gone out and done that kind of market research, I couldn't have gotten a more accurate result. They didn't have the persona for such a show. Very few people have it. Martha has it. And right now she's hot."

> *"Very few people have it. Martha has it. And right now she's hot."*

She was hot all right. There were predictions that 30 million people would watch the opening episode of her *Apprentice*. That may have been pleasant for Stewart and her acolytes to hear at that early stage, but it set an unusually high expectation for a new, basically untested television program. But few worried for her. Everyone assumed there were 30 million people out there who were curious enough to tune in to the first Stewart-hosted *Apprentice*.

Scores of newspaper and magazine stories appeared, describing her return. Mostly, the articles were favorable to her, crediting Stewart with doing a personality makeover, becoming softer and kinder, endlessly curious about how popular she would become. She could not have scripted the media coverage to be more positive. And yet, she regarded the media's new love affair with her with a degree of cynicism. She remembered all the nastiness and venom that had spewed from the media during the walk up to her trial. And now the same media was portraying her in heroic terms. Had she changed that much? She doubted it. Much more likely, she thought, the media loved to follow celebrities on the way down—and on the way back up.

She found it difficult to explain the new Martha Stewart to the public. Should she describe herself as greatly changed? Or should she suggest that she was really no different from the person who had gotten into all that legal difficulty? She seemed to have a hard time deciding how to project herself.

She wanted everyone to think that she had emerged from her legal difficulties, especially her prison experience, as a changed person, a better person. At the same time, she did not want to lose her loyal base of fans, and so she felt a need to convince them that she had not changed at all.

I'M NOT CHANGED

"I'm not changed," she told *USA Today*, "I'm the same Martha." On another occasion, she explained that she had adopted a new motto: "When you're through changing, you're through. We will continually change and evolve and be ourselves." And, to *Newsweek*, she argued: "Maybe it's time to think of me a little differently. In the last two years, people have tried to make me a dour, miserable human being, and I'm not."

> *"I'm not changed. I'm the same Martha."*

She hoped that few would quarrel with her over her obvious ambiguity. She wanted to leave her past behind her, but she knew that she could not ignore it completely; so, as she staged her comeback, she allowed fleeting, almost casual, references to her past legal troubles. For example, she permitted a rather unflattering courthouse photo of her to appear in the opening credits of her daytime show: She explained: "To avoid it (her legal difficulties) is avoidance. We're not going to avoid things."

On one of her daytime programs, she made a reference to her prison and home confinement. She told chef Scott Conant that when her company's board of directors met at his restaurant, she could not stay to have dinner with them. "I had to go home; it was during my bad time." The audience laughed, apparently in sympathy.

She made no mention of her legal difficulties during the opening *Apprentice* show on September 21st. The closest she came was during the opening part when she boasted about her business success and then added, as footage rolled of one of her exits from court, "I've faced incredible challenges."

It did not occur to her that she was taking on too much—two television shows, a radio program, the publication of a book, and a magazine column—and then there was all the planning that had to go into the effort to revive Martha Stewart Living Omnimedia. She acknowledged that she had been up at 4 a.m. editing the manuscript of *Martha's Rules,* her self-help book for small business entrepreneurs that was to be published in October 2005. But she never complained—at least publicly—that she was stretching herself too thin. She explained why she wrote the book: "I really do have rules for running and managing a business that have never been formalized before. To put them all down was a very good exercise for me. Thank goodness for home confinement." Writing a book giving business advice so soon after being released from jail and home arrest may have been the most audacious act in her comeback. Surely, she must have understood that she was opening herself up to the obvious criticism that someone who had been convicted of a white-collar crime so recently was in no position to offer business advice to anyone. But she ignored such thoughts, and made sure to get the book out as part of her fall 2005 comeback.

Her daytime show, *MARTHA,* debuted on September 12th. In some respects, the show resembled Stewart's earlier daytime television ventures: the recipes, the home projects, the gardening plans, and the craft ideas. But in other respects, it was totally different from her past television experience. For one thing, there was the huge pressure on her to regain her fan base. Of course, there was always pressure on the host of a national television show to succeed; but this time, Stewart had the extra pressure of knowing that the success of her comeback depended in part on how well this show did.

She could take some comfort from the fact that the television network, NBC, had invested far too much to allow her to fail. The ads for her programs were large and loud. One outside her studio proclaimed:

"Martha unsifted. Like you've never seen her before." The ad appeared in different parts of New York City with a beaming Stewart shining down on Manhattan. She also appeared on David Letterman's CBS late-night show as well as a host of other programs to promote her own television efforts.

Unlike her previous daytime shows, she planned to invite celebrities to *MARTHA* to engage in Martha Stewart-like projects: cooking and gardening. She did not want to turn the program into just another talk show. Hence, she banned couches from the set. She wanted guests to be doing things, not just sitting and talking. The guest she most hoped to book was actor Russell Crowe. He had offered her a quiet place to stay in Australia during her legal troubles.

There was another striking difference between past shows and this current one: The new show was to take place not in her Westport, Connecticut home, as in the past, but in a large New York City studio with a spacious kitchen replete with its own chefs and a glass-enclosed conservatory greenhouse.

STIFF AND FORCED

To her critics, she seemed just a bit stiff and forced in the first few episodes of *MARTHA*. They liked her poking fun at her legal difficulties, especially when she opened one show, proclaiming "I am unfettered. I am free! No ankle bracelets!"—then out came her producers and staff, all of whom wore ankle bracelets.

Critics felt that she was trying too hard to be warm and fuzzy; that she was working overtime to show her audience that she had gone through a personality makeover.

When *Desperate Housewives* star Marcia Cross gave Martha Stewart a few gag gifts, rubber gloves and an apron with leopard-skin fake fur, Stewart seemed uncomfortable as she uttered, "Oh, good! Rubber gloves with faux fur. Very cute—and an apron with faux fur. Very nice." She seemed, said one critic, to be gritting her teeth.

Though some of her guests seemed unfamiliar with the kitchen and incapable of doing much in it, Stewart never took on a haughty, know-it-all pose, perhaps hoping that her guests' faux pas would pass unnoticed. When Marcia Cross put butter in the bowl with the eggs rather than putting it in the pan, Stewart did not cringe; she said only, "I think it's good to cook scrambled eggs in the pan."

Aware that Marcia Cross possessed a graduate degree, Stewart asked, "You're a psychotherapist?"

Stewart then asked, "What made you go into that field?"

"The fact that I can't cook," the actress confessed.

Stewart introduced a regular taped segment of the show where she popped in on a family at home, offering to help them cook dinner. She chose a New Jersey family who were cooking an Italian meal for the first time; two sisters from the family then showed up live in the studio and revealed their secret for cooking meatballs.

During the early days of the daytime show, Stewart's celebrity guests gained all the headlines. More was written about them than about the content of Stewart's show. The media spent reams of copy on comedian David Spade showing up on Stewart's second show, dressed as Martha Stewart! He wore a blonde wig, gold clogs, and a poncho—and, of course, an ankle bracelet. He had played Stewart in a skit on "Saturday Night Live." "I thought you played me very well," Stewart told Spade. "My DVD is almost worn out from showing it. I show it to everybody who comes for dinner 'cause I think it's so funny." Later, Stewart taught Spade how to fold shirts and how to cook microwave dishes.

The first week Stewart hosted rapper Sean "Diddy" Combs, and provided her audience with the most memorable segment to date. While the hip-hop mogul watered plants in the background, Martha Stewart rapped some verses calling herself "Miss Martha from Jersey City", and poking fun at her prosecutors ("They thought they could stop me, but they must be silly").

Combs taught Stewart some hip-hop slang, as well as the lyrics from his 1997 hit, "It's All About the Benjamins." Stewart, for her part, taught him how to make Chinese dumplings and how to make personalized wrapping paper.

On September 20th, Stewart hosted a group of women all named Martha Stewart, bringing them to New York from around the country.

The live syndicated show drew 2.4 million viewers that week; those were the highest ratings for a new daytime show debut in syndication since self-help guru Dr. Phil began his television show. Stewart's show dipped slightly the second week. These were respectable figures for daytime television, but it was still a tiny number compared to the audiences for *Oprah* and *Dr. Phil*.

Yet, no one talked of canceling Stewart's daytime show. She was in her element on *MARTHA*. It was the closest kind of television program to what she had been doing in earlier years. It seemed likely that she would have a reasonably bright future on the daytime side.

The positive media coverage of Stewart's televised comeback included upbeat assessments of her businesses. *USA Today*, for instance, wrote an article on September 20th, noting that Martha Stewart Living Omnimedia's "comeback on Wall Street has been fast and impressive." Although the company had spent 14 percent of its cash in the past year, and although it had lost money in seven of the past eight quarters, the signs of a turnaround were in the air: Shares in Martha Stewart Living Omnimedia were four times what they had been before September 2002, trading at $30.36 compared to $7.80 three years earlier, even though MSLO was losing money in 2005. Advertising pages for Stewart's flagship magazine, *Martha Stewart Living*, were 35 percent higher than the previous year. The first issue of the magazine after the end of Martha Stewart's house arrest had sold 100 ad pages—more than any issue in the last two years.

When Mark Burnett met Martha Stewart for the first time, though her legal troubles seemed likely to marginalize her for years to come, he was convinced that she possessed the kind of spontaneity and sense of humor that would serve her well on television. He proposed to her that she consider a daytime show in front of a live audience, and a prime-time reality show. To Stewart, the proposals seemed far-fetched. She was about to begin serving a jail sentence. Still, she was pleased that someone envisioned a life and career for her beyond her legal difficulties. She was pleased that Burnett had come forward; the line of people asking her to stage a post-prison comeback was not that long. Out of the initial Stewart-Burnett conversations emerged the idea that Donald Trump would essentially franchise out his highly popular television program, *The Apprentice*, to Stewart and let her host a separate version starting in the fall of 2005. Trump and Burnett would co-produce the Stewart version just as they had done with the original *Apprentice*.

ROSY PREDICTIONS

Generally, the predictions for *The Apprentice: Martha Stewart* were that it would do quite well in its early episodes but could fade unless it possessed something magical. The worst thing that could happen, said some, was for Stewart to appear to be mean-spirited on the show. Donald Trump could get away with it. But she could not. Even Trump seemed somewhat worried about the public's perceptions of Stewart. He was quoted as saying: "You don't know what's going to happen when the lights go on. Martha may act very nice, and it may not come across as nice."

Stewart saw *The Apprentice: Martha Stewart* as the vehicle that would get her company back on its feet: "*The Apprentice,*" she said, "is meant to let viewers see, in addition to being a how-to teacher, that I am also a good boss-manager. I want them to see that part of our world—especially now, because it is very important to revitalize this fantastic company, to get people back on track about what we are and what we do here."

The Apprentice: Martha Stewart aired for the first time on September 21st.

The program opened with a mini-biography of Stewart. She told viewers that after she took her company public, she "became America's first female self-made billionaire." Americans had heard that phrase many times before, but never directly from the mouth of Martha Stewart. Making it clear that she planned to be in direct charge of the show, she also noted that the 16 *Apprentice* candidates were going to live in a loft down the hall from her office.

The show's theme song was "Sweet Dreams," originally sung by the Eurythmics.

Much like Trump's *Apprentice,* Stewart's show put the 16 candidates—10 women and 6 men—through a series of tasks, with Stewart eliminating one candidate each week. The winner was to receive a $250,000-a-year job at Martha Stewart Living Omnimedia. Stewart's daughter, Alexis, and Charles Koppelman, chairman of Stewart's company, served as advisers to Stewart on the show. Because the show had to be taped while Stewart was still under house arrest, Alexis Stewart and Charles Koppelman pulled extra duty, supervising the candidates while Stewart remained in confinement in her Bedford, New York mansion. She made it clear that she had relinquished none of her power or authority: "I will make the ultimate decision about who will stay and who will leave."

Much like Trump's *Apprentice,* the Stewart contestants divided into teams of eight. Whichever team lost the task for the week would be summoned to the conference room, and the losers would pick which one of them had to go.

With each show structured around a lesson, the two teams—Matchstick and Primarius—headed off as the show got underway to the giant publisher, Random House, for their first assignment: They had to adapt a children's book for a modern audience. As Stewart put it, they had to write a children's book that would "connect with today's children." One team relied upon "Jack and the Beanstalk," while the other based its work on "Hansel and Gretel."

The Matchstick team ran into personal differences. Jeff's idea was to give "Hansel and Gretel" an urban setting. The team picked Dawn to write the text because she had an MA degree in writing. When she asked for personal space, the team members were puzzled and appalled. Why would a writer need quiet to work? "My option," said Jeff, "is to marginalize her completely." Jeff wound up marginalizing everyone.

No one on the team thought it important to try out their efforts on children. Marcela, who had a child, suggested that it did not teach a good lesson. But Jeff was pleased with it, and that's all there was to that. He selected Dawn to read the story, but she said that she wanted a banana first. It was hard to believe how much chaos ensued over her request. Bethenny regarded Dawn's hunger as a disrespectful sign. Jeff demoted Dawn for asking for breakfast, and asked Shawn to be the reader.

The Primarius team fared much better. By the time the groups were supposed to read their books to kids, the members of Primarius already knew that their book had passed the test of one focus group. The children clearly preferred the "Jack and the Beanstalk" version (in which the beanstalk had grown down into the ocean) to Jeff's urban, edgy "Hansel and Gretel."

In the Matchstick's remake of "Hansel and Gretel," the siblings hated their names so much that they changed them and left home without their parents' permission.

In the conference room, Stewart told Matchstick members that, as a parent, she was surprised, as in disappointed, with the name-change ploy. She was also surprised that they allowed Hansel and Gretel to leave home without asking the parents—because she personally loved "Hansel and Gretel" as a fairy tale so much.

Stewart scolded the Matchstick members. "I saw some things in here that as a parent I couldn't understand." Charles asked, "What were you guys thinking?" Besides not liking the story, Bethenny took out her anger on Dawn, shouting, "Negative energy is like a poison and you have to get rid of it."

Primarius won and got the reward of dining with Stewart, with sushi as a main course. Howie was thrilled when Stewart noticed him: "I think I could possibly be falling in love with Martha Stewart." No *Apprentice* candidate ever said that of Donald Trump.

Matchstick returned to the loft to play the blame game. "She's negative, she's argumentative," Jeff said of Dawn. Jim wanted Jeff to be fired. "It's kill or be killed," said Jim, "eat or be eaten."

Stewart and her advisers dismissed everyone but Jeff, Jim, and Dawn. Jim and Dawn quickly realized they both wanted Jeff out. They ganged up on him. By the time the three left the conference room for Stewart and her advisers to deliberate, Jeff was in trouble.

WHAT PHRASE WOULD SHE USE?

For months, followers of the Stewart *Apprentice* show wondered how she would fire a contestant. Everyone recalled how Trump had off-handedly, but very chillingly, said to the first contestant on his show, "You're fired." And the phrase became part of the national lexicon. What phrase would Stewart use? That became a new national guessing game. Donald Trump had asked her what phrase she planned to use in one of their get-togethers as Stewart was preparing for the show. She assured him that she did not plan to use, "You're fired." She did not explain, but in the back of her mind was her wish to come up with a phrase that had a softer, gentler sound to it. Were she to use "You're fired," she could come off as arrogant and sullen, and she was hoping to keep those character traits on the shelf for good.

Back in the conference room, Stewart told Jeff with the utmost kindness, "We connect each and every day with messages that are trustworthy, with messages that appeal. And, Jeff, you didn't hear me when I said that the main business task was to connect. This story had to connect with parents, and it had to connect with kids. The message was really off, and it was your message. And I don't think you even connected with your own co-workers."

"So, Jeffrey. You just don't fit in."

"So, Jeffrey. You just don't fit in."

There it was, the new Martha Stewart phrase: a kinder, more diplomatic way of saying, "You're fired." (Other suggested phrases for Stewart to use: "Your goose is cooked!" and "Your soufflé has fallen!")

In the end, Stewart stamped her own identity on the dismissal process by doing something after she uttered those newly famous five words. She displayed her usual impeccable manners by writing Jeffrey a thank-you note:

"Good luck, travel safely, it was great to meet you. The next time you connect with your audience, I hope it is in a brawl at the local bar. [Just kidding about that last one!]

Cordially,

Martha Stewart"

When Trump fired a candidate, he sundered all connection with the person; but television cameras followed the person out of "Trump Tower" in New York and allowed the candidate to react to the firing while seated in the cab. It was all very embarrassing and sobering to the candidate. Stewart wanted none of that. She wanted her candidates to depart the show without getting banged up too much.

The media critics had mixed opinions of the show. Quite a number praised Stewart for getting back into the television game so quickly and so effortlessly. But some thought that *The Apprentice* as a franchise may have lost its appeal after several years on television. Some thought the behavior of the candidates beneath contempt.

The *Washington Post* wrote the next day:

"Naturally, the teams of would-be Martha acolytes fussed and feuded, mostly over trivia. Trump's *Apprentice* is all about backbiting, and so, it appears, is Martha's. The wormy substratum of society that churns out reality-show contestants seems to be filled with the kind of telegenic young nitwits who would argue, as two allied contestants did last night, over the fact that one ate a banana during a brainstorming session."

Then came the next dose of reality.

The ratings.

With all the media hype, with all the attention that the new Martha Stewart *Apprentice* show garnered, millions of people had been expected to watch the opening show—some predicted as many as 30 million. But the reception from viewers was chilly.

In her first week, only 7 million viewers watched Stewart's *Apprentice*. This was a disappointing figure. The only consolation was that the program went up against the highly popular *Lost* on ABC.

In her second week, Stewart had 6.2 million viewers, down 13 percent from the already-low debut. Was she not as big as people had thought? Had the concept of *The Apprentice* indeed run its course? No one could say for sure. Still, it was shocking. Why had all the notoriety surrounding Stewart's comeback not translated into large ratings? No one believed that the show was a dud; that is, that somehow people had tuned out because they had heard that Stewart's *Apprentice* was not very interesting.

What had happened?

It turns out that there had been warnings, but they had gone unheeded. Surveys for the networks in the summer had indeed shown huge awareness for *The Apprentice: Martha Stewart;* but among those surveyed, very few said they planned to watch the show.

As for the original Trump-centric version of *The Apprentice*, it too had suffered in the ratings, getting the lowest number of viewers ever, 9.9 million when it debuted in September. Some, including Trump himself, blamed Stewart's show for pulling down Trump's, a case of too many *Apprentice*s out there. But Trump's low ratings seemed to underscore the argument that the public, by the fall of 2005, was simply getting tired of *The Apprentice* as a television program.

Predictably, Stewart's allies put a good face on what seemed like very bad news. Mark Burnett predicted that the ratings would get better simply because the show was very good.

MY NEEDS WERE DIFFERENT

Susan Lyne, the former senior ABC programmer who was running Stewart's company, decided to put a positive spin on the low ratings. She credited Stewart's television exposure—even if it were only 7 million and 6.2 million the first two weeks, with helping Web traffic to grow and improving sales of Stewart's products at Kmart. "My needs were different from NBC's needs," Lyne declared. "They were disappointed by 7-plus million viewers. I think that was 7 million more viewers that were exposed to us. Anytime you can get 6 or 7 million people watching an hour of television that features your company and your brands, that's a good thing," Lyne said.

As if the Stewart version of *The Apprentice* did not need any further bad news, word came the day after the show's opening that MSLO's stock dropped upon the news that the show had disappointing ratings.

The shares fell $1.72 or 6 percent, closing at $27.16 on the New York Stock Exchange.

Would Martha Stewart turn mean-spirited on *The Apprentice* in an effort to boost ratings? After all, Donald Trump had gained a lot of viewers by having a tough, provocative demeanor on his *Apprentice*.

No, insisted Susan Lyne, Stewart would not do that. "That would not serve the long-term interests of the company or her," said Lyne. "She's not going to play a role that doesn't fit."

Most significant in all of this was the silence on the part of the NBC network. It issued no statement in support of the program, nor did it leak word that the show might not last the entire season. That was indeed good news to Stewart and Burnett. If the ratings did not improve in the coming weeks, surely there would be talk of not renewing the program for a second year. That seemed inevitable. But by early October, Stewart could still hope that the ratings would improve and things would get brighter.

Meanwhile, Stewart continued to defend *The Apprentice* against its less than impressive showing in its first three weeks. For the September 19-October 2 period, it came in 67th in prime-time household ratings. A reporter for *USA Today* noted that in her new book, *The Martha Rules: 10 Essentials for Achieving Success as You Start, Grow, or Manage a Business*, she talked about taking calculated risks.

The reporter then asked: "Given the difficulty of launching *The Apprentice*, why did she think the show was a good risk?"

"*The Apprentice*," Stewart replied, "has been a fantastic thing for the image of our company. ...To have 6 million eyeballs on your company in a very positive light every single week—that is invaluable."

As if Martha Stewart was not doing enough multi-tasking, her company announced on October 3rd that it was getting into the music business. Martha Stewart Living Omnimedia and Sony Corporation's BMG business agreed to form a joint venture that would be called Martha Stewart Living Music; MSLM was to release a number of compilation albums for holidays and special occasions. First to be launched would be "Martha Stewart Living Music: The Holiday Collection" by Epic Records, a holiday collection compiled by Stewart that would be released individually and as a three-disk boxed set. The individual releases would include a holiday recipe from MSO, and all boxed set collections would include 30 recipe cards, decorating tips, and craft ideas.

In a bizarre turn of events, Martha Stewart announced on October 4th—13 days after her low-rated *Apprentice* debuted—that she was planning to launch a third television program: a reality show on home improvement. It was bizarre given the tepid ratings of her *Apprentice* show.

This new show would deal with six women—either coming off welfare, bankruptcy, or out of rehab—who work together with mentors to renovate a house. The show was to launch sometime in 2006.

"Our new home improvement series will inspire and inform, while mentoring and teaching valuable life skills, from repairing brickwork, laying flooring, painting rooms, and installing a functional and lovely kitchen," Stewart said in a statement. Martha Stewart Living Omnimedia had already purchased a 125-year-old, 2,500 square foot house in Norwalk, Connecticut, for $700,000, which would become the setting of the show. The Martha Stewart Living staff was to choose mentors for the women.

In an interview on the *Today* show, co-host Katie Couric asked Martha Stewart if she had any regrets, presumably meaning did she have any regrets over any of her behavior since December 27, 2001. Again, Stewart had a choice in how she answered that question. She might have said that after all that had happened—the Federal probe, the indictment, the trial, jail—she certainly had regrets. She might have finally acknowledged that she wished she had reached some kind of settlement with the Federal authorities that would have kept her from going to trial and going to jail. She had decided to make a personality makeover, but she could still say none of this. So to Katie Couric, Stewart replied: "None. I went through a period of two years of great difficulty, came back with a passion, with a really guiding light behind me, trying to focus on making sure that every aspect of our business at Martha Stewart Living was great."

She could not have meant that she had no regrets. How could she not have been sorry for the collapse of her reputation, of her company, of everything that she had worked so hard for over three decades? Perhaps she felt that any expression of regret was tantamount to saying that she had been responsible, partially or completely, for what had happened to her. And she was still not willing to admit to that.

On October 13th, Stewart explained, in an interview with National Public Radio, why she wished to discuss her prison experience as little as possible. She had gone to jail, she said, "Without having gone to prison, I would be appealing and still waiting. That would have been an untenable situation to be in as a business person. Martha Stewart Living would not have two television shows on the air. We would not probably have the advertiser growth that we've had in the last seven or eight months. We would be suffering and suffering and suffering." So she noted that prison was nothing more than "a business decision that solved a problem."

For that reason, and others, she wanted to talk about her life there as little as possible.

"I'm really over prison," Stewart told NPR. "I can think about it privately. But to talk about it day in and day out is more tiresome than I wish. I am on with my life. I'm free. I am working. I am thriving. I feel really, really good. I'm glad to be home. And I am glad to be free."

The NPR reporter pressed Stewart to talk about what it was like inside Alderson.

"I was in what probably could be described as pleasant as possible a federal detention facility," Stewart said. "It was not as bad as anyone could imagine. It was not unsafe. I did not feel in danger."

Was she able to do anything to make her surroundings more pleasant, she was asked.

Stewart was amused by the question: "...There are no materials to work with in a place like Alderson. You are not allowed to receive decorative paper. You are not allowed to receive anything made out of fabric. You are really not allowed to receive anything other than letters, and a certain number of photographs and a certain number of books. So, if one could decorate one's room with five books and some writing paper and some colored pens that you could buy at the commissary, then you could do some decorating. But it was very impossible to do that. And I didn't want to spend my time doing anything like that. I read a lot. I had an opportunity to do a lot of thinking and reading."

The whole interview was Stewart's way of saying to NPR and the rest of the media: I'll talk about my prison experience, if you insist, but I'd prefer not to. I hope I don't get any more of these questions.

Could one declare Martha Stewart's comeback a success—even though it was early in the game?

In some respects, the verdict was already in: Just by lining up her television programs, her radio venture, her book, her magazine columns, and all the rest, she had staged an unprecedented, highly successful recovery. Her comeback was an undiluted success.

Interestingly, though the ratings for her television programs were hardly overwhelming, no one had suggested that her comeback was therefore a failure.

A quiet consensus appeared to be forming: 1) that her comeback stood on solid ground regardless of the ratings of her television shows; 2) she would be around, directing her businesses, appearing on television, for some time to come; and 3) she remained a unique cultural icon, flawed to be sure, weakened most certainly, but still a major celebrity whose every move would continue to be watched and dissected by the nation's media.

In the course of the nearly four years since her legal case developed, Martha Stewart wrestled constantly with the question: How do I want to project myself to the public? What persona can I convey that will help me get out of this mess?

At first, she chose to be arrogant and dismissive, but that did not work; then she sought the role of victim, and few had much sympathy for her. Finally, she relied on winning over the public by giving the impression that she was prepared to take her punishment, and she was 100 percent right that the public loved her for that.

But gaining public sympathy for going behind bars did not win her the support of all of her fans, only some. But she now had the media on her side; and she had major elements in the American culture (Donald Trump, Mark Burnett) in her corner. In the late fall of 2005, she was still hoping to win over the rest of those who had turned against her. She was trying to show that she was really the old Martha, a little bit more experienced, a little bit more understanding of the whole world out there. She had tried to change, and she had shown new traits that the public liked; but she could never, never acknowledge that she had misbehaved. Even if her stubbornness cost her some public sympathy, she was not willing to admit to anything other than that she had been victimized. The public would have to take her as she was. Still, she hoped to win over the remaining cynics because even at the age of 64, she did not want to leave center stage, not quite yet.

ENDNOTES

CAST OF CHARACTERS

"I will be back." Martha Stewart, speaking to reporters just after her sentencing, July 17, 2004.

"...A small personal matter..." Martha Stewart, speaking in court at the time of her sentencing, July 17, 2004.

CHAPTER 1

"L'affaire Martha isn't...," *Newsweek* magazine, The Insiders, July 1, 2002.

CHAPTER 2

"Hanging around..." Lou Colasuonno, interview with author, June 29, 2005. All other Lou Colasuonno quotes are from my interview with him, unless otherwise indicated.

"...A chubby plump..." "Martha Stewart: It's a Good Thing" biography, A&E Home Video, 1996.

"We all stood there..." Ibid.

"Got it from me..." Ibid.

"Fifty-something, well preserved..." Elizabeth Koch, notes from the trial of Martha Stewart, posted on Reason.com Web site, February 19, 2004.

"She did it..." Lisa Marsh, interview with author, April 21, 2005. All other Marsh quotes are from my interview with her, unless otherwise indicated.

"She had principles..." The Stewart associate asked not to be identified.

"If there had been..." Marvin Pickholz, interview with author, June 28, 2005. All other Pickholz quotes are from my interview with him, also unless otherwise indicated.

CHAPTER 3

"Anywhere in the law..." Elaine Lafferty, interview with author, March 31, 2005. All other Lafferty quotes are from my interview with her, unless otherwise indicated.

"It was a personal..." Andrew Ritchie, interview with author, February 10, 2005. All other Ritchie quotes are from my interview with him, unless otherwise indicated.

"Nobody sells the day..." Jake Zamansky, interview with author, March 18, 2005. All other Zamansky quotes are from my interview with him, unless otherwise indicated.

"Brilliant and arrogant..." Jeff Toobin, "A Bad Thing: Why Did Martha Stewart Lose?," *New Yorker* magazine, March 22, 2004.

Long before..." Robert Shapiro, "The Basic Rules of White-Collar Defense," *Wall Street Journal*, July 19, 2004.

"We all learn..." John Savarese, interview with author, July 28, 2005.

"She was one of the two..." Lanny Davis, interview with author, April 7, 2005. All other Davis quotes are from my interview with him, unless otherwise indicated.

"Can I go now?" Martha Stewart quoted by SEC lawyer in "Martha Stewart: Tip? What Tip?" CBS/Associated Press, February 11, 2004.

"I remember the first," Martha Stewart quoted on *Larry King Live*, CNN, February 2, 2001.

CHAPTER 4

"Cast his subject as a coiffed..." *BusinessWeek*, "Behind the Martha Mystique," April 22, 2002.

"It looks like Martha Stewart..." Alan Reynolds, Cato Institute, "Martha Stewart in Prison?" September 21, 2004.

"There really was this..." Jeff Toobin, National Public Radio, March 18, 2004.

"In a style more..." Richard S. Levick, Legal PR Bulletin, "Half-Pregnant, Ill-Begotten," undated.

CHAPTER 5

"Because you want people..." Martha Stewart, quoted on *Larry King Live*, CNN, July 19, 2004.

"A few days before Toobin's article..." "A Bad Thing: Why Did Martha Stewart Lose?"

"Public image has been..." Jeff Toobin, *New Yorker* magazine, "Lunch at Martha's," February 3, 2003.

"As I later learned..." "A Bad Thing: Why Did Martha Stewart Lose?"

CHAPTER 6

"What goes on in..." Knight Ridder Tribune Service, shopper quoted in "Martha Stewart fans solidly behind her as furniture lines introduced," May 2, 2003.

"Even if there is a favorable..." Ibid.

"Standing on the stock-exchange..." Sharon Patrick, quoted in *New York* magazine, "2 Blondes," February 1, 2005.

"Rang out like..." *Time* magazine, "Why They're Picking on Martha," June 16, 2003.

"It was just incredible..." "Martha Stewart: It's a Good Thing."

"Something happened," Ibid.

"I never hold it..." Eliot Spitzer, quoted in *The Legal Times*, "Litigating in the Limelight," 2004.

"I still cover the company..." Douglas Arthur, interview with author, March 10, 2005.

CHAPTER 7

"I don't do anything..." Martha Stewart, quoted on Academy of Achievement Web site, the Hall of business: "Martha Stewart Multi-Media Lifestyle Entrepreneur," June 2, 1995.

"I wouldn't have missed it..." Martha Stewart, quoted on *Larry King Live*, CNN, March 17, 2004.

"An elegant lady..." Martha Stewart, quoted on *Larry King Live*, CNN, July 19, 2004.

"She really does have..." Rochelle Steinhaus, interview with author, February 18, 2005. All other Steinhaus quotes are from my interview with her, unless otherwise indicated.

"It's a hard way..." Allen Dodd-Frank, interview with author, June 29, 2005.

"A tad condescending..." "Opening Statements," Elizabeth Koch's notes from the trial of Martha Stewart posted on Reason.com Web site, January 27, 2004.

"I was thinking..." Rosemary McMahon, quoted on *Dateline*, NBC, March 6, 2004.

"He is not physically..." "A Bad Thing: Why Did Martha Stewart Lose?"

"To set your...," Martha Stewart, quoted on *Larry King Live*, CNN, July 19, 2004.

"We were lined up..." Helen Lucaites, interview with author, May 17, 2005.

"We were all waiting..." Elizabeth Koch, interview with author, April 22, 2005. All other Koch quotes are from my interview with her, unless otherwise indicated.

"An egregious example..." Elizabeth Koch, Columbia Journalism Review, "Martha Guilty? Surely You Jest," May/June 2004.

"Out of laziness..." "Martha Guilty? Surely You Jest?"

CHAPTER 8

"Beanpole," Henry Blodget, Slate.com, "An Insider's View of the Martha Trial," February 4, 2004.

"A hypercompetent..." *People Weekly*, "The best revenge (life of Martha trial)," October 2, 1995.

CHAPTER 9

"Dumpy woman in her..." Elizabeth Koch's notes from the trial of Martha Stewart posted on Reason.com Web site, February 9, 2004.

"No wonder Stewart...," Ibid. "Lives in a tony..." *New York Post,* "Martha's Buddy Faces Legal Fight," January 29, 2004.

"That gets pretty close..." Martha Stewart, quoted on *Larry King Live,* CNN, July 17, 2004.

CHAPTER 10

"Stewart's best chance....," Karen S. Bond, Baltimore Sun, "Blunders that sabatoged her case," March 8, 2004. All other Bond quotes are from the Baltimore Sun article unless otherwise indicated.

"Devastated that..." Donald Trump, quoted on *Larry King Live,* CNN, February 27, 2004.

"She could have absolutely..." Dominick Dunne, quoted on *Larry King Live,* CNN, March 5, 2005.

"Looked like a well-dressed..." Knight Ridder/Tribune Business News, "Martha Stewart's Lawyer Argues She Wouldn't Risk Career with Stock Scheme," March 3, 2004.

CHAPTER 11

"It was their equanimity..." "Martha Stewart: It's a Good Thing."

"It might have been..." Alexis Stewart, quoted on *Larry King Live,* CNN, March 17, 2004.

"Incredibly saddened..." Ibid.

"That's not really..." *People* magazine, "'I'll Be Back.' Shaken But Defiant, Martha Stewart Braces for Prison—And a New Life," August 2, 2004.

"Well, we were..." Martha Stewart, quoted on *Larry King Live,* CNN, July 19, 2004.

CHAPTER 12

"Very, very sad—" Charles Simonyi quoted in *Seattle Times*, "Seattle-area friend says Martha Stewart calm but 'very, very sad,'" March 6, 2004.

"Rubenstein was taken aback..." Interview with author, June 27, 2005.

CHAPTER 13

"It's not a scary place." Chrisa Gonzales, interview with author, March 1, 2005. All other Gonzales quotes are from my interview with her, unless otherwise indicated.

"We asked the guards..." CNN/Money—Money.com Web site, "Martha, out and about," March 4, 2005.

"Never idle or..." Margaret Roach, *Martha Stewart Living*, Letter from editor, March 2005.

"Every time I..." Steve Gerard, quoted on *Larry King Live*, CNN, March 4, 2005.

"Some of the more light-hearted..." CNN/Money—Money.com Web site, "Martha's Homecoming," February 28, 2005.

CHAPTER 14

"Hot..." Donald Trump, interview with author, July 28, 2005.

"The article dealt..." *People* magazine, "Martha Stewart: Making the Best of a Bad Thing," March 21, 2005.

"...That I could go..." *New York Times*, "Martha Stewart, Unchained," August 29, 2005.

"It was by far..." *Vanity Fair*, "The Prisoner of Bedford," August 2005.

"You can't be sorry..." Ibid.

CHAPTER 15

"I'm not changed...," *USA Today*, Martha Stewart interview, "Martha Stewart coming at you.," August 25, 2005.

"I really do have rules...," Associated Press, "Martha's back," September 12, 2005.

"When you're through..." *Palm Beach Post*, "It's been quite a year for the world's most famous Domestic Diva.," September 12, 2005.

"Maybe it's time to think...," *Newsweek*, "She's Back!", August 29-September 5, 2005.

"To avoid it is avoidance...," "It's been quite a year for the world's most famous Domestic Diva."

"You don't know what's going...," *Newsweek*, "Martha Breaks Out," March 7, 2005.

"In addition to being...," CNN.com, "Everything is Coming up Martha," September 12, 2005.

"The Apprentice has been a fantastic...," *USA Today*, "Stewart shares business rules," October 10, 2005.

"None. I went through...," *Today* show, October 10, 2005.

INDEX

A

Ackman, Dan, 117
Adelphia, 8
Alderson Federal Women's Prison,
  xvii-xix, 195, 201-216, 229
ankle bracelet. *See* house arrest
Apfel, David, 138-139, 141
The Apprentice (television program), 163-
  164, 214-215, 232, 240, 245, 250
The Apprentice: Martha Stewart
  (television program), 223, 225, 228,
  232, 240, 242, 245-251
Armstrong, Ann, xiv, 136, 141, 157, 183
  importance of testimony, 175
  phone message log, 48-49
  Stewart's phone conversation with, 26
  testimony of, 143-148
Arthur, Doug, 107
Ashcroft, John, 62, 71, 116, 123, 161
"Ask Martha" (newspaper column), 103
Associated Press, 59

B

Bacanovic (mother of Peter), 173
Bacanovic, Peter, xiii, 9, 15, 22, 43, 50,
  61, 80, 82, 128-129, 160, 178
  Armstrong testimony, 143-145
  arrival at trial, 114
  background of, 15-18
  comparison with Faneuil, 21
  contact with Stewart prior to
    ImClone stock sale, 20
  conversations with Faneuil, 25-26, 41
  cover up with Stewart, 52
  Faneuil plea bargain, 70-71
  Faneuil sentencing, 193
  Faneuil testimony, 63-65, 133-142
  guilty verdict, 172
  indictment of, 94-98
  initial interview by federal
    government, 41
  investigation by Merrill Lynch
    internal auditor, 32-33

jury deliberations, 169
phone message log, 48-51
relationship with Martha Stewart,
  17-18
role in ImClone stock sale, 24-27,
  37, 39
sentencing, 186
sexual orientation of, 16-17
stop-loss order, 30, 33, 41-42, 50-51,
  71, 81
trial date, 103
Barnard College, 63, 86, 114
Bear Stearns, 15
Bennett, Kimberly Renee, 210
Birkin handbag, 127-128, 187
Blodget, Henry, xv, 117, 130-132, 134,
  172, 219
Bloomberg News, 117, 130
BMG, 251
Body & Soul, 103, 225
Bond, Karen S., 156, 159
Bonwit Teller, 63
Bost, Sara, 209
Branson, Richard, 240
Bristol-Myers Squibb, 11, 15
Brunswick Group, 68, 75
Buffett, Warren, 104
Burnett, Mark, xv, 163-164, 214-215, 223,
  227, 232, 238, 245, 250-251, 254
Bush, George, 223
BusinessWeek, 57, 117, 126
Byron, Chris, 57-58

C

cabbage-chopping incident, 67-68, 106
"Camp Cupcake." *See* Alderson Federal
  Women's Prison
Carl's Furniture, 92
Cedarbaum, Miriam Goldman, xiii, 96, 103,
  114-115, 119, 122, 134, 141-142, 146, 150,
  164, 169, 171, 184-186, 192-193, 195
Chanel, Coco, 4
Chanterelle (restaurant), 19
Child, Julia, 86, 100

N-O

P